The Jazz Problem

The Jazz Problem

Education and the Battle for Morality during the Jazz Age

JACOB HARDESTY

Cover image: Art adapted from the August 1924 issue of *The Etude* magazine, which was devoted to a discussion of "the jazz problem."

Published by State University of New York Press, Albany

© 2023 State University of New York

All rights reserved

Printed in the United States of America

No part of this book may be used or reproduced in any manner whatsoever without written permission. No part of this book may be stored in a retrieval system or transmitted in any form or by any means including electronic, electrostatic, magnetic tape, mechanical, photocopying, recording, or otherwise without the prior permission in writing of the publisher.

For information, contact State University of New York Press, Albany, NY
www.sunypress.edu

Library of Congress Cataloging-in-Publication Data

Name: Hardesty, Jacob (Jacob Whelchel) author.
Title: The jazz problem : education and the battle for morality during the jazz age / Jacob Hardesty.
Description: Albany : State University of New York Press, [2023]. | Includes bibliographical references and index.
Identifiers: LCCN 2022059347 | ISBN 9781438494630 (hardcover : alk. paper) | ISBN 9781438494654 (ebook)
Subjects: LCSH: Jazz—Social aspects—United States—History—20th century. | Music—Moral and ethical aspects—United States—History—20th century. | Moral education—United States—History—20th century.
Classification: LCC ML3918.J39 H37 2023 | DDC 306.4/84250973—dc23/eng/20221221
LC record available at https://lccn.loc.gov/2022059347

10 9 8 7 6 5 4 3 2 1

To Danielle and Eliot

Boy: Parents don't know anything about their children and what they're doing.

Girl: They don't want to know.

Girl: We won't let them know.

Boy: Ours is a speedy world and they're old.

—Robert S. Lynd and Helen Merrell Lynd
Middletown: A Study in Modern American Culture, 1929

Contents

Acknowledgments		xi
Introduction		1
Chapter 1	Chicago and the Urban Jazz Problem	13
Chapter 2	White Educators and Jazz: Moral Outrage and Musical Corruption	39
Chapter 3	Jazz and Black High Schools: Preserving the Spiritual and Promoting Racial Pride	59
Chapter 4	The "Jazz Problem" in Higher Education: Attitudes of College Students and Faculty	83
Chapter 5	The Dance Craze on Campus: Negotiations and Public Perceptions	107
Conclusion		135
Notes		141
Bibliography		181
Index		203

Acknowledgments

Studies of this length are impacted and shaped by more than a single author. I was and am fortunate to have family and friends who were generous with their time and read every word of the first few drafts of this study and offered invaluable suggestions. My friends from Indiana University, Abigail Gundlach-Graham and Daniel Dethrow, read the study chapter by chapter, helping me better draw out the historical significance of the narrative I was telling. My mom, Rebecca Whelchel, who even after three decades still has an amazing ability to find typos and improve my writing, promptly returned each chapter I sent her. Without your insights and encouragement, this book would look quite different.

I greatly benefited from a dissertation committee that from the start pushed me to think about this study as a book-length narrative, not a dissertation. Thank you Donald Warren for your encouragement, forthrightness, and, when I needed it, telling me "Keep your chin up." For decades, Don has thoughtfully challenged students and colleagues to consider how an inductive view of education is, in fact, a lived experience of education. I am honored to be counted among his students. Thank you Dionne Danns for continuing to help me improve my writing about race, seeing race in sources in ways I previously did not. Andrea Walton, thank you for sharpening my writing about higher education, particularly how gender was performed on campus. Luise McCarty, I am grateful for how you kept on me to draw out educators' implied or explicit philosophies undergirding their actions. And Lissa May, thank for keeping me honest in my explanation of the music I described. I greatly benefited from the unique perspectives each of you brought to our meetings.

My initial research at Indiana University was supported by the Indiana University School of Education Faculty Fellowship as well as the

DeVault Fellowship. The Beecher Dissertation Research Fellowship helped me collect sources and write the manuscript's first draft. As I was revising and updating the text, I also received financial support from the Rockford University Faculty Development Grants, as well as research support from DePauw University. For all that financial support, I am eternally grateful.

Archivists and librarians at various institutions gave their time graciously to collect various primary and secondary sources. Thank you Joyce Ann Powell (Manassas High School, Memphis), Robert Chester (Crispus Attucks High School Museum, Indianapolis), Rob Hudson (Carnegie Hall), Frank Villella (Chicago Symphony Orchestra), Susan Sutton (Indiana Historical Society), Beth Madison Howse (Fisk University), Ellen Swain and Lise Renee Kemplin (both University of Illinois), Jeremy Smith (University of Massachusetts, Amherst), Janet Harper and Laurie Lee Moses (both Center for Black Music Research, Columbia College), Andrea Jackson (Robert W. Woodruff Library, Atlanta University Center), and Andy Newgren and Andrew Johnson (both Rockford University). Dina Kellams (Indiana University), has been especially helpful, and patient, answering my many questions, large and small.

At SUNY Press thank you to Richard Carlin for helping with everything from my initial proposal submission to interpreting reviewer feedback. Thank you also to the three anonymous reviewers who read the manuscript and pushed me to see "the jazz problem" more accurately in terms of the cultural anxieties of the time. Thank you Susan Geraghty and your team for your copyediting expertise to this book and to Aimee Harrison for helping facilitate the creative cover design.

A *very big* thank you to Ronald Cohen for suggesting SUNY Press to me and making the initial introductions. I was lucky enough to be introduced to Ron during a History of Education Society meeting, and he has been a kind and thoughtful supporter of my work since. Ron always responded to emails quickly, with feedback that showed he had deeply thought through any questions I had. He was the very embodiment of a mentor. Where he thought my work could be improved, he said so. When something I wrote deserved praise, he said so. Sadly, Ron passed away while this book was in production. He leaves behind a wide body of historical scholarship, touching on areas including, music, education, labor issues, and how those topics can and should be in regular dialogue. I miss him greatly.

Other colleagues have offered thoughtful constructive feedback at various stages of this process. Jon Hale, Milton Gaither, and Kevin

Zayed also helped me prepare an earlier version of chapters 1 and 2 that appeared in the *History of Education Quarterly*. Kevin Zayed's ability to find primary sources is, frankly, otherworldly. He has been a loyal friend and supporter of this project for over a decade. Pax KZ. Thank you also to colleagues Ed Janak and Andrew Grunzke, two gentlemen similarly crazy enough to think music and popular culture might have something to say about educational history.

At Rockford University and DePauw University I have been fortunate to have received feedback from colleagues at various faculty research presentations. Thank you to all who attended those and helped me make the project as interesting to a wider audience as possible. Thank you as well to my department colleagues, present and past, for the ongoing support and encouragement.

To Mike Perry and Matthew Bork, please know I let you win at basketball on Fridays.

Thank you to my dean "partners in crime" at Rockford University, Drs. Deepshikha Shukla, Filiz Dik, and Jennifer Langworthy. I promise to "pay it forward."

Speaking of paying it forward, thank you to my parents, Becky Whelchel, Andy and Melody Hardesty, and Peter Gershefski for investing in my education early and often. That is a debt I will gladly repay, to Eliot.

To my sisters Susan Frigerio and Ann Gerschefski—Y'all are both "suffus," as are Nick and Sutton Frigerio.

Most importantly, thank to my family, Danielle and Eliot (and Bailey, Chloe, Remie, and Mo). You all have allowed me the space, encouragement, and love to finish "our book." I love-a you all.

An earlier version of portions of chapters 1 and 2 was originally published in *History of Education Quarterly* 56 (2016): 590–617. I am grateful to the editors for granting permission to publish those sections here.

Introduction

Bismarck and Agatha Biederbecke worried about their son and his interest in jazz music. Leon, known as "Bix" was a young, middle-class, white male from an upper-middle-class Iowa family, who had developed a habit of sneaking onboard the riverboats that traveled up the nearby Mississippi River. Aboard the SS *Capitol*, Bix listened to and occasionally joined performances by black jazz bands that had become increasingly common on riverboats.[1] Ever since his older brother bought the family's first Victor Talking Machine Company phonograph and a handful of records, jazz had been a sort of obsession for the young Davenport, Iowa, native: Bix had taught himself to play jazz trumpet by listening and imitating sounds he heard on the SS *Capitol* and on the Victrola. Though Bix was developing into a formidable musician, he also had a darker side. In 1921, Bix was arrested for committing a "lewd and lascivious act" with a five-year-old sight-impaired girl. Authorities ultimately dropped the charges after the girl's parents blocked her from testifying in court. Growing increasingly uncomfortable with his sneaking onto riverboats, and in order to avoid town gossip following his arrest, Bismarck and Agatha Biederbecke decided a major change was necessary. In September 1921, they shipped off seventeen-year-old Bix to Lake Forest Academy, a prestigious Chicago boarding school. His parents hoped the school would instill a sense of discipline in Bix, improve his academic skills, change his general behavior, and remedy his interest in jazz.[2]

The remedy Bismarck and Agatha Biederbecke chose—school—was one other parents have chosen when hoping to change their children's behaviors. Unfortunately for them, Chicago was one of the worst places they could have sent the young jazz musician. The Lake Forest classrooms were simply no match for downtown Chicago and its thriving jazz scene.

To improve his listening and playing, Bix regularly traveled to the South Side and to various dance halls in the Loop, often returning well past curfew. In one letter home, he wrote to his brother, "I'd go to hell to hear a good band."[3] Within a year, Bix was expelled for his poor class attendance, low grades, and general behavior problems. Bix frustrated educators by forming a campus band and performing "inappropriate" jazz music for at least one school dance. In essence, Bix introduced jazz to his new school, a connection I discuss in this book. The young trumpet player was also often caught drinking on campus, a major infraction during Prohibition. After missing curfew one too many times, the Lake Forest teachers voted to expel Bix in May 1922. One administrator wrote about Biederbecke, "We are . . . very sorry that he was in the school at all."[4] Freed from Lake Forest, and with his parents' begrudging approval, nineteen-year-old Bix worked odd jobs during the day and soaked up Chicago jazz at night.

A likable person as well as an excellent musician, Bix quickly built a reputation as a formidable trumpet talent in Chicago and beyond. Bix recorded some of the country's earliest and best-selling jazz records, some with his friend Hoagland "Hoagy" Carmichael. He toured relentlessly, traveling up and down the East Coast as a featured soloist for "King of Jazz" Paul Whiteman's group, as well as other ensembles. Within five years of his expulsion from Lake Forest, Biederbecke's popularity on college campuses rivaled that of any musician alive, a popularity perhaps due in part to Bix being the same age as his audiences. University administrators begrudgingly allowed Biederbecke and his bands to perform at various proms and college dances. Students could not get enough of Bix's "dirty tone." Unfortunately, his parents' concerns about the iniquitous behaviors surrounding the world of jazz proved to be valid. In addition to his success, Bix increasingly gave in to one of the vices widely associated with jazz: alcoholism. Certainly, drinks were easily accessible for jazz musicians. His friend Louis Armstrong would later recall, "Poor Bix, he would never say 'no' [to a party] . . . It's a drag!"[5] In August 1931, Biederbecke died alone in his New York City apartment at the age of twenty-eight.[6] In his death, Bix became the archetype of Jazz Age excesses, notably represented in the loosely fictionalized autobiographical novel and subsequent 1950 film *Young Man with a Horn*, starring Hollywood legends Kirk Douglas, Doris Day, and Lauren Bacall, as well as Bix's friend Hoagy Carmichael.[7]

Bix's short, famous, and ultimately, tragic life demonstrates the excitement and danger that swirled around jazz. Young people, by and large, embraced jazz as not only one of life's pleasures, but, indeed, one of life's necessities. "A college existence without jazz," one University of Illinois student quipped, "would be like a child's Christmas without Santa Claus. It would be empty, boresome, unendurable, exasperating. We couldn't stand it."[8] For some adults, this type of sentiment proved troubling. Indeed, a critic no less influential than Secretary of the Interior Hubert Work, countered that the "jazz spirit of the present day" was responsible for an increasing number of students becoming "criminals" due to a combination of "meager mentality" and wanting "moral stamina."[9] No period in American history, aside from the Jazz Age, is known by a musical genre.[10]

By 1924, the editor of the music magazine the *Etude* decided that educators' concerns about jazz had grown to a level that it warranted devoting a full issue of the magazine to the topic. James Francis Cooke assured his readers the magazine would handle the topic with nothing short of journalistic neutrality. In his editorial for the special issue, "Where *The Etude* Stands on Jazz," Cooke less-than-neutrally characterized the genre as an "accursed annoyance to teachers for years."[11] The front cover featured a circle of brass and wind instruments surrounding the caption, "The Jazz Problem: Opinions of Prominent Public Men and Musicians" (see fig. I.1).

The gradual decline of a Victorian worldview coupled with adults' unwillingness to embrace the jazz-drenched modern world that young people championed provides the backdrop for this study.[12] At its height, Victorianism rested on various identifying characteristics: a belief in a general superiority of Anglo-Saxon identity; considerable social emphasis on the immediate family, with parents doling out lessons in self-control and restraint; and clearly defined gender roles, such that boys were applauded for being diligent and stern while girls were taught to be modest and aim for simplicity of dress.[13] Certainly Victorianism had slowly been losing its "stranglehold on the national imagination," since at least the turn of the century.[14] Still, the Jazz Age systematically amplified the decline of previously cherished facets of Victorian identity—and critics amplified their responses. In *Cuttin' Up: How Early Jazz Got America's Ear*, Court Carney noted, "The shift from Victorianism to Modernism formed the context in which Americans reacted to jazz music. In general, Victorianism created a dichotomy separating controlled human instincts from natural impulses, and modernism strove to reunite these two forces."[15] Yet while historians have focused heavily on jazz's cultural impact and early performance history, schools have been seen an afterthought in this culture war. This seems surprising, given how students in the 1920s were spending more

4 | The Jazz Problem

Figure I.1. "The Jazz Problem," Cover. *Etude*, August 1924.

time in schools than ever before. Across the 1920s, just under 83 percent of elementary and high school students were attending school daily. At the turn of the twentieth century, the percentage of daily attendance was just 68 percent.[16] And students were not only attending schools more regularly, schooling was occupying a larger role in their lives.

In *The Jazz Problem: Education and the Battle for Morality during the Jazz Age*, I show how jazz was the vehicle for understanding the daily lives of students and educators, as both groups responded to the decline of Victorianism in the face of a new modern American culture. Schools were not secondary actors in the narrative about how jazz "got America's ear."[17] *The Jazz Problem* frames high schools and colleges as the primary sites of dispute between a wounded, though still influential, Victorianism and the emerging modern world, one synonymous with jazz. Schools were places where conflicting messages about jazz became the norm—where adults preached and where young people practiced.[18] Educators used a variety of curricular and extracurricular tools during school and outside school hours, in their efforts to dissuade their students from jazz. Such efforts were, at best, largely unsuccessful, and, more accurately, backfired. Young people saw their teachers' efforts as evidence that jazz was an exciting generational boundary line to embrace. And while young people routinely snuck into dance halls to dance the Charleston, it was in schools where they shared phonodiscs, clandestinely taught each other the newest dance steps, and made plans for the weekend. In short, in schools young people first learned that jazz was *their* music. As a major site of character formation where students came of age, high schools and colleges were the places where jazz was discussed, devoured, and deprecated. However, this is not merely a story of rebellious privileged children and their conservative parents. Nor is it a story as simple as "white parents feared their children listening to *black* music." Rather, the narrative I tell shows an interrelated set of conversations that transcended the racial boundaries enforced by a segregated school system. But one thing is certain, those conversations took place in, and focused on, high schools and colleges.

For critics and supporters alike, jazz represented something of a Rorschach test. Jazz's fluidity gave both groups the space to see what they liked and what they feared. A sense of increasing blackness on the white body politic? Jazz certainly delivered. Outrage about increasingly sexually active young people? Jazz's aphrodisiac qualities were well known, if not exaggerated. A sense of generational boundary that encouraged an increasingly evident youth culture? Here, young people cheered jazz, particularly young white people. Still, the "jazz problem" looked different in black high schools than it did on predominately white college campuses, where faculty and students alike largely agreed jazz should not supplant the spiritual, the primary source of musical pride. For all involved, students and educators, white and black, jazz's power was in its indefiniteness, that supporters and critics alike could see in it what they embraced or what they feared. "Jazz" meant more than music. Jazz was a *lifestyle*, one that operated as a useful metaphor for a whole host of concerns.[19] When speaking of jazz, critics routinely referenced the associated bare arms and legs of female jazz dancers, and the omnipresent possibility of alcohol and the increase in sexual activity. As the logic went, if they could dissuade young people from indulging in jazz, perhaps their interests in the other associated vices would also fall away.

Technology, Schools, and the Culture Wars of the 1920s

Historians have pushed back against the popular yet reductive depiction of the "roaring twenties" in favor of a more dynamic vision of the decade as "the roots of America's culture wars."[20] The 1920s was not a decade of unbridled "voodoo orgy," though that interpretation still pervades much of popular media.[21] Instead, scholars have cast the decade as the setting when an increasingly diverse range of character groups—party-happy flappers, the KKK and other "guardians" of supremacist ideals, evangelical Christians, liberal public intellectuals, African American and other minority groups—all waged a struggle for the "soul of America."[22] As Lynn Dumenil pointed out, "The depiction of the roaring twenties obscures the complexities lying beneath the surface, especially the considerable social tensions that permeated the culture."[23] I link this interpretation of the decade, one begun in the 1950s that eventually culminated in Dumenil's *The Modern Temper*, to the more recent specialized works that engaged black and feminist interpretations.[24] Jazz was not simply an idea argued by white Americans about progress and morality. It drew out variety regional and national anxieties about race and gender under the guise of the decline of Victorianism. In jazz, adults similarly saw a tangible villain they could point as the primary cause for a multitude of social ills—a supposed increase in "petting" (a purposefully vague term referring to any sexual contact), frenetic dance steps virtually synonymous with alcoholism, and an increase in prostitution. *The Jazz Problem* recounts how adults acted out those anxieties as they struggled to tighten a seemingly loosening grip on American youth. It was one thing when grownups with faculties wise enough ultimately embraced jazz; it meant something quite different when young people did. The former were considered irreparable, the latter could be "saved" or "rehabilitated."

Jazz in the 1920s was, without a doubt, black. Critics and enthusiasts overwhelmingly agreed the music had developed as the province of black musicians.²⁵ Though a universally agreed on creation story has eluded scholars, some general facts are clear. The music developed as black musicians in the south—particularly, though, not solely, in New Orleans—combined some semblance of African and European rhythm and harmony.²⁶ The Great Migration out of the south carried the music out of the south and across the country. Among these immigrant musicians, the pianist Jelly Roll Morton went to Chicago while the trombonist "Kid" Ory moved west to Los Angeles in 1919, three years later making what was likely the first instrumental black jazz recording at a studio on Santa Monica Boulevard. At least in terms of musical diaspora, such moves were not unprecedented. Since at least the early 1910s, black ensembles had toured across the Midwest and had sought employment on the thriving riverboat scene. Still, the Great Migration altered the musical dynamic by creating an increasingly permanent presence of jazz in regions outside the south. Large urban centers, destinations for such migration, became centers of jazz performance and dance.²⁷

Many white critics viewed this spread of jazz as cause for alarm. White critics used the emergent genre as evidence to justify their views of African Americans as both culturally and intellectually inferior. Terminology like "the Senegambian buzz-fuzz," "oscillatum Ethiopius," or even the tamer sounding "syncopated" were coded, racialized language to connect jazz with a stereotyped unrefined blackness.²⁸ In jazz, the idea of the sexually charged, unintelligent, and hypersexualized black man had a recognizable manifestation, an old idea with a new medium for re-presentation. Yet as Gerald Early has pointed out, such terminology was fundamentally reductionist in nature, meant to evoke the "form of black primitives."²⁹ The detractors who employed such language sought to define African Americans *writ large* as singularly culturally and intellectually underdeveloped, using a rubric that placed whiteness as the epitome of such organizational schema. In response, many black educators, musicians, and intellectuals who actively fought to dispel such myths distanced themselves from the music. As the reasoning went, if jazz acted in the minds of critics as another indicator of cultural and intellectual inferiority, then not being associated with it could serve as a sort of indicator of intellectual equality. A 1922 advertisement in the National Association for the Advancement of Colored People (NAACP) magazine *The Crisis* pushed back on this point that black musicians could only play, and therefore sell, jazz. He wrote,

"We believe the dealer is wrong. But unless we furnish him with what he has demand for, he will not handle our goods. . . . We have a special proposition for music teachers. Write for it."[30]

An increasingly sophisticated radio technology coupled with the increasing affordability of phonograph records in the 1920s helped account for jazz's rapid cultural diffusion.[31] The first commercial radio station, KDKA, in Pittsburgh, went on air in 1920. Eighteen months later, the number of commercial stations had risen to 220. By 1930, over 900 stations existed nationwide and over 40 percent of households owned radios.[32] Throughout the 1920s, young people increasingly turned to radio to listen to jazz, often at the expense of the phonograph. In 1927, 987,000 phonographs were sold; five years later, the number had fallen to 40,000. In contrast, radio production increased. Less cumbersome and cheaper than the phonograph, the radio easily filtered jazz into the home, much to critics' frustration. Station managers increasingly recognized that jazz's popularity among young people helped sell on air advertising space. One Dallas priest lamented in 1921, "Have you noticed how the modern young person, instead of sitting quietly in a corner to read, keeps a phonograph grinding out the latest syncopated tunes, and then goes on talking as though the music were not playing?"[33] A high school student wrote in her diary that she was listening to "damn good jazz on the radio" until her parents complained; her mother turned off the radio, saying, "They call that music!"[34]

Concerned Americans in the 1920s increasingly looked to schools to address a multitude of anxieties, at the same time that schools were taking on increasing enrollments of students. In 1900, just under 11 percent of fourteen- to seventeen-year-old students attended high school; by 1930 the number had risen to 51 percent.[35] Enrollment of black students remained much lower than for their white counterparts. African American students were 1.5 of high school enrollment in 1920, and just 3 percent a decade later, while representing roughly 10 percent of the total population.[36] Higher-education enrollment showed a marked improvement from the late nineteenth century. By the end of the 1920s, roughly 1,400 higher-education institutions served a national population of 122 million.[37] Over the course of the decade, the number of students attending college had nearly doubled, jumping from 600,000 to just over 1.1 million, with roughly 20 percent of college-age students attending some sort of secondary institution.[38] The decade witnessed an increase in the number of colleges serving black students, from thirty-three in 1915 to seventy in

1927 (years of federal surveys of black college enrollment). That increase in institutions also accounted for an increase in enrollment, from 2,600 to almost 14,000.[39]

As such enrollment statistics suggest, schools were also taking on an increasingly prominent role in society. Daniel Clark has noted, a college education in the early twentieth century, particularly for white men, was increasingly seen in popular imagination as a necessary stepping stone for later success in life.[40] By the 1920s, college became major sites of tension for those who sought to maintain a Victorian ethos and those who challenged that worldview in favor of embracing a yet-to-be-defined modern lifestyle. Like Bix Biederbecke's parents sending him to a Chicago boarding school, concerned adults looked to schools as a solution to young people's increasing jazz interests. At both the high schools and colleges, white and black educators joined in this battle, though their reasons differed. White teachers often spoke of jazz in racialized aesthetic terms, an unwelcome musical bastard of European harmony and African rhythm. As one educator told his peers in 1928, "Jazz, with all its unwholesome, wanton influences, takes the place of the sincerity and sweetness of the classics."[41]

Given the increasingly prominent role schools were playing in the 1920s, those institutions became a logical ally in the fight to quell such cultural anxieties. The Jazz Age was a moment when educators—newly tasked with the health of the "whole child"—employed new tools to protect, legislate, and teach morality to students. High schools were not only increasing in enrollments, but services, capabilities, and expectations as well. Reformers took steps that broadened the roles those schools had in young people's lives, including an increasing set of responsibilities for the mental, emotional, physical, and spiritual well-being of the students. Educators also sought to instill a sense of racialized, often eugenic, Americanism, among an increasingly pluralistic student body.[42] Others sought to make schools more physically accessible and less intimidating to students requiring additional assistance.[43] In higher education, enrollments swelled, in loco parentis was being challenged, and colleges tried to find out more about students in order to guide their moral development.[44]

Taken together, scholarship on Jazz Age and schooling at the time explains much about curricula, programs, philosophies, architecture, budgets, and enrollments, but relatively little about the cultural lives of students. However, historians have yet to go inside schoolhouse doors to understand how educators and students responded to the decade's cultural changes that elicited exultation and existential dread in seemingly equal parts. Paula S.

Fass alluded to the need for that lived experience in her seminal text *The Damned and the Beautiful: American Youth in the 1920s*. She pointed out, "Educators were suddenly confronted by new social problems concerned with residence, recreations, youth organizations, and only casually related to academic concerns."[45] Ultimately, the case studies I discuss add greater texture and more of an on-the-ground lens to the young people that the actors in policy-oriented curriculum and policy histories were trying to impact. Such a social history-infused approach explores not only the goals of those who viewed schools as a counterbalance to the decade's cultural changes, but explains how the people in those buildings, mostly young people, responded to that counterrevolution.

Book Organization

Much of my inquiry, particularly when discussing higher education, is a national story with a Midwestern regional interest, a region supposed to be, in the words of *Ladies Home Journal* editor John McMahon, "a citadel of Americanism and righteousness."[46] Yet it is not my thesis that the "jazz problem" was a regional manifestation—in fact, I would strongly argue that it was not. Instead, the number of large land-grant universities, as well as smaller religiously affiliated liberal arts colleges, provides multiple cases that demonstrate how university officials and students in different types of institutions in different regions reacted to jazz. Because the vast majority of historically black colleges were (and are) below the Mason-Dixon Line, I focus more on the south when discussing those schools to draw on as large a sample size as possible. Similarly, I shift to the Northeast when discussing single-sex women's colleges. Still, the general focus remains what campus bon vivant and white jazz musician Hoagy Carmichael unironically called the "mystic Midwest response to jungle beat."[47]

This study develops over five chapters, an organizational structure that highlights the differences in jazz responses between high schools and colleges. While educators at high schools and colleges were increasingly concerned with the morality of their students, they diverged in their answers to the "jazz problem." This first chapter sets up the differing responses of educators at both levels. It focuses on how high school and college officials reacted to the threat jazz believed posed to young people in Chicago, one of the country's most "toddlin' towns."[48] Certainly, a palpable degree of concern over student well-being existed for both high school and college students. Still, Chicago high school administrators took comparatively drastic measures to minimize students' contact with and interest in the music while their higher-education counterparts took a more hands-off approach. Building on this discussion of institutional response, chapter 2 explains why educators felt they had to take such drastic actions by breaking down the racialized argument against jazz itself. It argues that white music teachers were quite outspoken about the genre, both for its supposed musical and moral shortcomings. Much of this chapter focuses on the Music Supervisors' National Conference, a white music education group whose members offered up various solutions to solve the "jazz problem." As chapter 3 explains, the reasoning for this racialized opposition to jazz differed for black educators. Unlike their white colleagues, black educators rarely discussed jazz. Instead, they pointed to the spiritual as the most important recognizable black contribution to music. Black music educators worried above all else that jazz could "corrupt" the spiritual—that students would musically combine the sacred and secular. In those rare instances when jazz was discussed, black educators dismissed it in terms that were often stronger than those of their white counterparts.

The final two chapters turn specifically to higher education, a major progenitor of jazz-crazed young people. Colleges in the 1920s were taking up the role of morality on campus, with an old guard defending more straightforward moral critiques to reformers pushing greater social science–driven method of diagnosing and solving problems.[49] Chapter 4 places jazz in the middle of this debate by examining the attitudes of students and faculty in higher education. Without a doubt, white college students overwhelmingly praised jazz. In fact, jazz was audibly the background of higher-education life in the 1920s, enjoying a sort of hegemonic popularity among white college students. Still, a vocal minority of white students critiqued the genre on aesthetic and religious grounds, while most black students expressed little interest in jazz, preferring to identify musically with the spiritual. White higher-education faculty, like their secondary school colleagues, largely took a dim view of jazz. Yet while they dismissed jazz in professional publications, higher-education faculty typically did not feel they should attempt to shape students' musical tastes. Instead, it fell to deans of men to attempt to stem extramusical consequences associated with the music. The final chapter turns to the problem of jazz dancing on campus, easily the most popular form of recreation during the decade, and a tangible, discernible target for the prescient sexuality surrounding jazz. The chapter initially focuses on university-sponsored events, such as proms and balls, and how they served as events around which students and faculty could negotiate what was socially acceptable and what was forbidden. Colleges placed minimal restrictions, despite grumblings from alumni, administrators, and professors' own inclinations. Even relatively conservative institutions, such as historically black and evangelical colleges, dropped their dancing bans by the middle of the decade, largely in response to student interest. Chapter 5 then turns to the central role dancing played in Greek life. While many Panhellenics were genuinely interested in jazz, others found themselves drawn to the music for another reason—the chance to dance with "the coeds." Concluding with a discussion of the pianist Hoagy Carmichael, chapter 5 explains how colleges served as fertile breeding grounds for jazz musicians.

Finally, I should explain some points about terminology. First, though other synonyms were used at the time, unless otherwise specified in direct quotes, I use the word *spiritual* because it implies a connection with the sacred, a point black music educators often included when critiquing jazz. Other possible terms used during the Jazz Age included "Negro folk songs," "black folk songs" or simply, "our music." Second, though historians and musicologists can point to notable differences between jazz and its antecedent, ragtime, critics of the genres in the 1920s either did not recognize such distinctions or did not acknowledge them. As a result, some of the quotes I include use the terms *ragtime* and *jazz* in a seemingly interchangeable manner. Not appreciating the real musical differences between the genres points more to an unwillingness among critics to recognize any musical validity. Third, the term *European classical music*, while imperfect, I believe is the best available option for this study.[50] The issue of who owns music, or at least who can make historical ownership claims, is a necessary question for other studies. For purposes here, I simply ask readers to see my best intentions, one that acknowledges all genres' lineage, creates space for musical collaboration, and acknowledges a history of race-based musical exploitation. Finally, I use the terms *predominately white institutions* and *historically black institutions* throughout the text in an effort to avoid normalizing whiteness in higher education. I also recognize that other types of institutions have historical and current significance, including, though not exclusive to, tribal colleges and universities as well as Hispanic serving institutions.

Chapter 1

Chicago and the Urban Jazz Problem

Writing in 1922 for the *Ladies Home Journal*, editor John McMahon complained of the "Jazz Spotted Middle West." McMahon reminded readers of the "ancient axiom" that "big cities are wicked but small towns and rural districts are clean." Blaming African Americans for the spread of jazz, he referred to the "unholy marriage of the civilized and the savage" and went on to lament how "college and high school students in Chicago have been largely drawn into the maelstrom of the ultradance." McMahon then reviewed policies of various schools and their attempts to address jazz. He applauded one high school in which teachers had begun taking ballroom dancing lessons to better monitor and identify illicit jazz dance steps. Educators reasoned that they would be familiar enough with appropriate dances that they would become more vigilant if their students attempted the "shimmy" or other jazz dances. McMahon also reported how one university dean of women disapproved of, yet allowed, jazz dancing on campus. He wrote, "[the administrator] tries to be tolerant and think the youngsters do not get the harm that seems obvious to the elders."[1] The famed Russian ballerina Anna Pavlova also made precisely this point in Chicago on a 1922 United States tour. Urging jazz resistance, she called on educators to "Start them young. When they are old enough to go to dances they will love the beautiful and graceful movement and jazz will be distasteful to them."[2]

Chicago had performance and financial appeals to young black jazz musicians. Beginning in the late 1910s, Chicago developed a reputation as one of the country's prime destinations for those hoping to develop a career as a jazz musician. Realizing such hopes came at the expense of formal education. Buster Bailey, a young black clarinetist and saxophonist from Memphis, could not resist the pull Chicago had on this new breed of performer. He would later become one of the most respected session musicians of his era, though in his secondary school years Bailey put jazz ahead of schooling. He would later recall, "I was in such demand in Memphis during the time I was going to school that I was working all the time, but I only got paid two-sixty a night for dances and five dollars out of town for expenses. So I wanted to go to Chicago to get some of that money. So I left even before I finished those last two weeks of high school."[3] Alberta Hunter, a young jazz and blues singer, also from Memphis, ran away to Chicago at twelve with the assistance of her music teacher. Once there, she worked as a potato peeler before being hired at the Dreamland Ballroom, one of the most prestigious venues for African American performers in the city.[4] And Lil Hardin dropped out of Fisk University after one year in favor of life as a jazz performer. After an impromptu performance in a Chicago music store for the leader of the famous New Orleans Creole Jazz Band, King Oliver, she quickly quit that position and left school. Hardin later said, "The New Orleans Creole Jazz Band hired me, and I never got back to the music store—never got back to Fisk University."[5]

A city with just under sixty thousand students in public school, Chicago was the booming center of the jazz world by the late 1910s. Getting to Chicago was the goal for jazz musicians leaving New Orleans, Louis Armstrong and Sidney Bechet among them. Musicologist Eileen Southern has described how "the jazzmen from New Orleans who migrated to Chicago during World War I made that city a capital of classic jazz in the New Orleans tradition."[6] In his noted study on the Great Migration, James Grossman concurred, "The sounds of New Orleans jazz and Mississippi blues; styles of worship; patterns of speech . . . reshaped both their cultural heritage and their new environment. In Chicago's Black Metropolis, newcomers adapted to urban life and helped to create an Afro-American urban culture."[7] In a city of 2.7 million people, the black population during the 1910s had grown from roughly 45,000 to nearly 110,000.[8] Despite such demographic changes, Chicago remained a "city of neighborhoods."[9] City commissioners did not view this demographic change as a citywide phenomenon, at least in terms of housing, perhaps because many new Chicagoans immigrated to the South Side, creating a new "black belt."[10] Where Chicago's population change was undeniable was in the city's ubiquitous dance halls. In a decade when recreational dancing reached its nadir, dance hall managers hired black musicians to play for dance-hungry patrons. White young people in particular flocked to dance halls, while their parents looked on aghast, at least when they actually knew where their children were.

This chapter centers on the efforts of white educators and their allies in Chicago to keep young people out of the city's ubiquitous dance halls, particularly the efforts of jazz critics in the first half of the 1920s, the years in which racialized opposition to jazz was at its peak. And while both secondary and higher-education students frequented public dance halls, critics overwhelmingly spoke out about the dangers they believed such institutions posed to younger high school students. Concern among jazz critics focused primarily on secondary school students, with considerably less emphasis, and dialogue, on students in higher education. White city leaders used their positions of prominence to speak out about the moral and physiological dangers they believed dance halls posed. This criticism was often subtle, though unavoidably race-based, a response to this recognizably black genre newly carried into the city. As Amy Absher made clear in her study of migration, music, and race in Chicago, "Black music—and by extension the black musician—were seen as the accomplice of vice."[11]

Attitudes toward Jazz in Chicago: An Overview

Speaking to Chicago high school teachers in 1922, University of Wisconsin professor Michael Vincent O'Shea sounded a rallying cry among his education colleagues about the dangerous influence jazz was having on secondary students. O'Shea reported the results of a recent study he had undertaken in twenty-two American cities about the recreational habits of young people. He concluded that jazz dancing, movies, and driving in automobiles had "an emotionalism on the part of boys and girls which has cut short their intellectual development." O'Shea further rebuffed any suggestion that jazz dancing had any elements of beauty. Instead, "I contend it is simply a pose in which two persons are stacked up together with nothing but their feet to move." As a solution, O'Shea ended his talk on a nostalgic note, referring to the "gymnastic, callisthenic, and dramatic . . . dances of our forefathers" and said, "the sooner we can get back to those dances, the better it will be."[12]

While O'Shea's claims that jazz could "retard" students academically may have been met with some degree of skepticism, his larger antijazz position was common among Chicago educators during the first half of the 1920s. Critics pointed to the sexualized nature of jazz dancing and the ease with which young people could find outlets for dancing as a uniquely dangerous urban condition. Not only were the black bottom, the shimmy, and the Charleston seen as lewd and inappropriate acts, dance halls also provided opportunities for additional iniquitous behaviors. Edith L. Hilderbrant, a high school music teacher in Harvey, Illinois, a Chicago suburb, made this argument to her colleagues when she suggested the following:

> One wonders if much of the looseness in speech, morals, dress and conduct that characterizes the modern age is not directly traceable to the degradation of one of the fine arts, a universal art—music. Consider the popular music of today. It consists chiefly of ragtime and jazz.
>
> Music and dancing are so closely allied that the degradation of one means the degradation of the other. Jazz music means jazz dancing. It is difficult to say which proceeds in the process of degeneration. In all probability the two move downward together.
>
> Jazz dancing means the taking of liberties. Any inclination of the dancer to be bold and reckless is increased by the noisy, wild, simple *beat, beat* of the tantalizing music designed to appeal purely to the physical. The natural accompaniments of jazz dancing are slang, immodest dress, and the general lowering of moral standards.[13]

Lamenting such a social condition, Hilderbrant absolved students of much of the blame they may face. Instead, she pointed to teachers as bearing the real responsibility for such declines in morals and manners. She suggested, "But are not educators in some sense responsible for these conditions? Youth hardly can be blamed for them. The ignorant and uninformed cannot be held altogether accountable." Tellingly, Hilderbrant did not pretend that students had no interest in jazz, willing to acknowledge the challenge and responsibility educators faced. She did not argue the music had no appeal or that it could never attract listeners, that there could be no appealing side to jazz. Indeed, Hilderbrant was more than willing to concede the point that jazz has the ability to draw listeners in. The answer, for her, rested in an education that cultivated aesthetic taste. Youth were "ignorant and uninformed," attracted to jazz principally because they had not learned how to appreciate better music. Jazz preyed on the uneducated and unrefined. For Hilderbrant, jazz was a "tantalizing" music and children could be especially susceptible to its lure.[14]

Hilderbrant's analysis highlighted a common refrain among jazz critics, the perceived black-initiated sexualization of white girls. Like other critics, Hilderbrant coded her language as black. Her reference to the "wild, simple *beat, beat*" was certainly a value statement about musical competency, but also left little doubt about the black musicians to whom she was referring. Her critique also extended beyond aesthetics, certainly pointing to jazz as a musical bastardization at the base, though also extending the critique to extramusical consequences. In particular, young girls came across as helpless against the pernicious, "natural" decline in morality that accompanied jazz dancing. The music's appeal to the "purely physical" did away with any possible rational decision-making. Stripped of rational thought, and physically aroused, some form of sexual activity became the natural consequence. The "natural accompaniments of jazz dancing" were predictable results of the torrid thoughts jazz dancing created. And while Hilderbrant viewed them as victims, girls were also singled out for their "immodest dress," a criticism not equally leveled a high school boys.

Educators like Hilderbrant had allies in the orchestra world seeking to rid young people of their interest in jazz. During his thirty-seven year tenure as Chicago Symphony Orchestra (CSO) conductor, no musician loomed larger in the city than Frederick Stock. As one biographer noted, "Stock was *the* leader of musical culture in Chicago."[15] Stock, born in the small German town of Jülich, sought to develop a uniquely American traditional of music education. He recognized the need to further develop music education in Chicago's public schools and established alliances with the city's music supervisors to satisfy young people's "good musical cravings," though the conductor's interest in education went beyond concerts aimed at young people.[16] Stock actively worked to improve opportunities for music education. As early as 1920, the conductor lobbied the city's board of education to have the Civic Orchestra of Chicago perform regularly in public schools.[17] That ensemble, which he founded, was the first of its kind in the country: a training orchestra for high school age musicians. Stock conducted the group himself from its initial 1919 season until his death in 1942. Also in 1919, Stock, with the help of his public school music education colleagues, developed the CSO's Young People's Concerts in part to, as the *Chicago Tribune* editorialized, "wean school children from their affection for jazz."[18]

Speaking about the Young People's Concerts in 1922, Marion V. Cotton, head of the city's music supervisors said, "The problem is to satisfy good music cravings of children who have been surfeited with the excitement of degrading jazz."[19] Stock collaborated with the city's music educators to align the concerts with the city's music education curriculum. The concerts—held at 3:45 p.m., immediately after the school day ended—generally featured lighter classical works orchestral arrangements of folk-songs such as "Molly on the Shore."[20] The printed programs included helpful material for young students and their parents, such as a picture of the orchestra setup and descriptions of what the various instruments sounded like. Stock played to his audience, showing stereopticon slides of the composers and transcribed melodies the orchestra was playing as well as staging impromptu music memory contests.[21] Reviews in the newspapers often commented on how the normally stoic Stock appeared considerably more genial onstage during these concerts.[22] The conductor would allow roughly one hundred students of the twenty-five hundred which often attended onstage as his personal guests. References to jazz in the Young People's Concerts program notes were rare, perhaps an attempt not to tempt fate and provoke student interest. When they did appear, they were negative. One such instance was a 1925 concert that included a Johann Strauss waltz on the program. Describing the historical popularity of the dance, assistant conductor and program notes author Eric DeLamarter wrote how, in Strauss's day, the waltz was "as popular as jazz—and a great deal better music."[23]

Chicago Herald and Examiner music critic Glenn Dillard Gunn wrote how the Young People's Concerts "represent an important part of the anti-jazz movement."[24] Gunn described the concerts as "feasts of good music" and was clearly delighted to report young people—almost exclusively white young people—attending saw the concerts as entertainment, not education. The critic reported one boy said, "Mother, I don't know if I am supposed to learn something here, too, but I am enjoying these concerts very much." In addition to the music, Gunn praised DeLamarter's footnotes, saying they represented an "astonishing understanding of child psychology" and further praised DeLamarter's humor and ability to avoid being "prosy" in his writing. Financially, Gunn reported that the Chicago Symphony Orchestra generally lost money on the concerts, depending on the levels of attendance. Still, the orchestra justified them as a sort of civic responsibility to the city's young people. Finances aside, Gunn's real pleasure with the concerts was simply how much the students enjoyed them. He reported they often sang along "lustily" when a melody being played was projected on the large screen, writing, "The youngsters come again and again because they have a good time." For Gunn, not only were young people learning about music that was better than jazz, they were enjoying themselves while doing it.

Concerns of Chicago teachers like Hilderbrant and Maestro Stock were based on an obvious assumption: white young people in Chicago loved jazz. In 1922, in an effort to increase their revenue, the American Society of Composers and Publishers began requiring that radio stations pay a royalty fee when playing recordings that used their copyrighted music. Secondary school students responded with alarm that stations might have to limit or eliminate the amount of airtime devoted to jazz.[25] One fifteen-year old boy suggested students need jazz music as a corrective for boring algebra lessons. Jazz music at the end of the school day provided an adrenaline rush after the drudgery of classes. The student went on to swear the next day's lessons went much better after "listening to a bass drum beat the rhythm of a popular song."[26] Another boy reported he was "frightened to death" after hearing that stations may replace jazz fox trots with speeches and jokes. He said listening to people talk on the radio did not provide any needed relief after listening to people talk all day during school.[27]

Still, as critics recognized, the much more widespread appeal was not passive listening, but dancing. Chicago's ubiquitous dance halls were a draw for young people and a cursed annoyance for their parents.[28] While a student at the University of Chicago in 1928, a young Saul Alinsky, along with coauthor Constance Weinberger, studied the city's public dance halls and the clientele they attracted. Alinsky, like other jazz antagonists, saw jazz dancing as a catalyst for social ills, especially regarding the young and impressionable, though was sympathetic to the need for physical exertion and recreation.

Among other dance halls, Alinsky explained that the Dreamland Ballroom, a hall on the West Side, was a favorite for students at nearby Lane Technical High School.[29] A cavernous one-story barnlike building, the Dreamland was a white-owned dance hall that catered to a mostly Jewish and Italian clientele. It was there in 1916, that a group led by Charles Elgar became the first black jazz orchestra to play a long-term engagement in a white West Side dance hall.[30] Similar to other dance hall proprietors, Dreamland owner Patrick T. "Paddy" Harmon was certainly not above serving alcohol, despite the constitutional amendment banning its sale. After a successful undercover raid, the Dreamland closed briefly in late 1923 for violation of the Volstead Act. For his part, Alinsky made no effort to disguise the dancing he saw at Dreamland, simply calling it "immoral" and complained about how the Dreamland staff made no efforts to stop such behavior. The high school students Alinsky spoke to saw little problem with the jazz dancing taking place. One boy told Alinsky they just came to "dance and monkey around, that's all." Upon further questioning, he explained that he and his high school friend each hoped to "just take a good-looking woman out on the floor and squeeze a little, like they're dancing over there at the side." The boys then pointed out a woman who "comes there early every Sunday evening, picks up a fellow, goes out with him and comes back later for another fellow." Before returning to the dance floor, the boys told Alinsky more than half of the boys at Lane frequented the Dreamland.[31]

Speaking in 1927, Dreamland owner Harmon would tell the International Association of Policewomen, with little apparent irony, "You can't keep fifteen-year-olds out of the dance halls. If you do, they'll go to cabarets where they get liquor . . . a fifteen-year-old girl is a problem when she's full of liquor."[32] Still, Alinsky had been assured by staff during his visit that no girls under the age of sixteen were allowed, though Alinsky noted the only required evidence included each girl's word. Alinsky also pointed out the age range of female dancers while researching the White City Ballroom, a primarily white dance hall on Chicago's South Side, off Sixty-Third Street. Alinsky wrote, "The girls vary in age from naïve youngsters in their early teens to vicious middle-age looking women who make no attempt to conceal their purpose." Certainly, a major attraction of public dance halls was the freedom to share a dance with new people, what Alinsky called the "freedom of making acquaintants" that was a major appeal about social dancing. Still, skeptics like Alinsky worried that high school students could be dancing with partners their own age, or with the man in his mid-twenties who bragged that there would be "no virgins left in Chicago" if he had a car. Regarding six girls visiting from nearby Berwyn visiting downtown Chicago for an evening of jazz dancing, Alinsky remarked, "They seem very respectable and extremely stupid."[33]

In contrast to his treatment of high school students, Alinsky expressed little concern, or even annoyance, about the college students he saw at Dreamland. His major frustration rested in the widespread view that college boys were only interested in jazz dancing as a means for sexual conquest. He complained they do "all manner of queer and incomprehensible things."[34]

Alinsky even playfully mocked them, pointing out how many are unable to get a dance. In a coy reference to perceived sexual motivations to such men, Alinsky wrote, "The girls here are looking the men over with an eye to possible matrimonial intentions, and they have no time to waste on college boys, except perhaps a few of them who may believe in Santa Claus and stories about rich men's sons."[35] Yet, aside from briefly noting that one unnamed University of Chicago fraternity was on the White City Ballroom mailing list, Alinsky spent little time on the dance hall exploits of college students. His concern focused on secondary school students.[36]

Alinsky's disdain for college students was not unheard of among jazz opponents. In contrast to high school students, students in higher education were more often seen as guilty of spreading jazz and its associated vices. Edwin L. Miller, Detroit assistant superintendent, explained as much at the 1927 meeting of the North Central Association of Colleges and Secondary Schools, held in Chicago. He complained that jazz, along with Greek life and coonskin coats, were responsible for the academic failures of many first-year university students.[37] The assistant superintendent complained that the social life on campus, for such students, had developed into a priority over academic study. Miller's comments, especially compared to critics like high school educator Hilderbrant and other jazz critics, point to the contrasting attitudes about jazz for secondary and tertiary students. Whereas secondary students required oversight and a degree of protection from jazz's "hot rhythms," college students received a combination of discretion and blame for their interest in the genre.

Such disdain aside, Chicago was an enticement for higher-education students interested in jazz. A 1925 article in the magazine *College Humor* described Chicago as one of the country's most "syncopated cities," along with New York, Nashville, and "Pittsburgh." The article noted, "But do forgive us—we almost forgot Chicago!—'famed in song and story,' the wickedest city of them all, with its 'College Inn,' 'Bert Kelly's Stables,' and Rush Street Bridge."[38] The accompanying image, somewhat abstract, shows a fairly standard setup for dance halls in the 1920s: well-dressed students are sitting around tables while a jazz orchestra plays in the background, with a large dance floor in between. The Chicago dance halls were not only full of university students from that city, jazz enthusiasts from around the region also made the pilgrimage to Chicago for an evening of listening and dancing. In his memoir *Being Lucky: Reminisces and Reflections*, longtime Indiana University president and former student Herman B Wells recalled how Indiana University students made the roughly 230-mile drive to Chicago in the 1920s. He wrote that students would drive to "South Side Night Spots" to go dancing and listen to "great jazz."[39]

For their part, higher-education faculty in Chicago at predominately white institutions did not express the same level of outrage as their secondary school colleagues regarding the influences of jazz on their students, though some showed personal and professional disgust at the genre. In 1923, one University of Chicago professor equated jazz with William Randolph Hearst's "yellow journalism." He suggested both were corruptions of the more authentic, more discerning ideals of their respective fields.[40] Yet unlike their high school colleagues, higher-education faculty in Chicago rarely spoke out against the dangers they felt jazz held for their students. And while secondary school teachers often looked at jazz and worried, some higher-education faculty did not hide how much they personally enjoyed the music and dancing. At the Chicago College of Dental Surgery, a school in downtown Chicago associated with Loyola University, some of the faculty felt comfortable enough at the 1926 prom that they joined in the dancing, along with the students, to the music of a "red hot ten piece band." After the prom had ended, one faculty member reported, "Everyone left with a good taste in his mouth."[41]

In addition to Alinsky's work, other studies pointed to the preponderance of young people in city dance halls, often presented as a hazardous social practice. Paul Cressey's study, *The Taxi-Dance Hall: A Sociological Study in Commercialized Recreation and City Life*, verified Alinsky's claims about young people in dance halls. *The Taxi-Dance Hall* was originally Cressey's dissertation, conceived as a study of youth and social deviancy and later published as a book in 1932. Cressey began his study in 1928, telling his University of Chicago adviser, Ernest W. Burgess, he wanted to explore how dance halls served "young toughs looking for sexual stimulation."[42] Unlike Alinsky's study, which focused on recreational dancing for both dance partners, Cressey examined primarily the scenario of girls who danced with men for money. He asked, "Who are the young girls who at such an early age have been drafted into this dubious occupation"?[43] Cressey focused his research on Chicago's "taxi-dance halls" that used a pay structure in which men were eager to pay usually ten cents for a single dance with a female "teacher."[44] Many of the "teachers"—a clear misuse of the term, meant to hide the reality that dancers were paying for female companionship—were often teenage girls and young women in their early twenties, some of whom Cressey believed also worked as prostitutes. According to Cressey, after the final "blare from the jazz orchestra" of each song, the teachers moved to the next patron.[45] Noting such realities, Cressey's research was read as a sort of cautionary tale. In his preface to the book version, Juvenile Protective Association Executive Director Jessie F. Binford concluded that Cressey's study demonstrated the need for "wholesome acceptable social centers, commercial, as well as private and municipal, to meet the recreational needs of young people."[46]

Cressey focused part of his study on the Gaelic Park Ballroom, a non-taxi-dance open-air pavilion about five miles west of the University of Chicago. Like Alinsky, Cressey identified the public dance hall as a major attraction for high school students. Less restrained than in *The Taxi-Dance Hall*, Cressey expressed the common anxiety about what he saw taking place on the dance floor and afterward. Like the Dreamland and the White City Ballroom, Gaelic Park attracted, in Cressey's phrasing, "groups with quite different mores and folk-ways."[47] He described one girl, "presumably about age fifteen and very obviously of Slavic lineage," as dressing relatively appropriately. She wore a "dress of the form-fitting waistline-less variety which reaches the floor." In contrast, another girl wore a brown silk dress with "a prominent slit down the side." The dress of "older girls"—in their early to mid-twenties—was less of a problem for Cressey. Instead, he focused more on how they were more socially adept than the teenager girls. He noted how they waited until later in the evening to enter and generally seemed more comfortable dancing with and interacting with the boys. Cressey avoided discussing age and dress of boys at Gaelic Park altogether, though.[48]

As in other dance halls, Cressey observed young people in the mid- and later teenage years dancing together while the band "[ground] out elemental rhythm in the form of the recent jazz hits." The "twisting of the hips" of high school–age girls, for Cressey, was an evocative presentation of sexuality, one unsuitable for the public and especially for people of that age, writing that such behavior "has a tendency to excite many of the young men spectators."[49] Referring to the differences between how young and older girls behaved, he wrote, "The younger ones make the boys exert themselves considerably and so the young men appreciate these favors more before they receive their reward. But the older ones, as soon as the music stops, collapse in the arms of their partners, putting their arms about their necks. The boys endeavor to 'make hay while the sun shines' and so the periods between dances become periods for 'loving up' much more than during the dances."[50]

Despite his disgust at what took place inside the dance halls, the young University of Chicago researcher believed even greater threats lay ahead. Cressey was particularly perturbed that boys and girls who had just met hours earlier would leave in cars together at the end of the night. He remarked the "cave man lover catches his prize." In an exasperated and overstated deduction, Cressey intoned, "Jazz dancers were either whores or whore chasers."[51] In this analysis, the music and dancing were not ends in themselves; Cressey identified them as conduits for baser instincts. And while he was certainly not alone in his view, Cressey's analysis emphasizing sex was not universal. Some highlighted aesthetics, while others pointed to corrupted racial pride as jazz's primary sin. The "jazz problem" for critics, Cressey included, spoke more to their priorities and fears. This particular young scholar emphasized postdance intercourse, a perhaps overestimated realty, though a reality nonetheless.[52]

Studies such as those by Cressey and Alinsky highlight the enjoyment and frustration public jazz dancing caused in young people and adults, respectively. Responding to the general notion of physical danger, Chicago doctors also spoke out about the possible physical effects they believed jazz dancing could have on young people. Their view of the "jazz problem" did not highlight sex, but the possible physiological consequences jazz had on young people. In 1923, pediatrician Robert A. Black opened what he described as the city's first sanitarium designed specifically for children and young people on the outskirts of the city on South Marshfield Avenue. Black observed, "With the age of the flapper comes the age of the nervous child." The problem, the pediatrician observed, did not reside in the jazz clubs alone, as parents shouldered some of the blame for the mental anxiety of their children. Instead, "The arrival of father at home is the signal for an uproarious romp with jazz music on the phonograph. The child presumably is put to bed at 9 o'clock in such an excited state that 11 rolls by before the eyelids close."[53] Black saw the sanitarium as providing an antidote for a widespread problem, needing considerable medical treatment. To this end, the doctor did not mean the sanitarium to be an exclusive resting place for children from well-heeled families. Instead, parents were free to pay what they could afford.[54] The previous year, Dr. Lee A. Stone, chief of the Division of Hospitals, Social and Industrial Hygiene at the Chicago Department of Health, leveled a similar critique, though focusing more on inappropriate physical relationships the music could engender. Stone conceded that kissing, and even some "petting," was not necessarily bad between boys and girls—if properly chaperoned.

However, the doctor told his colleagues at a medical conference that jazz acted as an unacceptable aphrodisiac. He argued, "The sex problem and the teaching of social hygiene must be regarded in a common sense way. I hate jazz. It is deadly—simply perverted music used for the sole purpose of arousing the emotions." Stone willingly acknowledged young people do not always act responsibly, treating such indiscretions as an unavoidable part of growing up. However, including jazz in the question of young people and their physical desires represented an unacceptable scenario. He concluded, "No decent minded boy or girl will resent a chaperon as an intruder, if she uses common sense."[55]

The city's newspaper opinion writers and critics also lent their voices to the problems of jazz and young people. Like the city's doctors, they highlighted their occupational-specific concerns. Writing for the *Chicago Tribune*, music critic Edward Moore was an outspoken critic of the genre's influences on young people in the 1920s. Though he was steeped in the classical music world—his most read book was *Forty Years of Opera in Chicago*—Moore was no ideologue.[56] As a critic, he acknowledged that his opinions of various performers or concerts were precisely that, professional judgments, not absolute truths. Moore also had a sense of humor about his work. Regarding the number of negative responses he regularly received for his reviews, he wrote, "Let me but express an opinion, no matter how cautious and guarded, and I am quite certain to be severely castigated by letter for not having expressed another. . . . It would seem as though I had not wit enough to avoid being run down on a street crossing."[57] Yet despite his self-deprecation, his position as music critic for the *Chicago Tribune* allowed him considerable opportunity to shape conversations about music throughout the city and beyond. Moore was, quite simply, one of the most widespread and influential voices in the city's music world. He came out early in the 1920s as opposing jazz with a multifaceted criticism: a sense of nostalgia for "more uplifting" popular music, faulting jazz as being inferior given its development by black musicians, and the implications of jazz for young people. Writing in 1921, he optimistically suggested that "Jazz is dying," since publishers were selling less jazz sheet music. Moore did not attempt to hide his delight at this possibility, gloating, "The Senegambian buzz-fuzz will crawl into its canvas cover for a long silence"; in another, he described the genre as "imitation orientalism."[58] Still, Moore's primary critique of the genre rested on music terms. He complained that "one jazz number has sounded like another, and it is only with difficulty that one can remember the tune of any of them."⁵⁹ Regarding the genre's popularity among young people, Moore did not warn about any extramusical consequences that would inevitably befall them; his criticism did not include dire warnings about drinking gin or "petting parties." Instead, Moore lamented how listening to jazz's origins necessarily lowered musical standards for future generations. His baffling juxtaposition for jazz's geographic origins, citing both Africa and Asia, seemingly mattered little. What mattered was pointing out how jazz was coded as not white. Perhaps not surprisingly, as a solution Moore suggested teachers include more folk songs, particularly those from white European countries, in their lessons.⁶⁰

Moore's counterpart at the *Chicago Defender*, the city's most prominent black newspaper, did not share his views. If Moore's critiques about jazz were inflexible—jazz was inherently a musical degradation and should be keep away from young people—Dave Peyton's were more nuanced. In his history of early jazz, Court Carney has characterized Peyton's newspaper work as traditionalist: "Conservatism—in finances, in behavior, and even in performing—marked Peyton's columns in the newspaper."⁶¹ In his regular column, "The Musical Bunch," Peyton agreed with critics that jazz could be, in his words, "filthy, discordant."⁶² His critique was not with the genre per se, but with unrefined and crass "clown jazz." Though "clown jazz" was something not specifically defined (and perhaps did not need to be), Peyton did leave some space for jazz to have positive outcomes.⁶³ Unique for the time, Peyton held up the genre as a valid source of racial pride. At one point he suggested, "Let us show Gershwin that we, the originators of syncopation, can write jazz operas, which will very soon be as popular as the old standard operas." Yet while he had relatively moderate reservations about the genre itself, Peyton cautioned teachers not to allow their students to play popular tunes too early. In one column he wrote, "Once you get the training wrong, it is seldom that you get back on the right track" and reminded educators that students should be technically proficient with rudimentary exercises like scales.⁶⁴ Despite Peyton's temperate view of the genre, he acknowledged that jazz was not the "right track" for young people.

Superintendent Mortenson's Crusade

Especially in the first half of the decade, moderate views such as Peyton's stood in stark contrast to many in the Chicago Public School officials, none more so than the city's highest official in education, Superintendent

Peter A. Mortenson. Mortenson made student morality a focus of his 1918–1923 tenure as school chief, albeit a morality very much responding to current affairs. Among his earliest recommendations, Mortenson acted to eliminate the teaching of German from schools during World War I. In 1918, his first year in the position, Superintendent Mortenson persuaded the school board to avoid a full ban on teaching the "language of the Hun," initiating instead a compromise that reduced the amount of German taught in Chicago schools, but not eliminate it fully.[65]

While Mortenson saw the German language as an external threat, jazz was a home-grown menace, and the superintendent used his bully pulpit to ensure his message was heard. At the first 1922 Board of Education meeting, Mortenson took full advantage of that opportunity. Following an announcement about extending emergency authority for Chicago Public Library branches in high schools, Mortenson spoke passionately about the need to address "generally accepted principles" of student behavior. What followed was a list of regulations meant to rid students of their "modern" tendencies. The proposal, Mortenson added "evolved" from his discussions with deans and high school principals about problems in student behavior, both during the school day and outside of school hours. These included restricting use of automobile, "joy riding," not allowing students to smoke, forbidding jazz dancing, and limiting "dress extremes." To outline the various criticisms, Mortenson proposed a "Statement of General Principles." Specific to jazz and jazz dancing, Mortenson said: "We feel that no effort on our part can counteract this evil unless the parents realize the danger and help up maintain the standards. . . . we believe that jazz music has done much to corrupt dancing and to make it impossible for young people to learn the more refined forms of dancing, at the same time violating their taste for good music."[66]

The board unanimously accepted the statement. Mortenson, again, with the deans' and principals' input, suggested that students "keep early hours" and only attend school-organized dances. To help with implementation, the superintendent proposed, and the board approved, some 45,000 fliers be made up and taken home for students and parents to review and 500 additional posters be placed in secondary schools.[67] Mortenson made a point of appealing to parents to help recognize and curtail inappropriate dancing, asking them to educate themselves to the vices that swirled around jazz. This included forbidding students from going to cabarets he had not approved and chaperoning school dances so appropriate decorum could be maintained there as well.

White parents in Chicago reacted positively to Mortenson. They favorably reacted to the superintendent's multifaceted "war on jazz music, 'petting parties,' cigarate [sic], and extremes in dress, as indulged in by high school students."[68] Part of the problem Mortenson saw was the general lack of oversight of student behavior. Left to their own devices, the Superintendent reasoned young people would engage in any number of wicked acts, from "spooning parties" to drinking. Parents were quick to acknowledge the role home life must play in the return to previously accepted norms of dress and decorum. While not disagreeing with the superintendent's claim that schools were "the greatest source for good," parents welcomed the call for greater involvement in the home, the space they could influence the most. To further involve parents, and perhaps to verify some level of parental accountability, Mortenson sent out "pledge cards," which "thousands" of parents returned, according to the *Chicago Tribune*.[69] Such cards were meant to require parents to forbid jazz dancing or "petting parties" at their houses. The president of the Illinois Parent Teacher Association praised Mortenson's morality campaign, saying, "The solution of the problem lies even more with the parents than with the boys and girls themselves. She then added, "Excesses in dress, recreation and social life" should all be scaled back.[70] In another instance, a supporter sought an architectural solution to the moral problems believed to be plaguing the city's youth.[71] One *Chicago Daily Tribune* editorial writer applauded Mortenson's stand against jazz and went on to suggest the construction of a greater number of smaller high schools, with fewer spaces for students to sneak out for nefarious deeds. The editorialist went on to say that "a remedial agency would be a change of building policy in favor of more and smaller high schools, and the addition to the present buildings." The current "mammoth building" was poorly suited to help the child, "mentally, morally, or physically." This less "factory-like" approach, with closer contact between students and teachers would lead to less "dancing, jazz music, joy riding, and so on."

The superintendent's suggestions were also positively received by the school board, which declared there existed "too much jazz dancing, too much auto riding, and too much cigarete [sic] smoking among high school students."[72] Following that January 1922 speech, Mortenson sought to continue alerting the public to the danger jazz posed to young people. A pair of photographs published the same week as his speech in the *Chicago Tribune* demonstrated the difference between acceptable and lurid dancing. Mortenson himself oversaw the appropriate dancing technique for young people. In one photo, Mortenson observes as two students exhibit appropriate technique—visible space between the two dancers, no "hugging," and no "cheek rubbing," with the caption below reading, "AS THEY SHOULD DANCE" (below, on right). The other photograph shows a different scenario. In it, the two dancers' bodies are touching, and their arms are slightly lower than the other pair. The caption beneath reads, "NAUGHTY! NAUGHTY!" and continues, "The school board says students who dance as this picture shows are not nice" (below, on left).[73]

Mortenson did not direct his criticisms at boys and girls equally. Instead, the superintendent singled out girls in his call for reform. In his speech to the Board of Education, Mortenson asserted that jazz dancing "has done much to break down the respect for womanhood," though he did not say anything about the implication for masculinity.[74] The superintendent also went on to call out high school girls for "dress extremes" and questioned why their mothers would allow such immodesty. Yet Mortenson did not make that claim for boys and their fathers. The task for minimizing sexual activity was uniquely the responsibility of girls. Mortenson

Figures 1.1a and 1.1b. "NAUGHTY! NAUGHTY!" and "AS THEY SHOULD DANCE." *Chicago Daily Tribune*, January 27, 1922, 26.

would also stop short of calling for any universal set of rules—such as the acceptable length of a girl's skirt—instead appealing for "common sense" on the part of parents, teachers, and students.

As Kelly Schrum has pointed out in her history of girls' culture across the twentieth century, a generational conflict about appropriate dress also became apparent. In particular, the changes in Jazz Age clothing created a major rift between girls and adults about appropriate clothing choices. As girls made their dressing choices more independently, "conflicts between parents and teenage girls about clothing reflected larger tensions related to sexuality, femininity, age-appropriateness, and peer culture."[75] Both male and female adult critics pointed to the responsibility high school girls were shirking in presenting themselves according to their own ideals of beauty. The problem of new dress styles marked a restriction shared unequally by the sexes. When critics such Mortenson spoke of "immodest dress," they did not reference male students. Instead, the complaint about student dress was firmly grounded in notions of female sexuality; the notion of physical corporeal display was not felt equally by boys and girls. New trends in attire and grooming for young men were comparatively modest in the 1920s. Besides occasional references to "slickers"—based on the practice of boys slicking their hair back—reactions to the changes in male dress paled in comparison to girls and young women. Raised hemlines so often associated with the Charleston and other jazz dances, held up by critics as clear markers of social decline, uniquely resided in changes in female dress, not men's. High school boys were not critiqued for "immodest dress."[76]

Perhaps not surprisingly, girls in Chicago Public Schools complained that they were being unfairly singled out in the superintendent's critique, that similar charges were not leveled against boys. Confirming the increasing gap between youth and adults, high school girls countered that the superintendent misunderstood constructions of morality in students' lives, that he had no real basis to make such claims. One Hyde Park student argued, "Because a dance is freakish doesn't make it immoral." Others seemed genuinely hurt by the superintendent's argument and characterizations. One girl simply said, "Girls aren't wicked." The *Chicago Tribune* reported students responded by collectively saying such required dance-related changes were "bosh."[77]

However, long-term implementation of Mortenson's campaign was limited. His tenure as superintendent became increasingly politicized and ended acrimoniously in 1923, only a year after his speech.[78] Without leadership from the superintendent's office, no sustained campaign against jazz and its moral laxity remained possible. Four years later, a Chicago assistant superintendent briefly spoke out against the genre. At a speech for the International Council of Religious Education, Charles D. Lowry complained how "he recently turned the dial of his radio thirteen times and heard nine jazz selections." Unlike Mortenson, Lowry did not follow up his complaint with any action, nor did he express any concern about how such music may be influencing young people.[79] Why the lack of continued interest in condemning jazz for Lowry? Certainly, all superintendents operate, to some degree, like politicians. Lowry may have been trying to read the political tea leaves after the firing of his predecessors. Or like many educators, by the mid-1920s he may have recognized that jazz was not going away. Or perhaps both.

Social Reformers' Antijazz Efforts

Other prominent Chicagoans also lent their voices to the cause of minimizing jazz's impact on the city's youth. Jane Addams, the urban reformer and cofounder of Hull-House, used her position and influence to try and minimize young people's interest in what she called "the spirit of youth and the city streets."[80] Following the kidnapping and murder of fourteen-year-old Bobby Franks in 1924, by two University of Chicago law students, concerns about what the *Chicago Tribune* called "jazz spirit and youthful cynicism of modern boys and girls" reached a fever pitch.[81] Addams sat on a committee of prominent citizens—including conductor Frederick Stock and University of Chicago Settlement House founder Mary McDowell—tasked with starting a "save the children" campaign. The group came up with a musical solution to the social ills they believed were plaguing young people. Beginning in the suburb of Wheaton, communities were called on to hold "community sings and welfare meetings" in churches, assembly halls, and schools. The group reasoned such public performances would help instill in participants, especially the youth in attendance, the sense of community they believed the Jazz Age threatened. Unfortunately for Addams and her colleagues, the measure seems not to have generated much support.

Addams also served as a board member of the Juvenile Protection Association (JPA), the organization that had heartily endorsed Cressey's taxi-dance hall study. The JPA was highly critical of city officials for, they argued, allowing a litany of such immoral temptations to exist in a city full of young people. In 1928, the JPA issued a report highly critical of Mayor Thompson, arguing that Chicago's politicians were primarily beholden to "liquor, gambling, and vice interests" and not the interests of young people. JPA head Jessie F. Binford argued that the ultimate result of such depravity was a generation of "erring youth" and concluded by calling on the mayor to build "a school system that will abolish child labor and meet the needs of the children."[82] The JPA was also one of the few social agencies to draw attention to problems higher-education students faced, at least when circumstances favored their agenda. Binford spoke out after the 1925 death of Robert Allen Preston, when the Northwestern student shot himself in the head and collapsed into Lake Michigan. The *Chicago Tribune* noted, "Social workers, protectors of the young and ministers" believed Preston's death was caused by "the whirl of youth's jazz mania" and questioned whether his experiences were typical of "young college life." Yet while the *Tribune* and others emphasized that Preston's death should be seen as an individual case, Binford placed the blame on school authorities. She wrote, "It is pure hypocrisy . . . when well-informed people appear shocked at such revelation as were made by Preston. . . . The delinquency is among the adults, the fathers and mothers and teachers of the young."[83] Still, aside from the Preston affair, the JPA did not generally focus their criticisms on higher-education students.

A more aggressive organization, the Illinois Vigilance Association, headed by Rev. Philip Yarrow, also worked to rid the city of jazz and its associated social ills. In his 1954 obituary, the *Chicago Tribune* summed up his calling as a "vice crusader," an apt description of which Yarrow himself would have likely approved.[84] A British-born Congregationalist minister, he stepped down from the pulpit in 1920, partly for financial reasons, though his retirement did not mean Yarrow spoke out any less forcefully. In fact, while he had been involved with the Illinois Vigilance Association for nearly a decade—in 1916 he warned about the need for a "dry Chicago"—his 1920 clergy retirement allowed him to devote more time to critiquing the city's moral laxity. Though a middle-aged former minister, Yarrow argued he was uniquely qualified to study how young people spend their free time. He cast himself as the omniscient and tough "MAN WHO KNOWS."[85] And Yarrow espoused a particularly outspoken approach as he sought to alert Chicagoans to the dangers jazz held for young people. In Yarrow's view, all adults had the responsibility to monitor the city's youth, and he did not shy away from calling out those he thought did not live up to that responsibility. During a series of lectures to parents at Woodlawn Baptist Church in 1922, Yarrow criticized the parents in attendance as being "thoughtless, careless, and indifferent" when it came to youth and the city's jazz dance halls.[86] He went on to call for those "cesspools of vice" to be banished from the city. Yarrow was equally forthright discussing the direction he saw young people headed, or, more accurately, young girls headed. In one fictionalized short story, "Mabel's Downfall: Or, The Jazz Route to Ruin," he described the experiences of a wholesome white girl who had just turned eighteen and went out on the town with friends to celebrate. The "sex infuriating strains of the discordant jazz orchestra" lured the tragic character in and aroused sexual desires.[87] Having become addicted to jazz dances, Mabel also became accustomed to the overly sexualized nature of their gestations. Eventually, Mabel must "Display Her Charm for Money."[88]

Yarrow's actions were not outlandish in one sense: white clergy beyond Chicago also used their positions to speak out about the dangers they believed jazz posed for young people. In 1921, the Episcopal Bishop of Kentucky, Charles Edward Woodcock sanctioned a clericus resolution to ban jazz music and jazz dancing in Louisville churches, since "such forms of pleasure lead to jazz manners and jazz morals among the younger members of the church."[89] The clericus, the diocesan clergy's primary decision-making body, went one step further than condemning the music and called on adults to be vigilant and "examine rigorously" whether couples were sneaking out of church dances for what one newspaper report called "auto-spooning."[90] Accompanying this charge was a sort of apology that the diocese had been too lenient in dealing with jazz previously, a mistake they vowed not to repeat. That same year, the Methodist Episcopal Church, South, passed a similar resolution urging evangelists, pastors, congregations, and Sunday schools to abandon "jazz jingles so popular right now."[91] The clergy's concern did have some legitimacy to it. A handful of churches had brought jazz into the worship space, though such cases were more the exception than the rule. The two-person committee who put forward the resolution further suggested returning to the sole use of the hymnal, as it was "by far the greatest collection of songs in English." And one year earlier, a group of Missouri Sunday school teachers spoke out about how young people in their classes were increasingly talking about jazz, while simultaneously complaining clergy did not incorporate enough music into services.[92]

Still, Yarrow espoused an especially antagonistic approach to countering jazz dancing and other vices, even testing the limits of legality. In

1931, he was convicted of entrapment and served a six-month prison term. At issue was the book *A Night in a Moorish Harem*. Yarrow had one of his associates enter a North Side bookstore asking to purchase a copy. The store's owner, Walter Shaver, responded that he would have to order a copy and the man could return the following day to pick it up. When Yarrow's associate returned, he was accompanied by Yarrow himself and a squad of detectives who promptly arrested Shaver. Shaver was found not guilty in trial, but was bankrupted by the litigation. He countersued and Yarrow was found guilty of setting up the bookstore owner who was awarded $5,000. Meanwhile, sales in Chicago of *A Night in a Moorish Harem* doubled.[93]

Yarrow also edited the book *Fighting the Debauchery of Our Girls and Boys*, an indictment of young people's interest in jazz and its consequences. The nearly 500-page tome included chapters with titles like "The Peril of Jazz Music," "Hazel—A Victim of White Slavery Today," and "The Primacy of Prayer and Preaching in Saving Our Girls and Boys." Like-minded critics working in a variety of fields contributed chapters, each giving different perspectives on why young people should be separated from the iniquitous music. Notably, Yarrow included Superintendent Mortenson's full speech before the Chicago Board of Education in the chapter titled "Immoral Conditions in High Schools." The retired priest commented that it "ought to be read by every teacher and parent in America."[94] Chicago Bureau of Hospitals chief Lee A. Stone, the medical doctor who had previously spoken out about jazz as "perverted music" and the necessity of chaperones, likewise contributed a chapter.

Fighting the Debauchery of Our Girls and Boys also included a Yarrow-written chapter on the culpability of higher-education students. That piece, "Are the Moral Standards of the Colleges Low?," focused on why the social activities of college-level students, especially men, required condemnation. Certainly no progressive, Yarrow was unique among jazz critics for emphasizing the lived experiences and responsibilities of young men. He wrote, "When college men's minds are filled with lewd and vulgar thoughts concerning womanhood, the moral leadership of the coming generation is in rather questionable custody," and on one page he showed college women dressed in flapper dresses as examples of the "smut" of college magazines.[95] The chapter included tales of lust-filled male students stalking around university campuses in search of sexual conquests. Still, the retired pastor did hold out some measure of sympathy, quoting one university faculty who asked, "How can we impress boys and young men with a realization of the dangers that threaten them?"[96] Yarrow also cited portions of a lecture from University of Wisconsin professor Michael O'Shea—who had previously spoken to Chicago teachers about the dangers of jazz—on the pernicious influences of jazz as well as a secondary concern, motion pictures. O'Shea reported that he spoke to a student who could not study Latin because he could not get the "vamp" he saw in the motion picture out of his mind, continuing, "Dancing is so different now. It reminds me of the catch-as-catch-can hold."[97] For his part, the retired Congregationalist priest responded with a surprisingly moderate solution. Since "preaching" and "moralizing" would likely prove ineffective, activists must lecture to college men about the prostate gland and the possible sexually transmitted diseases they would eventually acquire if they didn't reform their behaviors.[98]

Yarrow's text also brought another instance of critiques leveled specifically at female students. In addition to bobbed hair and raised hemlines, Yarrow lamented the appearance at dance halls of "Check Your Corset" signs. As the reasoning went, unencumbered of such restraints, girls were able to move more "naturally" or "sensually" depending on one's opinion. Certainly, the relative freedom of movement that came with the black bottom, the shimmy, and the Charleston must have come as quite a shock to parents. This was a terrifying new reality Yarrow gladly exploited, exclaiming, "Mothers and Father of America-Awake!"[99] In one particularly overwrought example of the dangers associated with jazz, following a night of jazz dancing and "sex" a young man and woman took their own lives after realizing they were actually siblings.[100] For Yarrow, death was the logical conclusion of a proscriptive jazz-driven trajectory he saw young people facing. Where did this depravity begin? His story, "The First Step to Ruin," highlighted two places: the ice cream parlor and fruit stands.[101]

Changing Attitudes

Whether he recognized it or not—and he likely did not—Yarrow was fighting a losing battle. In fact, signs of that decline had begun somewhat earlier in some high schools. In 1924, C. D. Isaacson, a manager of the Chicago Civic Opera (CCO) visited the city's Marshall High School to promote the upcoming CCO production of *Aida*." Isaacson told students they did not need to know the "technical side of music" to enjoy the production and recounted stories of his boyhood when he attended opera performances. He went to contrast opera with jazz and "cheap books," telling students, "You are judged by what you like and if you like cheap things you are cheap; if you like fine things you are fine."[102] Unfortunately for Isaacson and other jazz critics, Marshall students had adequate opportunity to hear jazz. The same day of Isaacson's visit, the *Marshall Echo* reminded students about the upcoming "dance week," a two-week judged jazz dance competition. Providing the music for each round was the Marshall Jazz Orchestra, which also played for the school hop, among other events.[103] In fact, between 1924 and 1929, Marshall students organized additional school-based jazz ensembles, including the student-run, four-person "Parisian-Apache Orchestra" and the much larger faculty-sponsored "Social Orchestra."[104] By 1926 the latter was playing for students each Friday night. Indeed, while many educators, especially music educators, would hold their positions about it not being musically inferior, the permanency of the music in the late 1920s was becoming difficult to question. Jazz had longevity beyond a passing fad. The head of the Illinois Music Teachers Association may well have been trying to find a silver lining in the public's increasing acceptance of jazz when he said in 1927, "superheated jazz is on the wane."[105]

Even Maestro Stock's condemnation had abated by the middle of the decade. While he may never have been "temperamentally attuned to jazz," the Chicago Symphony Orchestra conductor did develop some appreciation for its musical validity. Speaking to the magazine *Musical America* in 1926, he said, "When [Stravinsky] came to Chicago to conduct . . . I introduced him to the first real Negro jazz music that he had ever heard . . . [He] went with me one evening to one of Chicago's 'Black and Tans.' We heard some excellent music . . . of an order entirely new to Stravinsky."[106] Still, acknowledging that jazz could have musical validity and arguing it had a valid place in music education were not the same. Stock, who regularly commissioned new compositions, was eager to help develop a uniquely American composition style. He may simply have become increasingly comfortable directing composers to jazz and what he called, "real American Negro songs" as a way to broaden the toolkit available to composers.[107] Such a mind-set would be consistent with the research, albeit limited, done on him as a curious and innovative musician. Regardless, by the middle of the 1920s he seems to also have moderated his earlier goal of minimizing or eliminating young peoples' interest in jazz. The slight about jazz included in the 1925 Young People's Concert program—that the waltz was similar to jazz, but "much better music"—had been removed when the orchestra performed the piece again in 1927.[108]

Superintendent Mortenson and other jazz critics in Chicago felt they were, in essence, fighting a musical invasion, one born in the South and carried into the Upper Midwest through the Great Migration. White critics foregrounded race in their opposition, often attaching a view of hypersexualized blackness to jazz dancing. The jazz problem, as critics in Chicago understood it, was made all the more daunting by a widespread ubiquity of urban dance halls. And the widespread interest white young people in Chicago had in dancing was certainly not synonymous with some interest in civil rights. Instead, jazz gave these young people a sense of self, members of a newly recognizable youth culture. White educators and their allies responded with measures to separate secondary school students from the plethora of dance halls Chicago contained. Yet that strategy backfired, making those jazz-drenched public spaces all the more enticing.

Chapter 2

White Educators and Jazz

Moral Outrage and Musical Corruption

A 1922 Mount Sterling, Kentucky, newspaper article rhetorically asked, "Will Jazz Kill School Music?" The author, a boys' school principal from Louisville, lamented the general impressionability of children and how a music from the "harems of the Barbary Coast" had become so popular among young people. He then evoked the decline of ancient Rome and identified jazz as a marker of impending national demise. Though bombastic in its presentation, the article must have found a sympathetic audience among those concerned about jazz's influence on the younger generation. Like many critics, the principal saw jazz not solely as a musical genre, but as a lifestyle, and a dangerous one at that. Emphasized here was jazz's inherent blackness, with the principal suggesting that origin was necessarily associated with sexual promiscuity. Jazz, in this imagining, was born out of African harems, and therefore young people must be protected from such hypersexualized blackness. Other educators, perhaps hopefully, viewed jazz's popularity among young people as a temporary craze and focused their critique on nostalgia, though not a nostalgia for some distant past. As one Chicago band teacher wrote, "[Jazz] is a disease that will have to be rooted out of the young folks if we are to return to the safety and sanity of pre-war years. And the School Band can be largely helpful in this."[1]

White educators recognized an external pressure, if not responsibility, to keep jazz out of their students' lives and teachers, especially music teachers, took up the charge. One prominent music educator wrote of the "grave responsibility" schools in general, and music teachers in particular, had in keeping further growth of jazz in check.[2] In his study of the KKK and conservative 1920s culture, Felix Harcourt argued that "Even those white Americans who celebrated jazz frequently tended to do so in a way that reinforced racial tropes."[3] For young white jazz fans, this racialized view of jazz meant meeting their friends at white-owned dance halls for music performed by black musicians (or, increasingly throughout the decade, white musicians imitating sounds of black artists). These young white jazz enthusiasts were typically not interested in some larger civil rights agenda; they enjoyed dancing. Yet this racial dichotomy was also true for white educators, who similarly framed jazz's aesthetics in racial terms, though less charitably. For those educators, jazz was often "bad" while European classical music was "good"; jazz was "syncopated" while its opposite was "beautiful." As Stanley Coben correctly has pointed out, "Most white American adults of the 1920s had been persuaded at an early age the Western symphonic music was the epitome of high culture, superior to any other, especially to what sounded to them like savage black 'jungle music.' "[4] And that racialized aesthetic distinction created a permission structure to keep young people away from jazz, using school hours to instill in their students what was "beautiful" in music.

Race and the Aesthetic Case against Jazz

In his 1922 address to the Music Supervisors National Conference (MSNC) meeting in Nashville, the French-born music critic Carl Engel presented a view of jazz that was impressively balanced, given the overwhelming opposition among educators at the time. Engel, head of the Library of Congress Music Division, presented his overwhelmingly white audience with a generally positive interpretation of jazz, one based on his reading of music history. On the one hand, he discussed composers who would have been widely accepted by the conference's attendees as being the highest quality, most notably J. S. Bach. Bach had long been a favorite of music teachers. Engel then considered musical dances, scandalous in their day, which Bach and other composers had appropriated into their scores. Engle reminded the audience—or perhaps taught them—that the "slow and stately" sarabande most commonly associated with Bach and Handel's music actually had "Moorish origins."[5]

Engel used Bach to criticize what he likely saw as a less-than-critical response to jazz by music educators. Engel used this sly reference to comparatively draw his audience's attention to the obvious characterization of jazz as a genre that had been developed by black musicians. By evoking the sarabande's "Moorish" early history, Engel pointed to race as an extramusical criterion that would have shaped many attendees' ideas about musical quality. The music critic was pointing out that genres not initially viewed in the most positive ways by white critics, often due to the race of their composers, in time came to be seen as more respectable. While citing the historically near-scandalous reception of various forms and dances (such as the sarabande), his audience would have seen as rather tame, Engel reminded them that the case with jazz was not the first time musical innovations were seen as scandalous. Quoting Byron, Engel went on to make similar cases for the waltz and other musical developments that were similarly shocking in their day. Without having to be directly accusatory, which may well have lost him any sympathy from his audience, Engel could point out such criticisms were, in part, products of a uniquely Caucasian viewpoint about race and musical aesthetics among nonwhites.[6]

By comparing the genre relatively favorably to European classical music, Engel argued that jazz had real musical merits. He attempted to tie the two genres together by arguing that they were essentially made up of the same components—pitch, rhythm, and harmony. Certainly, this was a relatively generic point, one that could be applied to the popular tunes and Broadway "hits" Engel *did* feel were in poor taste. Still, Engel's larger argument was emphasizing how teachers should not make wholesale indictments of the genre, but critically attempt to understand the techniques and skills required to play jazz. Engel attempted to strike some note of mutual interest with his audience. In his words, "Like any other type of music, jazz can be either good or bad."[7] That is, difference itself, race conscious though it was, should not be the sole criterion for musical value. Simply being dissimilar should not make jazz bad, since it required a unique skill set and its own performance standards. It is in this relativistic view that Engel made perhaps the most controversial argument of his speech, that good jazz is better than "the bad playing of Beethoven."[8]

Not surprisingly, Engel's speech did little to sway attendees' opinions. He faced an audience critical of his history-infused and relatively positive discussion of jazz and its merits. The official *Music Supervisors National Conference Journal* conference review confirmed how poorly received

Engel's lecture had been. After heaping praise on various aspects of the conference—the talks were "interesting," the banquet was "cordial," and the official photograph turned out well—the tone turned quite sharply on Engel's speech. Specifically, one reviewer noted the widespread attitude among music educators that "there is no proper light for jazz" and the talk "did not seem to throw any satisfactory 'new light' on the subject for [teachers]."[9] For his part, Engel was well aware that his speech was not well received, a point of some frustration. Writing later that year, he would decry the "puritanic sanctimony" of the audience, and referred to the music educators present as "self-appointed apostles of musical righteousness." Still, Engel held out hope he may have "smoothed the wrinkles on some of the prettiest foreheads in the assembly."[10]

On that count, Engel knew his audience. Prominent white music supervisors frequently spoken out against jazz, using language designed to help widen the gap between European classical music and jazz. Edward Bailey Birge, a music supervisor and "Professor of Public School Music" at Indiana University, shared an editorial with his music education colleagues from his hometown Indianapolis newspaper that highlighted its association with black musicians by evoking a caricatured black dialect. It read in part, "Let our mothers resolve t' slow down against th' pitfalls of o' jazz music. The' first impulse when a jazz orchestry begins t' mumble an' squeak an' rattle is t' kick up, or hug someone, or shimmy, or git fresh."[11] As such, jazz's blackness barred it from being included in any discussion of musical quality. In other cases, quasi-militaristic language often characterized their charges against jazz, with music educators casting jazz as an enemy to be conquered. The emergent musical genre was cast not as any sort of musical innovation, but as a military foe to be conquered. One Texas music teacher informed his colleagues, "The public schools, in the closest touch with the millions of children and younger people, are the strategic point of attack."[12] The editor of the popular music educator-focused magazine the *Etude* wrote about the "battle of jazz." Minimizing jazz might be an encumbrance to music educators' other professional responsibilities, but was one they were called on to take on as a certain sense of duty.[13]

No music supervisor wrote more passionately about jazz than Will Earhart. Earhart worked to spread and professionalize music education throughout his career. In the late 1800s he founded one of the first high school orchestras in Richmond, Indiana, and later moved to Pittsburgh, where he served as the city's first music supervisor.[14] In 1915 he served the standard one-year term as MSNC president. Earhart critiqued jazz for its musical failings, rarely mentioning any of the vices adults feared it brought out in young people. Yet unlike Bailey, Earhart was unwilling to discuss jazz based on musical components. Earhart refused to acknowledge that jazz was even music, as doing so would have given it at least the appearance of musical legitimacy. Instead, he opted for a more holistic critique, arguing that jazz was a sort of drug that caused "abdication of control by the central nervous system." Refusing to provide any music-based argument, Earhart had simply described jazz as a "disgrace" the year before Engel's MSNC conference speech, which he almost certainly attended.[15] Earhart was unwavering in his convictions. Even as late as 1930, when such full-throated critiques had fallen out of favor, Earhart continued to complain about the "ultra-modern" jazz.[16]

Yet as a music supervisor, and one of MSNC's most vocal advocates for public school music, Earhart recognized a certain silver lining in the genre's very existence. It gave instrumental programs a renewed sense of purpose. Never before had "good" music been under such a sustained and widespread assault as in the 1920s. Responding to such conditions, the music supervisor argued that school instrumental music programs were well suited to "safeguard against the ragtime and jazz that disgrace our age."[17] Earhart argued that the music educator should not "fit the pupil into a musical life, but to fit music into the pupil's life"—a call to have school music programs be the primary influence of young peoples' musical tastes.[18] Jazz's mere existence and appeal to young people meant public school education became more necessary than ever. As the reasoning went, music teachers needed to teach students what was musically acceptable and unacceptable before they learned it somewhere else.

In 1922, Earhart reviewed a new play, *The Reveille*, for the MSNC music teacher periodical, *Music Supervisor's Journal*. The publisher, Eldridge Entertainment House ("The House that Helps") had run advertisements in the magazine, asking music teachers, "Are You Fighting Jazz and Cheap Popular Music?"[19] If anyone had the qualifications to answer in the affirmative, Earhart was that person. In an effusively positive review, Earhart applauded the message the play would leave behind for students. Though he conceded that the play makes "no attempt at profundity," Earhart commended the simplicity and lack of technical requirements, suggesting the play's message would come across clearly, unencumbered by a convoluted plot.[20] In his less than one-page review, common in *Music Supervisor's Journal* at the time, Earhart noted the "powerful lesson" the play would leave behind, presumably among the students as well as their parents.

Concluding his review, Earhart implored his music education colleagues not to consider any other operetta or play without first reading *The Reveille*.[21]

The Reveille author Alice Brockett, herself an assistant music supervisor in East Orange, New Jersey, did not shy away from her larger purpose in writing *The Reveille*. In her introduction to the play, she wrote: "The General Federation of Women's Clubs has adopted the slogan, 'Make good music popular and popular music good.' This play is an attempt on the part of the author to present this idea in dramatic form and to aid in the campaign against jazz and cheap popular music; making an appeal to the youth of the day to choose the best music."[22] Indeed, the play's mere existence—that a music administrator took the time to write it—attests to the level of concern Brockett and her counterparts felt about jazz. It also hints at a certain lack of knowledge and oversimplified position music supervisors and teachers held regarding jazz. Read today, the play seems like a racialized caricature of music educators' greatest fears and wishes about the music and its effects on young people.

Brockett personified various musical components and some extramusical iniquities. That is, she cast musical ingredients like rhythm and harmony as human characters that could speak to and articulate the role they should play in music; she anthropomorphized music. The play revolves around a handful of characters, all seemingly young boys and girls: Music (the Queen of Sound); her friends Melody, Rhythm, and Harmony; Syncopation ("a relative of Rhythm by adoption"); Youth ("a boy of today"); Jazz ("a character of today"); and the ten imps who follow Jazz (including Vanity, Frivolity, Boisterous, Lawless, and Don't Care). When the play begins, Jazz has just stolen Harmony, and her friends are looking for her. Youth shortly appears, and confesses he has started to develop an interest in Jazz. This worries Music, Melody, and Rhythm, who Youth had loved and been devoted to for so long. Meanwhile, Jazz expresses his delight in the potential loss of Harmony, gloating, "Music won't be worth a thing without those treasures—they make her powerful."[23] After being told "The choice is yours alone," Youth realizes Jazz's true evil nature, and chokes him, thus freeing Harmony. Afterward Syncopation pulls off Jazz's shirt, exposing his various tattoos.[24] Syncopation then tells the others, "[Jazz] ruled the savage tribes in the South Seas before he ventured here. His was the voices that urged them to the worst, with incoherent cries and hideous, spine-chilling sounds."[25] Having reunited with Music, Rhythm, Harmony, and Rhythm, Youth affirms his loyalty to them as the play ends. Jazz is banished, never to be heard from, or perhaps simply heard, again.

One theme in *The Reveille* that overlapped with teachers' understanding was the role of the city as a sort of jazz incubator. As Brockett's play suggests and many teachers believed cities were not only considerably more welcoming places for jazz than the countryside, but urban life embodied a sort of artificiality that distinctly contrasted with the more natural and idealized rural life. In the play, part of Jazz's plan to co-opt Youth involves keeping him so busy that Youth will not have time to "leave the city."[26] Part of Jazz's plan was the keep Youth away from the presumably more idealized countryside and overwhelm him (Youth) with the cacophony of noise the city offered. Unable to escape to the country's idealized natural goodness, Youth would become addicted to the unnatural frenetic pace of the city and its jazz.

Certainly not a candidate for the canon of great plays, *The Reveille*'s general tenants were consistent with what white music teachers thought about the genre, especially its origins and diffusion. Brockett ended her play with the revelation that "Jazz" (the character) had emigrated from the "South Seas." As Youth himself acknowledges, jazz was "of Savage origin."[27] This revelation acted as a key point in Brockett's argument, one that would not have been lost on her audiences. Jazz's distinct lack of social restraint, its inability to adapt to contemporary standards of dress and decorum, embodied a sense of nonwhiteness in the worst way. Jazz, the character and the music, had failed to culturally evolve and, by implication, whites had. Instead, jazz represented a sort of primitivism, imported from the global South. Jazz was not only loud and grating on the ears, but its color embodied a distinct lack of décor and acceptable contemporary behavior.

Many agreed. At the 1921 National High School Conference, one music educator complained of jazz's "imitation orientalism."[28] Another teacher referred the jazz's "syncopation" and deemed it "unnatural."[29] Similar references to jazz were common among critics ranging from physicians to magazine and newspaper publishers. In an article on how the Italian island of Trieste could "cure" the jazz habit, the one *Chicago Tribune* journalist referenced "oscillatum Ethiopius," though denied the term was prejudicial. Instead, it was excused as the term scientists used when discussing jazz.[30] And writing in *Cayton's Monthly*, a Seattle-based Republican-leaning monthly, Madge R. Cayton similarly articulated such prejudicial views when she wrote, "[Jazz] is a result of the savage musician's wonderful gift of progressive retarding and acceleration which is guided by his sense of ewing." Cayton went on to argue that jazz, which came to

America from West Africa, was kept in check during slavery, but found an audience in "impatient youth."[31]

On those rare occasions when educators discussed jazz in musical terms, jazz's association to a caricatured sense of unrefined blackness lay just beneath the surface, widely enough understood that it did not need to be acknowledged. Though educators assigned various pejorative adjectives to jazz, the genre was most often contrasted simply with "good" music. A music school director from New Jersey suggested in 1923 that student interest in listening and dancing to jazz "does not decry at all the learning and hearing of good music in school."[32] Such a Manichean dichotomy—jazz as "bad," European classical as "good"—was typical in early 1920s music educator rhetoric. Jazz, characterized in such a way, was an inherently inferior genre to virtually any other, and the musical opposite of Western classical music. A Texas music educator similarly articulated the need to turn jazz devotees into "serious music lovers" who attend "good concerts" and listen to "good music." He went on: "The widespread hearing and buying of good music is necessary as a stimulant for the stimulation and publication of good music."[33] Anne Shaw Faulkner, the prominent music appreciation proponent and textbook author similarly exemplified this approach. Writing in the *Ladies Home Journal*, she argued that jazz brought about "degraded . . . musical opportunities" for students. Such qualitative statements among educators dominated much of the discussion about the genre in the first half of the decade, as teachers avoided any substantive discussions about jazz and its musical merits.[34]

This emphasis on jazz's imagined origins also found its way into cartoons. A drawing appearing in a popular music educator magazine the *Etude* rhetorically asked, "Will our dance orchestras come to this?," and the accompanying picture shows an all-white dance orchestra playing in the jungle (see fig. 2.1).[35] A sense of incongruity saturates the image. While the orchestra is neatly dressed in tuxedos, percussionists play on pots and pans, the conductor uses a gun to lead the orchestra, and one musician holds a shrieking black cat. Though no black musicians are present, the jungle serves as a convenient, if not more indicting, substitute, as it slowly consumes the white orchestra it surrounds. The text underneath—"Will our dance orchestras come to this?"—makes the same claim regarding music, while reinforcing a clearly racialized dichotomy. White orchestras are "ours"; jazz belongs to the Other. Thus, the cartoon spoke not only to present conditions, but also a possible dystopic future, one in which the primitive becomes modernity's undoing.[36]

White Educators and Jazz | 47

Figure. 2.1. "Will Our Dance Orchestras Come to This?" *Etude*, May 1925, 322.

Viewed today, the image seems inconsistent, or, at least, contradictory. How could two concepts—jazz, a recent musical development, and the jungle, a historic referendum of humanity's progress—coexist? Yet this juxtaposition, connecting the primitive and modern, was an increasingly recognizable feature of early-twentieth-century life. In fact, that tension between modernity and primitivism, real or imagined, played on a larger sense of unease throughout the decade. In her study of the imagery of evolution in the Jazz Age, Constance Areson Clark suggested the two archetypes were not designed to be consistent, writing, "For many people— and not only anti-evolutionists—images of simians suggested grotesque caricatures of humanity, and the images of 'primitive' people seemed to confirm deeply felt anxieties about the modern."[37] As Clark suggests, the inconsistency was the message, one that drew out fears among those who identified with a wounded, though certainly not extinct, white Victorian worldview. The science-driven sense of encroaching blackness also overlaid with worries among parents that their children frequented dance halls to dance to "primitive" music. That is, "In the confusion of modern and primitive, in the symbolic universe of that uneasy decade, when old verities seemed to slip into uncertainty, jazz was a potent symbol."[38]

Though there many have been limited student readership of the *Etude*, young people did encounter similar descriptions in music education texts that included less-than-flattering references to African Americans, the Chinese, and other groups. Marion Bauer's and Ethel Peyser's *How Music Grew: From Prehistoric Times to the Present Day*, originally published in 1925 and intended for high school students, took a distinctly evolutionary approach by noting, "The African shows us the steps from the primitive . . . to . . . music as an art." Further, "Our American Jazz is the result of our desire for strong rhythms and shows that we, for all our culture, have . . . in us . . . the savage's feeling for movement."[39] Bauer and Peyser were not alone in drawing on the theme of the primitive. The description of multiple nonclassical genres—and their performers as "primitive"—was a common theme in such texts. Anne Shaw Faulkner wrote in her high school text, *What We Hear in Music: A Course of Study*, that "As all music developed from primitive man, and as America is possessed of folk music derived from two primitive races, the Indian and the Negro, it is but natural that American musicians should feel that our great national music comes from these sources."[40] Like Faulkner's prose suggests, race operated as the clearest dividing line for such characterizations. Whites were cast as clearly more evolutionarily developed, a condition their music embodied. Louis C. Elson exemplified this music/evolution connection in his work. In his *The National Music of America and Its Sources*, he describes Native Americans as existing "on the lower savage plane." In contrast, Elston described the English folk song, and its composer, with the more dignified "yeomanry" of a "well-defined type."[41]

And such characterizations existed outside music education as well. As Zoe Burkholder has pointed out, many educators in social studies, history, and English classrooms during the interwar period adopted various techniques for incorporating discussion of race into the curriculum, generally conflating race with nationality. For example, Italians were taught as a distinct group since they came from a distinctly defined country, what Burkholder terms "Race as Nation."[42] *What We Hear in Music* and similar texts adopted a parallel organizational schema. Faulkner divided her book into four sections, the first of which was "Learning to Listen: National Music." She then proceeded to describe the characteristic music of various European countries, attributing given musical characteristics to homogenous characterizations of general deportment and attitude. The Irish "have ever retained their love of music, but their songs are a strange mixture of joy and sorrow, which is characteristic of the Celt."[43] Yet as Burkholder correctly observes, such a characterization conflating race with nationhood presented a major obstacle for describing African Americans, regardless of the subject. The default racial view of the United States in the texts Burkholder analyzed as well as *What We Hear in Music* was Caucasian. As a result, African Americans become a "Nationless Race."[44]

Speaking at a 1923 MSNC conference about a high school music class she observed one New Jersey teacher recount how a student responded to listening to European classical music: "After a few minutes one boy said: 'Ah, come on! Cut this out! Give us some Jazz! I like the real stuff!' [The students] all agreed, and were very obviously having a good time while the 'jazz' was going on."[45] Recognizing young people's interest in jazz, educators were occasionally willing to incorporate the music into their classrooms for various reasons. Certainly, such teachers represented a minority in their profession as most found jazz crude, indecent, and a corrupting influence on young people's lives. Yet those who found a use for jazz in the classroom embraced the faster tempos and seemingly "frenetic" pace of the music, with relatively little concern that it could musically or morally debase their students. As early as 1919, an Ogden, Utah, typewriting teacher had students practice their typing exercises while playing jazz in the classroom, arguing that the relatively fast tempos served as useful background listening as students tried to quicken their typing exercises. Contrasting jazz with "canned music," she also noted how the popularity of the genre among young people meant students looked forward to and enjoyed her class.[46] Luise Freer, director of physical education for Women at the University of Illinois, suggested a similar approach in girl's physical education classes, having experimented with it herself. Here, the music could invigorate and energize girls as they go through their exercises. At one high school conference, she told her colleagues, "In a corrective gymnasium today . . . you will see a girl in one corner standing on her head, another swinging on a trapeze, a third using a punching bag, all to a jazz tune on the Victrola."[47] And toward the end of the decade, some female teachers also slowly began to physically appropriate jazz culture into their own dress styles. Students at Shortridge High School in Indianapolis were pleasantly surprised when they came back to school in August 1927 from summer vacation and found two of their teachers had their hair "bobbed" over the break, the quintessential flapper haircut.[48] And a New York City substitute teacher made headlines for similar transgressions, playing jazz in classes for "relief" after math, Latin, and other courses.[49]

Pedagogical Efforts to Dissuade Young People from Jazz

Still, condemnation was not enough. Educators understood jazz's pull on young people, and sought to strategize its demise. Critics and proponents of jazz agreed on at least one point. Jazz was meant as dance music. Francis Elliot Clark, once an Iowa music teacher and longtime education director for Victor Talking Machine Company, referred to jazz as the "syncopated clap-trap that appeals only to the heels."[50] Similar to music educators, though fewer in number, dance teachers—often termed "Dance Masters"—saw jazz as a threat to their profession. Dance Masters worried young people would lose interest in learning the waltz and other dances as jazz became an increasingly popular alternative. And like music educators, though not affiliated with public schools, dance teachers greatly feared how such changes would affect their profession as young people incorporated jazz steps into more conservative dances or lost interest altogether. One Chicago Dance Master aptly summed up the attitudes of his colleagues when he said, "Jazz music has had a marked effect of degenerating the dance."[51] Dancing Masters recognized two culprits in their public education campaigns to discredit jazz dancing: women and the city. During a 1921 convention of two dancing education organizations, one female instructor told the *New York Times*, "I firmly believe that 80 percent of the faults of position on the dancing floor are chargeable to the girl. . . . It seems as if the girl of today cannot dance unless she has a death grip on the neck of the man with whom she is dancing." Another spoke of how "Close dancing, a product of the cities, was due to the crowded ball room and dance hall, where it [is] impossible to spread out."[52] Encouraged by the success of the implementation of the Eighteenth Amendment making alcohol illegal, in 1922 a group of New York City dancing instructors even lobbied unsuccessfully for the revival of the "Duke Bill," legislation that would have regulated dancing and made most jazz dances illegal.[53]

Folk dance advocates also saw the disgust over jazz as a problem folk dancing could possibly address. Drawing a clear distinction with salacious jazz dancing, European heritage folk dancing was promoted as good and natural self-expression, an example of natural beauty, a cure for "bad health," and even, somehow, "a cure for broken hearts."[54] And, not coincidentally, folk dancing overwhelmingly involved dances originating from European countries. The American Folk Dancing Society itself was organized in 1905, with the assistance of New York City physical education supervisor Dr. Luther Gulick. Dr. Gulick enthusiastically supported folk dancing, thinking it could teach "large body movement" as well as help students understand individual and group dynamics.[55] The "folk dance movement," as its proponents called it, also had success beyond the northeast. Gulick's Portland Oregon counterpart, Professor Krohn, instituted folk dancing in that city's public schools in 1915, again with the aim of providing students with exercise while participating in a more "wholesome" form of dance. One supporter of Krohn's compared the benefits of folk dances to the increasingly popular jazz dances. He wrote, "We have bartered the courtly minuet for the syncopated rhythm of a voodoo orgy . . . the nasal whine and blare of the musical monstrosity known as 'jazz.'" Referring to an event at a public park in which up to one thousand Portland students participated, the unnamed editorial writer again praised folk dances as "revelations of sheer, unsullied beauty."[56]

Elizabeth Burchenal was undoubtedly the most prominent proponent of school folk dancing. The chair of the American Folk Dance Society as well head of the Committee on Folk-Dancing of the Playground Association of America, Burchenal began teaching New York City students and educators how to perform such "aesthetically pleasing" dances in the early 1900s. In the Preface to Burchenal's signature text, *Folk-Dancing and Singing Games*, physical education supervisor Gulick praised her efforts, saying, "Miss Burchenal's work has been a definite, concrete force making this language in America speak the word that is true and wholesome" and praising her for teaching "school children in congested areas in New York City."[57] Gulick's comments allude to the particularly urban justification for school folk dances. Proponents such as Burchenal and Gulick believed folk dancing allowed students living in cramped New York City conditions a proper outlet for exercise and youthful energy. Images included in *Folk-Dancing and Singing Games* also provides visual, if also anecdotal, evidence for Gulick's numerical claim. The original 1909 text also includes instructions for each dance, pictures to indicate how portions of each dance look when properly carried out, song texts, and music arranged for the piano as accompaniment (the book was subsequently republished in 1913 and 1922).[58]

Burchenal saw in jazz, as well as its negative reception among educators, a potential opening to help solidify folk dancing in schools.

In her work to promote folk dancing, Burchenal emphasized what she saw as its relative whiteness, contrasting folk dances with the universally understood blackness of jazz. Burchenal's understanding of musical and moral ethics stopped at the color line. Speaking to music educators at a 1918 MSNC conference, she carefully pointed out how the folk dances she taught young people were necessarily white: "If there is to be the great American School of Dancing, it must be the school of dancing that incorporates the folk dances of the nation, and it is not the Indian dance and it is not the Negro dance that we build the American folk dance upon. . . . We have this great tremendous wealth of treasure that has been brought to us by other countries, which we must absorb if we want to take advantage of it."[59] Burchenal drew on that inherent whiteness as sufficient justification of the dances' wholesomeness. Indeed, the second part of the title of *Folk-Dancing and Singing Games* belies its necessarily European focus—*Twenty-six Folk-dances of Norway, Sweden, Denmark, Russia, Bohemia, Hungary, Italy, England, Scotland and Ireland, with the Music, Full Directions for Performance, and Numerous Illustrations*. As if to underscore this point, she had young girls in her instruction manual clothed in white dresses, perhaps to further highlight the natural purity of the dances included. Referring to jazz, she was especially pointed in her critique, arguing that it inevitably led to the "mongrolization" of American society.[60]

Burchenal's European-heritage based views aligned with other educators seeking to connect European classical music to a ruralized, wholesome, and natural whiteness and jazz, by extension, its opposite. Music educators largely agreed with Burchenal's assessment of the countryside as a sort of idealized bucolic landscape, though not one without hardships. While educators were quick to acknowledge problems of staffing and funding in rural schools, they simultaneously bragged about the lack of penetration the believed jazz had made into rural areas. Contrasting with the artificial nature of the and the urban environments in which it flourished, such educators argued that European classical music contained some natural properties that would naturally interest students.[61] Many teachers in rural communities were gleeful that the "jazz problem" had not yet reached them, even bragging about its lack of penetration. One educator who taught in rural Arkansas boasted that his students, and rural people in general, enjoyed "better music, not jazz."[62] A teacher at Iowa State Teachers College would point out, "A farmer is very closely associated with nature, and nature doesn't jazz much."[63] Indeed, educators saw jazz as exemplifying the artificial and unnatural. The countryside, relatively untouched by modernity, acted for critics as a sort of gauge of how far contemporary urban society had devolved. Carl Withers (writing under the pen name James West) found that, at least in rural Missouri, such attitudes had changed relatively little by the late 1930s and early 1940s. One Missourian told him, "Jazz music and swing interest only a few of the young. Adults often say, "I can't stand that *jerkin'.*""[64]

Unfortunately for Burchenal and her allies, the school folk-dancing practice was noticeably on the decline just as jazz was gaining popularity among young people. Despite earlier success in New York City in the 1900s and 1910s, folk dancing never gained widespread traction among music educators. Burchenal's 1918 appeal to the MSNC did not spark the widespread implementation she had hoped. She continued to speak and write about the importance of folk dancing in the 1920s, though the practice slowly fell out of favor. Burchenal also offered up folk dancing as a solution to the less wholesome dances young people overwhelmingly preferred. In 1926, Burchenal wrote in the *National Education Association Journal* about "Reviving the Folk Dance" and emphasized the dangers of jazz dancing—and offered up folk dancing as the answer. She argued, "The Dance Evil has many phases. The dangers of improper dancing are more numerous and subtle than is implied in most condemnations of the commercialized public dance hall."[65] Still, the time of Burchenal's message effectiveness had passed. Perhaps most importantly, the danger and excitement many young people associated with jazz simply did not exist in folk dancing. Not coincidentally, folk dancing also did not appeal to students as much, since any adult endorsement of the genre likely lessened the thrill. Though not universally accepted, the predictability of folk dancing, with its set dance patterns, did not have the pull that jazz did. The risk of being caught practicing jazz in schools, of being involved in something new, a level of unchartered musical territory, only made jazz more enticing. Any adult sanctioning of folk dancing likely intensified the relative apathy students felt compared to jazz's alluring tunes.

While folk dance proponents offered a ready-made solution, among music educators, efforts among music educators to stop the spread of jazz were often haphazard. Despite rumblings about the genre, there was no "official" MSNC policy about jazz or methods to stop it. Yet this lack of an organized strategy certainly did not mean that educators were not taking the matter of jazz seriously. At the school and district levels, teachers implemented various methods to instill in their students acceptable musical values and to persuade them of jazz's iniquity. Perhaps most directly, many teachers and school administrators altered their music programs. In some cases this meant essentially meeting students where they were musically. One Illinois teacher noted that she had to put away the "beautiful music she had selected" for her glee club and begin the school year singing "college tunes" with the students as a sort of compromise. She blamed "jazz" for the need to change her lessons plans and vowed that her "first goal" was to wean students off it and only then toward better music.[66] Mabelle Glenn, who taught and supervised in Kansas City, Missouri, urged her colleagues to take advantage of newly available technology to combat the "jazz problem." She allowed her students to check out educational phonograph records, just as they could borrow books from the library. She boasted, "As a result, there is very little demand in Kansas City for the jazz type of records."[67]

Some music educators and administrators sought to ban the music from schools altogether. Such prohibitions included anything from practicing jazz on school property to listening to jazz records on the school Victrola. A survey by the Texas Federated Music Clubs, likely carried out in 1922, found some fifty-four schools out of the seventy schools surveyed had in place some policy prohibiting jazz in which under no circumstances could the music be heard in schools. Before being published in *Music Supervisors' Journal*, the music clubs' findings were presented at that state teachers' convention, bringing together educators from different disciplines, informing a cross-disciplinary discussion of solving the "jazz problem."[68] Similarly, administrators in Chicago's Senn High School received considerable newspaper coverage when they vowed to eliminate "jazz, immodest dress, joy riding, etc."[69] Though the school's teachers grimaced at the implication that student morals had slid far enough that such action was necessary, they did not disagree about the general need for reform. The Senn jazz ban was cast as an exercise in "citizenship" and a discussion of students' responsibilities to their school, community, and each other. Still, neither of the cases in Chicago or Texas rose to the level of one Spokane music teacher's efforts. He attempted to sue, unsuccessfully, the leader of a popular local jazz orchestra, claiming it was "perverting the ideal of classical music held by the people."[70]

Part of any necessary strategy to lessen jazz's appeal to students was replacing it with "better music" in such a way as to ingratiate it to students. Speaking at a conference for high school teachers, one educator complained about jazz as "pernicious to high ideals and . . . the Symphony Orchestra." He then offered up a solution, that "the greater the appreciation [for classical music], the greater the inspiration."[71] As one music teacher pointed out, "You must make them want something else and give them something else they can appreciate before you take away what they already have and can appreciate."[72] Hoping to instill this desire, teachers also fought against jazz with a relatively new pedagogical tool, the music memory contest. Such competitions, many educators hoped, would not only engage students in a more refined genre of music, therefore combating jazz's influence, but would also positively appeal to students' natural competitiveness. The formula for music memory contests was simple. Local newspapers would include a list of works that may appear in the competition itself, which was often separated between elementary and high school levels. One such list in the Portland-based *Oregonian* included some relatively popular works alongside the standard classical canon; "Swing Low, Sweet Chariot" was included alongside Mozart's G minor symphony. Students would have the week to "practice" listening, generally on a phonograph at home or school, carefully noting various identifying characteristics of each piece.[73] Students did not necessarily have to be able to play an instrument to be involved in music memory contests; they only needed to remember the advertised pieces during the competitions. And, as the above comments suggest, students could learn to "appreciate" the music without having to learn to perform it.

The competitions themselves were often much publicized events, and, if possible, held in auditoriums with various music businesses serving as sponsors. In Detroit, the final round of the contests was held in Orchestra Hall with the city's symphony orchestra providing the music as students who achieved perfect scores competed for awards. These included trophies, small financial prizes, gift certificates, as well as public recognition with the winners having their pictures and names in local newspapers. Giving out awards was seen as a way to further draw students' interests away from jazz since they served as tangible motivation. Teaching students to identify and appreciate "better" qualities in music partially through such motivations was understood as less cumbersome—and ideally more successful—than attempting to directly change their opinions about jazz.[74]

Some of the first such competitions, albeit rather informal, were organized as early as 1909 by Indianapolis music supervisor and later Indiana University Public School music professor, Edward Bailey Birge. Mabel E. Bray held what was in all likelihood the first organized music memory competition in 1916 in Westfield, NJ, and made a point of inviting the media and encouraged community attendance. The contests spread quickly. In 1922 there were 405 such contests nationally; two years later as many as 1,193.[75] An estimate from that time suggested three-fourths of states had at least one music memory contest during the school year.[76] And, of course, such competitions also happened exclusively at white secondary schools. If white educators had considered the relative financial privilege of being able to afford such competitions compared to their counterparts in black schools, they never acknowledge that reality.

Over time, though, it was precisely the emphasis on competition over music that, along with the increase in instrumental music, precipitated the decline of the music memory contest.[77] Ironically, the criticism that precipitated the decline of music memory contests was similar to the critiques often heard regarding jazz. The amount of class time devoted to "listening drills" was increasingly viewed with suspicion throughout the second half of the 1920s. As the decade progressed, the idea of advertising in the newspaper, which students won $1 at a weekend memory contest appeared to be in increasingly poor taste. Teachers worried that the desire to win money, trophies, or other prizes for their students and school was increasingly driving music education, not student interest in music. Music educators also began to consider what effect such competitions would have on the music they were ultimately trying to promote, that external motivations conflicted with, not complimented, the larger goal of teaching students to appreciate classical music. Percy Scholes, the famed English music appreciation champion and music memory contest advocate likely cast the death knell when he wrote in 1935 that the overemphasis on competition over music would eventually lead to "desecrating music."[78]

A Changing Reality

Though many likely did not develop personal interests in the music, professionally, white educators shifted from a policy of blatant opposition toward one that emphasized containment through the second half of the decade. Instead of continuing to try supplanting young peoples' interest in jazz with "better music," teachers increasingly began discussing what they could do in their classrooms to minimize jazz's effects on their students' performance of European classical works, a sort of acknowledgment that jazz was more than simply a passing craze. At conferences and in professional publications, educators shared ways to counteract jazz-influenced performance traits that increasingly appeared in their students' classical lessons. Such suggestions could sometimes be rather technical, a sort of "shop talk" among professional colleagues. One piano teacher wrote to the *Etude* contributor Clarence Hamilton, piano professor at Wellesley College, asking how to respond when students inquired about *chording*, a term she confessed she had not previously heard. Hamilton replied he also had not heard the term before, though it likely "refers to a mannerism of jazz players," of one hand improvising a melody line while the other supplies backing harmony. Hamilton then provided a handful of exercises the student could play that would satisfy an interest in "chording" without resorting to jazz.[79] Hamilton's colleague and fellow *Etude* contributor Russell Gilbert, similarly worried about the jazz influence on classical music. Gilbert advised another precollege piano educator to remind his students that jazz and classical music were distinctly different genres and that they should "deport" themselves at the piano accordingly.[80] Such advice also existed for instruments other than the piano. In response to a judged band performance at Chicago's 1925 Midwest Band and Orchestra Contest, one reviewer suggested that avoiding the "jazz band style" of playing a cymbal with a snare drum stick and using a gong instead. The judge did not say jazz acted as a poor influence on students' musicianship, simply that it was not appropriate in this particular musical genre.[81]

Other signs in the music education community similarly pointed to a shift in attitudes. Writing in the *Music Supervisors Journal* in 1925, music publisher C. C. Birchard argued that the genre had undergone a noticeable musical evolution, writing, "It isn't so long ago that Paul Whiteman, of Jazz fame, was pretty completely discredited in high-brow musical circles. Not so now. There are composers of the first rank preparing manuscripts in hope of acceptance by Mr. Whiteman."[82] The next year, in an article on jazz and its prominence on the radio, William Arms Fisher, later to be Music Teachers National Association president, reported to readers that he had it on good advice of an unnamed source at a "big" radio station that "Jazzy jazz is on the wane, but well played syncopation is rising."[83] Fisher also pointed to Paul Whiteman, the self-proclaimed "King of Jazz," as the best example of this more refined and "symphonic" approach to jazz.[84]

The fact that white musicians Birchard and Fisher cited the white musician Paul Whiteman as embodying the appropriate musical embodiment for jazz was not coincidental. As the decade wore on, this "sweet jazz" approach convinced previously skeptical white adult audiences that jazz could be defanged from its necessary blackness and, therefore, be enjoyable. Whiteman was not alone in his approach. Other white jazz band leaders trafficked in symphonic jazz, merging jazz musical elements with a symphony-like musical presentation. Theirs was not the jazz of South Side dance halls. Drawing on the widespread view of white Americans that the symphony orchestra was the embodiment of high culture, they placed jazz in the orchestra hall, where audience members sat and clapped politely between songs. This musical reimagining by Whiteman, like those of Isham Jones and Fred Waring, also helped convince skeptics that jazz was more than a passing phrase. Whether their approach was musically creative or musical thievery, like many questions of taste, depended on who was asked. The famed band leader Benny Goodman later remarked, "The white big bands like Whiteman, Isham Jones and the rest didn't play what musicians considered real [hot] jazz. They used 'symphonic' arrangements, with fiddles, and all sorts of effects."[85] What was indisputable, however, was the fame and financial success such "sweet jazz" musicians enjoyed, particularly in the second half of the decade.

As the Progressive Era drew to a close—one at least symbolically capped off by President Harding's 1920 famous pledge of a return to "normalcy"—a new menace had emerged to threaten young people's morality and musical standards.[86] Though "normalcy" may have been politically attainable, educationally and culturally the decade presented white educators with fresh challenges. Helped particularly by the interest among white young people, jazz became a major cultural force, with its characteristically "syncopated" or "primitive" rhythms. That racialized aesthetic distinction created a permission structure for white educators to attempt and keep their students away from jazz, using school hours to counteract a vision of hypersexualized blackness jazz presented. Yet the wish that young people would lose interest in jazz looked increasingly remote by the middle of the decade. Educators responded by moving away from the policies of outright bans and condemnation toward a sort of containment.

Chapter 3

Jazz and Black High Schools
Preserving the Spiritual and Promoting Racial Pride

Speaking at a National Association of Negro Musicians conference in 1922, Harry Pace of Black Swan Records complained to a sympathetic audience, "The truth is, no [record] company has given our artists a fair chance no matter what their training or ability." He continued, "the prejudice of the white people of this country would not permit Negroes singing anything else than ragtime, comic songs, or blues. It would ruin their business to have a colored person making records of high class music, etc." Pace also took out a 1922 article in *The Crisis* with the headline "'Colored People Don't Want Classic Music!'" It went on, "So our Dealers write us. 'Give 'em Blues and Jazz. That's all we can sell.'"[1]

A black phonograph company executive, Pace's claim that many African Americans in the 1920s looked at jazz with suspicion would have found widespread support among black secondary school teachers in the 1920s. These teachers worried about jazz's possible influence on their students, a criticism similar to their white colleagues. In the most general sense, concerns among black and white educators played out along similar lines. Jazz was musically and morally corrupting influence on young people. Jazz led young people toward a life of drinking, lewd dancing, and general debauchery. Still, where white educators saw only music and moral corruption, black educators feared being associated with a genre they had no hand in creating and often palpably disdained. Jazz's emergence out of the instruments of black musicians, coupled with its rapidly increasing popularity in the 1920s, created an atmosphere in which black educators had a uniquely difficult task—propagating a uniquely black aesthetic in schools, albeit one that excluded the omnipresent jazz. Like their white counterparts, black music teachers programmed works by Mozart, Rossini, and Beethoven in their school concerts. Yet the aesthetic among black educators extended beyond the European classical music canon to include spirituals in their school concert programming.[2] In both high schools and colleges, "negro" spirituals were held up as the musical embodiment of the black experience in the United States. Educators voiced concerns that secular jazz could corrupt the sacred spiritual, the primary musical source of racial pride. Or, as one Indianapolis educator wrote, concerned educators lamented that students increasingly "jazzed up" the spiritual.[3] And, in many ways, jazz and spirituals were opposites. Spirituals were old; jazz was an emergent genre. Spirituals were typically slow and mournful; jazz was fast and exciting. Spirituals spoke to a history of struggle; jazz was built on pleasure. Spirituals were unquestioningly sacred; jazz was undeniably secular. Yet both genres were widely understood to have been developed by black musicians, a point not lost on educators. And that recognizable blackness helped fuel concerns that young people would irreparably "jazz up" the spiritual, robbing it of its significance.

More than any other organization, the National Association of Negro Musicians took up the mantel of spreading gospel of the spiritual. While the overwhelmingly white Music Supervisors National Conference had been founded in 1907 in Keokuk, Iowa, no nationwide music education organization for black musicians existed until the NANM's founding in 1919. The organization's founding, as well as the first decade of its existence, included the first discussions on a national level of what was musically appropriate to teach and why, which genres should be taught and held up as embodying characteristics of the African American experience. While white educators could write the music off as the work of unrefined and crude black musicians, black educators were unwilling to make such racist statements. Instead, many opted to only minimally talk about the genre, preferring to discuss the positive characteristics associated with the spiritual. Referencing that institutional history here serves to position the spiritual as simultaneously a point of both pride and concern for black music educators. Educators frequently cited the spiritual as an educational tool, one that referenced lessons of the American black experience. At the same time, these same teachers worried that jazz would corrupt the spiritual. For the music educators in the NANM, jazz seemed unrefined, crude, and unworthy of being included in any discussion about racial pride.

Aesthetics in Black High Schools in the Early Twentieth Century

High school remained both an elusive and exclusionary institution for many teenage African American throughout the 1920s. At the beginning of the decade, only 1.5 percent of the nation's high school students were black, roughly 28,000 students. By the end of the decade, the proportion of black students in high schools had only risen to 3 percent, despite roughly 8,000 high schools being founded in that time.[4] In Indianapolis, a city "teaming with racism and white supremacy," the percentage of African American population in the 1920s grew from 34,678 to 43,967.[5] This represented increase of 11 percent to 12.1 percent of the city's total population. Crispus Attucks, the city's all-black high school, opened in 1927, and was situated just off Indiana Avenue, the largest of the three recognizably black neighborhoods.[6] Yet the decision to open the Attucks was no act of educational benevolence. Instead, Attucks' existence was the result of a political effort by a newly resurgent KKK and their desire to racially segregate students.[7] As Kyle Steele thoroughly documented in his study of Indianapolis high schools, white education authorities in the city were systematically and ruthlessly creating a two-tiered system of schools. Among other inequities, the school board reported spending $43 per pupil at the city's white schools though only $23 per pupil at Attucks.[8] When Attucks opened in 1927, many African Americans sought a balance of realism and optimism. Speaking to the newly segregated school, a piece in the *Indianapolis Recorder* opined, "But forced upon us, many degrees of happiness may accrue to us as a result of it."[9]

For many black educators, the possibility that the comparatively small group of high school students could be corrupted by jazz served as justification to minimize student contact with the genre and, if necessary, dole out harsh punishments. Such was the case at Crispus Attucks High School, Indianapolis's only black secondary school. Russell Lane, the school's principal, exemplified the type of educator who despised jazz: scholarly, disciplined, and demanding. By his early thirties Lane had earned a doctorate in education from Indiana University, as well as a law degree from the University of Dayton. Prior to his appointment as principal, Lane taught law at Wilberforce University near Xenia, Ohio. In 1930, at the age of thirty-two, Lane took over the three-year-old school as its second principal, seeking to develop it as a community pillar for African Americans living in Indianapolis. Lane worked to establish a relationship between Indianapolis black churches and Attucks; he regularly spoke at various Colored Baptist and African Methodist Episcopal (AME) Church services and arranged for various church events to be held at the high school.[10] For the 1932 citywide Mother's Day event at Attucks, Lane allowed participants to borrow his car for, as the *Indianapolis Recorder* reported, "the purpose of taking the aged mothers to and from the program."[11] The young principal also worked as a sort of unofficial guidance counselor to graduating seniors, urging them to consider teaching as a profession.[12] The Crispus Attucks class song after his first year as principal summed up his expectations of students: that they not become "slackers."[13] Not a musician himself, Lane also financially supported the performing arts at Attucks and served as patron for various concerts held at Mount Zion Baptist Church, among others.[14]

By all accounts a caring educator and civic leader, Lane did not hesitate to confront his students when necessary and sought to make Attucks a particularly inhospitable environment for jazz. As Lissa May has pointed out, "Support for students wanting to play jazz . . . was nonexistent in the early years of the school."[15] Punishments were especially harsh, as the dangers the genre posed to those relatively few young African Americans in secondary school education could not be overlooked. In 1934 Lane caught one student, thirteen-year-old Jimmy Coe, practicing tenor saxophone in the school basement during the school day.[16] Retribution for that insubordination was swift. Lane promptly lectured the high school student for playing "that kind of music" and reminded him of the "evils" associated with it. He then suspended Coe for two weeks.[17] As the incident with Coe suggests, while the genre was universally wrapped in notions of blackness, jazz was far from welcome within school walls. Lane's order for his student not to engage with "that kind of that music" was part of a wider concern, inside schools and not, about the effects jazz could have on young people.

Articles in the black press similarly spoke to the sense of unease many felt about the genre's potential influence on young people. Similar to white critics, many wrote about potential physiological consequences, particularly for young people. Writing in the *New York Amsterdam News*, Dr. E. Elliot Rawlins lamented, "jazz music intoxicates; it affects the brain through the sense of hearing, giving the same results as whiskey or other alcoholic drinks taken into the system by way of the stomach. It has the same effect as a drug and one may become addicted to its use." While he did not explain his research or how he came to such conclusions,

Dr. Rawlins concluded, "To the young and inexperienced, jazz music is dangerous."[18] Two years later, Rawlins would shift his position slightly, arguing that humans were capable of retaining corporeal control when exposed to moderate amounts of jazz.[19] Others pointed to the difficulties associated with jazz's universally acknowledged origins from black musicians. Writing in the *Pittsburgh Courier* in 1926, managing editor William G. Nunn suggested that jazz, despite being "originally Negro," was luring young people away from the church. He complained how "jazz fervor of modern youth presents a serious problem."[20] Writing in the *Journal of Negro Education* in 1933, the poet and folklorist Sterling A. Brown used even harsher language. He brilliantly critiqued the view among many whites about the significance of black musicians and their capabilities: "A stereotype exists between this stereotype and the contented slave; one is merely a 'jazzed-up' version of the other, with cabarets supplanting cabins, and Harlemized 'blues' instead of the spirituals and slave reels."[21]

The complicated relationship black educators had with jazz similarly resonated a generation earlier with its antecedent, ragtime. Nowhere was this more pointed than the first attempt at creating and funding a New York City music school for young African American musicians. In 1911, David Mannes, a white violinist and concertmaster of the New York Symphony Orchestra, had grown frustrated over the segregated policies of many music schools and hoped to develop an alternative model.[22] Mannes, who had studied with the son of a freed slave as a boy, planned to found a school that catered to young black musicians and partially helped offset the cost of lessons through charitable donations.[23] That year he gave up the prestigious position as the New York Symphony Orchestra concertmaster, a post he had held since 1898, to help found the Colored Music School Settlement, a precollege music school specifically for young African American musicians. Mannes also convinced W. E. B. Du Bois, Lyman Beecher Stowe, and the prominent black singer and composer Henry Burleigh to serve on the settlement school's board. To secure and maintain funds for the project, Mannes and his colleagues organized a series of concerts at New York's famed Carnegie Hall. Mannes reasoned that having listened to talented young black musicians, white concertgoers would be willing to donate to the obviously worthy cause of their musical education.[24] These concerts, which ran from 1912 until 1919, sometimes on a monthly basis, were designed partially as showpieces for white audiences about the "peculiar" musical genres associated with black musicians and partially to demonstrate the musical potential of young black classical musicians.[25]

The Colored Music School Settlement concerts were typically a combination of works by both white and black classical composers—works by Samuel Coleridge-Taylor and R. Nathaniel Dett, were featured prominently—as well as chorus and solo arrangements of spirituals. Famous singers, including Roland Hayes and Harry Burleigh also performed. Mannes also reached out to James Reese Europe, a New York–based conductor at the forefront of incorporating ragtime elements into the orchestra, to perform in the first three 1912 concerts. The former New York Symphony concertmaster reasoned that including Europe's orchestra would be a provocative choice, and ideally one capable of drawing a large audience.[26] Indeed, his decision to include Europe and his Clef Club Orchestra drew considerable attention from the white concertgoing public, and Mannes confirmed at the first concert of his decision to include ragtime was not "a joke." Combining musical praise and a measure of faint haughtiness, Mannes reasoned that "music can be a great lever to raise these people, to whom harmony is natural and who have made the only original contribution to music that has come from America." One of Mannes's associates echoed that sentiment, speaking of the "educational appeal of the Negro through a particular talent, which is a distinct racial."[27] Reviews in publications like the *New York Times*, *New York Age*, and *Musical America* also emphasized Europe's race over his musical abilities, routinely referring to the performances as "negro music."[28]

Reviewing Europe's first Carnegie Hall concert for the *New York Age*, Lester Walton summed up both the prevailing attitudes among whites both before and during the concert.

> Many white composers and writers do their best to disparage syncopated music, commonly known as ragtime, and do their utmost to show wherein this brand of music does not even merit passing consideration. Yet I noticed that not until the Clef Club had played "Panama" did the audience evince more than ordinary interest. White men and women then looked at each other and smiled, while one lady seated in a prominent box began to beat time industriously with her right hand, which was covered with many costly gems.[29]

R. Nathaniel Dett, a composer and music instructor at the Hampton Institute, would later express mixed feelings about the Mannes-organized concerts. To be sure, the concerts raised needed funds so young black musicians could further their music education, which Dett applauded. And Mannes's efforts emerged out of a real concern about the widespread lack of music education, at least European classical music education, in many black communities. Yet they also were a major force in making the white public in general more aware of secular music written by black musicians. In his Bowdoin-winning prize essay written while a student at Harvard in 1920, Dett pointed out, "It was through the direction of the directors of the Music School Settlement for Colored People in the city of New York that something of what is possible in the development in the secular music of the Negro was brought conspicuously to the attention of the American public."[30] Dett recognized how white jazz critics grew to blame black musicians, not white promoters like Mannes, for spreading such lurid music. He noted, "That the Negroes made the most of their 'opportunity' is proven by the face that New York was literally 'taken by storm.' The unheard-of instrumentation of Europe's orchestra . . . and irresistibility of the ragtime . . . marked this concert as distinctive. . . . The effort received nation-wide notice through newspapers and magazines."[31]

Almost two decades after the fund-raising concerts, Mannes reflected in his memoir, *Music Is My Faith*, about the mixed feelings many African Americans had about jazz at the time. He wrote, "I was always comforted by the thought that the Negro's idea of music in his native sense was intensely religious, and that the majority of them, especially the women, deplored the existence and popularity of jazz music." He went one to recognize the musical importance of the spiritual, though did not fully grasp the embedded narrative of communal struggle it carried for African Americans. Mannes wrote, "The high artistic value of the spiritual attests to the fact of their fine sense of musical proportion and a naïve devotional quality." Regarding his own experiences working with black students, Mannes recalled how he learned "the sheer love of imparting knowledge to a poor, unguided boy who dreamed and loved music." He also recounted how his white friends had attempted to discourage his efforts to improve what Mannes termed "the cause of education among the Negroes." The violinist and fundraiser recalled being told, "colored man was incapable of realizing advantages because of physical and intellectual barriers that were the biological inheritance of the race." Absent from his memoir was any developed recognition that he, as a prominent white musician in New York, progressive as he was, had the capacity to organize the Carnegie Hall concerts, unlike the performers onstage. As it turned out, the fund-raising aim turned out less successfully than Mannes had hoped. The school closed in 1919, due largely to lack of funds.[32]

Similar to such criticisms among upper-class African Americans, much of the resistance to jazz among black educators, as well as ragtime before it, was first articulated by early music education advocacy organizations, an opposition baked into such organizations' ethos. The earliest attempts to form an African American music organization were by Harriet Gibbs Marshall, an 1889 Oberlin alumna and the first black musician to complete a music degree in an American conservatory. After teaching briefly in Kentucky, Marshall moved to Washington, DC to serve as Music Education Supervisor of Colored Schools. In 1903, she left that position to found the Washington Conservatory of Music. Three years later she wrote the country's prominent black musicians, trying to gauge the level of interest among her colleagues in founding a yet-to-be-defined organization. Unfortunately for Marshall and her aspirations, response to the letter was minimal. Marshall had decided to contact exclusively conservatory-trained musicians; only forty-one years after emancipation, this number remained relatively low.[33]

Expanding the classification of musicians beyond just performers helped grow participation numbers. In 1916, Washington Conservatory of Music and Paul Laurence Dunbar High School teacher Henry L. Grant called a meeting of local African American musicians to discuss setting up an organization for African American music educators. Given the positive response of that meeting, Grant and his group sent a nationwide letter, inquiring about the level of interest in forming some sort of black music advocacy organization on a national level, though the response was minimal. In late 1918, he sent out letters again, but with a different strategy. Grant invited musicians to come to Dunbar's music festival in April 1919, both to perform and begin planning a permanent organization. The Dunbar Music Festival, the second of its kind, took place over three days in May 1919, and laid the organizational and philosophical seeds for the NANM.[34]

Grant's music selections for the festival were emblematic of music education curricula in segregated schools, built largely around European classical music—with a particular eye toward music by black composers—and spirituals. The Dunbar festival featured performances from various segregated area schools and groups, including the Dunbar High School Glee Clubs, the Afro-American Folk Song Singers, the Washington Conservatory of Music, the Howard University Girl's Glee Club and pupils from the Howard University Conservatory of Music, among others. Grant raised funds for the event, in part, through revenue of program advertisements from mostly black-owned businesses, including drug stores, magazines, and tailors. Typical of performances at black high schools and colleges at the time, the music performed included a combination of European classical music and spirituals. On Saturday evening, the final night of the festival, a Saint-Saens aria from the opera *Samson and Delilah* was followed by a set of five spirituals, including the perennially popular "Nobody Knows the Trouble I've Seen" and "Weeping Mary." Jazz—like the spiritual, universally associated with black origins and performers—was not only absent from the concert, but may well have been the last genre Grant considered including. Instead, concerts included primarily European classical music, with sets of spirituals integrated into the program throughout the evening. The sense of racial pride Grant and his education colleagues found in spirituals and with black composers simply did not extend to jazz.[35]

The music festival took place over three days, beginning with a Thursday evening program and concluding with matinee and evening concerts on Saturday. Following the Friday evening concert, the visiting musicians and Grant met to discuss preliminary ideas and actions for setting up some kind of music advocacy organization specific to African Americans. That meeting began with Grant outlining his vision for the organization to the roughly fifty musicians who received his letter and could attend. Attendees warmly received Grant's plan, as the meeting's minutes note, "Such an organization was in the minds of persons North, East, South, and West, though none had materialized."[36] Indeed, the conference drew attendees from locations as distant as New York, California, Alabama, and Michigan. Clarence Cameron White, a composer and violinist from Boston, informed the group about a similar organization being formed in Chicago. After discussing the possibility of attending that meeting, already slated for the end of July 1919, the group decided attending that conference could provide a welcome opportunity for some sort of collaboration or merger. The Washington conference attendees agreed to postpone any major decisions and instead meet again two months later with the Chicago group. In the meantime, the group elected Grant temporary president and Alice C. Simmons, head of the Tuskegee Institute Department of Instrumental Music, secretary. They also chose the name "Temporary Organization of Musicians and Artists."[37]

One proposal, however, notably irritated some of the attendees. Grant suggested limiting membership to solely to "artists," or conservatory-trained musicians, echoing earlier efforts by Harriet Gibbs Marshall. But surprisingly for Grant, that proposition found relatively little support. Carl Diton was particularly adamant speaking out against the measure. Diton, a composer, pianist, and baritone who later in the decade served as the group's president, represented the majority of participants who spoke out for a more inclusive membership. Likely aware of how a similar declaration severely hampered establishment of Harriet Gibbs Marshall's proposed group a decade earlier, Diton pushed for and obtained the more inclusive membership criteria of "musicians and artists" rather than simply "artists." Wellington A. Adams, who wrote the "Musical World" column for the *Washington Bee*, did not hide his frustration at the "artist" designation for membership: "Who support[s] these artists, anyway? The common people, they of music-loving interest, the thousands of insignificant music teachers, choir directors, choir members, local choral[e]s and the like. Then is it reasonable to set up a strictly "artist" organization and ignore the very forces that make them tangible assets?"[38] Grant's proposal called for—or at least strongly implied—an organization that emphasized performance, minimizing any responsibility the group would have with music education. Instead, the "artist and musician" designation that Adams and Diton championed, which eventually won out, framed a more generalist orientation for the budding organization. Adams and Diton's "artist and musician" classification helped guarantee the NANM would also be active in multiple musical areas.

The National Association of Negro Musicians and Protecting the Spiritual

While Adams and Diton's "artist and musician" classification did solidify the involvement of an array of African American musicians ranging from educators to composers, it was not meant to expand the notion of acceptable music beyond the extant canon of spirituals and European classical compositions. Though the group was an important step forward for prospective black musicians, organizers were reluctant, if not in outright opposition, to including genres seen as lower-class art, less refined, or musically invalid. In their eyes, jazz was, at best, a crude musical approximation that deserved no place in music education. In his study of the yearly NANM conventions, Willis Patterson addressed the musical implications of exclusion, writing the following:

The perception that the National Association of Negro Musicians was begun to address the needs and concerns of "artists" in the western classical music sense of the word, and those who aspire to that status, has created a serious problem for N.A.N.M. This problem, in large part, accounts for its relatively low profile among black musicians who specialize in jazz, blues and gospel music. Though it had the early and active support of prominent men of jazz such as Will Marion Cook, W.C. Handy, and William Grant Still (who would later prove to be a musician of great ability in Jazz, Western Classical, and popular radio music), the organization did not, and has not succeeded in gaining the wide support and involvement of the "common people."[39]

Two months after the initial meeting Grant organized in Washington, DC, the first official meeting of the NANM took place in Chicago, although under rather auspicious conditions. That 1919 summer, racial tensions in the city had swelled to levels previously unseen, in what James Weldon Johnson would call the "Red Summer." Two days before the conference began, a black boy had drowned in Lake Michigan after being stoned by a white swimmer after drifting over into the "no-man's-land" swimming area. The boy's friends found a black policeman and indicated the perpetrator, but a white officer prevented any arrest. Word of the incident quickly spread across both white and black beaches, inflaming racial tensions, and shooting quickly followed. Four days of riots followed, only eventually slowed by a combination of massive rain storms and the state militia. Even then, smaller but still violent mobs, primarily Irish, roamed the streets for at least another week. Thirty-eight people, twenty-three of whom were African American, died. One NAACP report at the time found that fifty black Chicagoans were charged with serious crimes, while whites were charged only with lesser offenses.[40]

Still, there was little, if any, recorded discussion among conference attendees of canceling, though the riots did create logistical and travel problems within Chicago. Fortunately for conference attendees, the Wabash Avenue YMCA where the meetings took place was outside the most dangerous neighborhoods of that summer's racial violence, though the printing company who had prepared the conference program was unable to deliver the programs to the convention site. As a short-term solution, Grant, in his role as temporary president, read the program aloud. Much of that meeting was devoted to the logistics of setting up such an organization and the question of membership criteria that had elicited debate at the Washington, DC meeting two months earlier—whether to allow just "artists" or "musicians and artists"—did not reemerge. Notably, attendees did formally adopt the name, National Association of Negro Musicians.[41]

Unlike the Music Supervisors National Conference, which was overwhelmingly white, the NANM focused more broadly than music education alone. The NANM's Jazz Age leaders were a combination of composers, editors, and practicing professional musicians. Many, like Henry Grant, worked primarily in all-black secondary and tertiary schools. Part of the goal of that first meeting involved drafting a constitution, the second article of which specified the group should strive for "educational betterment" and "foster[ing] Negro talent" (the first article identified the group's name).[42] The NANM also allocated financial resources, admittedly limited at this early stage in the group's history, to assist promising young artists offset some of the costs of musical study. Marion Anderson, then a young contralto voice student living in Philadelphia, was awarded the first scholarship prize and gave a performance at that first convention which elicited "a chorus of Bravos from all parts of the house."[43] A review of the second conference, in 1920, in the music magazine *Musical America*, reflected this multifocus approach by noting the convention's attendees as "teachers and supervisors in Negro schools and colleges, conductors of private studios, heads of Negro conservatories of music, well-known concert artists, as well as promising young Negro students of music."[44]

Though not intended *solely* as an educational organization, from the start the NANM members saw education as their highest priority. Indeed, education emerged as clearly the most frequently discussed subject at conferences and in the group's journal, *The Negro Musician*. Part of this education focus stemmed from the goal of promoting musical literacy in each successive generation. Writing in *The Negro Musician* two years after the group's founding, Grant passionately argued, "Organization, promoting intercourse, education and fellowship, prepares all alike for higher aspiration and endeavor."[45] Much of the discussion revolved around the problems of establishing and developing public school classical music programs as well as pedagogy questions. Conference papers included titles such as "Credit towards Graduation in School for Study in Music," "The School Orchestra," "Teaching of Voice," and, "Tuition of Pupils." Members criticized public school music programs on a number of grounds: general working conditions, extracurricular status of music education, teacher pay, and the lack of music by black composers often included in concerts. At the first conference, President Grant authorized a committee on music education to begin addressing such problems endemic to the music education of black students with Lola Johnson, a music supervisor at Minor Normal School in Washington, DC, serving as the first chair.[46] By the second conference the role of education in the NANM increased further as two similar committees had formed: the Committee on Music Teachers and Organizations and the Committee on Private Schools Having Music Teachers.[47]

From the organization's inception, music-based racial pride was a motivating factor, as NANM members devoted themselves to the promotion of some, though not all, musical contributions of African Americans in schools. In their conferences and publications, N.N. members identified two primary examples of "Negro genius" to support: European classical compositions—especially those written by African American composers—and spirituals. "Negro genius" did not extend to jazz. Instead, European classical music and spirituals dominated conference papers and performances. Like the music festival Grant had organized at Washington, DC's Dunbar High School, NANM conference performances throughout the 1920s were a combination of the two genres, an arrangement easily agreeable to members since the first conference. The Thursday afternoon session of the first annual meeting began with all in attendance singing the spiritual, "Steal Away." The next day, members were treated to a collection of classical art songs by Saint-Saens, Kreisler, and Tchaikovsky.[48] A concert at the fifth annual concert featured an arrangement of the spiritual "I Stand on the River of Jordan" and a group singing of "Bye and Bye" with a Chopin fantasia and Beethoven's "Bagatelle in E Flat." For the NANM, as with Henry Grant and the Dunbar Music Festivals he organized, the spiritual and European classical music fit together comfortably in the concert setting.[49]

From their 1919 inception to the middle of the decade, NANM members only rarely discussed or condemned jazz. Instead, the organization's participants seemed to relish the success of forming such an organization, and spoke optimistically about future implications for music education. A 1919 article in the *Tuskegee Student* characterized the optimism within the group at the time, applauding the organization's efforts to "to promote fellowship, economic and educational betterment, to foster and preserve Negro talent, and to stimulate Negro expression."[50] Conference sessions addressed methods of effectively incorporating the spiritual into the music classroom, easily the most popular topic. Papers such as "Uses of Negro Folk Music in Schools" (a title used multiple times) and "How to Create a Keener Appreciation for the Compositions of Negroes" dominated official NANM meetings. Some discussion even revolved around the possible usefulness of jazz in composition. Carl Diton—the composer who had previously resisted the "artist" criteria for NANM membership—was one of the few to bring up jazz at the early NANM meetings. He discussed how prominent classical composers like Darius Milhaud had begun incorporating the genre into large symphonic works and discussed whether the practice could be part of a beneficial future trend. Of course, importing jazz to the rarified world of symphonic music was far from synonymous with ratifying its use in the classroom, and the group's reluctance to discuss the genre was not synonymous with approval.[51]

When dealing with works by black composers, NANM members emphasized encouraging those compositions, especially ways to share such works with their students and the general public. At the organization's first meeting, Henry Grant pointed to school concerts as an effective way of promotion. Dett, the Hampton Institute faculty member, was one of the leading composers and arrangers, and using his work was a sort of gauge.[52] Grant suggested, "If Percy Grainger, a modern master, is always to include a Dett composition on his program, we should include one number of each of our most representative composers" on each program.[53] Others brought up different promotion strategies such as "us[ing] more Negro music for teaching" and "provid[ing] each teacher with a list of compositions on hand produced by race musicians." To further institutionalize this advancement, the Composition Committee also reported on new pieces by African Americans at the yearly conference. Still, Grant would draw on the wider racial uplift narrative, lamenting in 1921 the general lack of black composers: "We want, but have not yet developed, Kreislers, Rachmaninoffs, Galli-Curcis, or Dubussys, nor have we more than a few who measure up to the standards of lesser lights in the world of musical arts. But we haven't had the opportunity, you say. Exactly!"[54] Jazz proved little threat to developing a repertoire of composition by black composers and was rarely mentioned.[55]

In contrast to this emphasis on greater awareness by African American composed European classical works, NANM members expressed a palpable sense of alarm when discussing the spiritual. Harriett Gibbs Marshall, who had initially suggested an NANM-like organization in 1906, set the tone for much of this discussion when at the second convention she said, "If the spiritual be not nourished and cultivated, the soul becomes warped. And now that the members of our race, urged by wrongs trials and sufferings, are drawing closer and closer together each day, we have a glorious outlook in our music."[56] Writing in 1921, Henry Grant called for a sense of unity in black educators based their concerns largely around the spiritual, how the genre spoke to a sense of community, and of continuity. He passionately wrote, "*Folk expression*, the advent of genius is traceable. . . . Individualism would fail us."[57] H. Lawrence Freeman, a music teacher in New York, similarly argued at the 1922 conference, "The aboriginal Negro Folk Songs, Spirituals, etc., should be preserved in their primitive and elemental form throughout all the ages."[58]

By the middle of the decade, as any wishes about jazz to be a passing craze had become increasingly unlikely, NANM members trained their sights more on the increasingly popular genre. Much the antagonism emerged from the widespread concern that jazz was musically corrupting the spiritual, posing a sort of existential threat to the genre. Nowhere was this more evident than the revised 1926 NANM Constitution. The initial 1919 constitution made no reference to any specific musical genres, beyond "sound musicianship" and "foster[ing] Negro talent."[59] In the intervening years, teachers increasingly worried their students would attempt to merge the two genres, to "jazz up" those folk songs and secularize the sacred. Following the second annual conference, held in New York City, *Musical America*, a trade magazine focusing mainly on live performances, referenced jazz influences in the article "Negros Urge against Perversion of their Songs at Second Convention." Conference attendees also passed a resolution calling for the "true and correct interpretation" of the spiritual.[60] The revised 1926 document called on the organization "To resist the desecration of Negro spirituals," "To spread abroad the love and appreciation for Negro music," and "To foster a larger appreciation for and education in good music as a preparation for the advent of the real Negro genius."[61] Without mentioning jazz by name, references to "good music" and "real Negro genius" left little doubt about the genre being referenced. The constitutional revision was not the first time the NANM attempted to preserve the genre.

Though only minimally associated with NANM, Henry Burleigh held the similar position on the subject as members of that organization. Professionally, Burleigh served as the baritone soloist at the wealthy white St. George's Episcopal Church for some fifty years between 1896 and 1946. He also worked as a private teacher, with students including Marion Anderson, Paul Robeson, and Roland Hayes and by the 1920s had developed a reputation as "father figure" to the upcoming generation of black musicians.[62] In 1922 the *Chicago Defender* carried a letter written by Burleigh on the problem of jazz and the spiritual. The *Defender* described his missive on the spiritual as a "letter to the public." It read, in part,

> The growing tendency of some of our musicians to utilize the melodies of our spirituals for fox trots, dance numbers and semi-sentimental songs is, I feel, a serious menace to the artistic standing and development of our Race. These melodies are our prized possession. They were created for a definite purpose and are designed to demonstrate and perpetuate the deepest aesthetic endowment of the Race. They are the only legacy of our slavery days that we can be proud of—our one priceless contribution to the vast musical product of the United States. . . . [Jazz musicians'] use of their melodies debases the pure meaning of the tunes, converting and perverting them into tawdry dance measures or maudlin popular songs.[63]

The Fisk folklore professor John W. Work acknowledged such themes in 1923 conference paper, redundantly titled "The Negro Folk Songs of the American Negro." Speaking to the assembled crowd, Work held up the Spiritual as a sort of return to a more pure and natural musical ethos, as "Civilization wears away the spirit and conditions which give birth to folk songs." He then articulated the sense of beauty that emerged from pain embodied in the genre: "The sorrows of slavery pierced [the Negro's] heart and it poured itself out in such lamentations as 'Nobody Knows the Trouble I See,' 'I'm Troubled in Mind,' 'Before I'd Be a Slave,' songs of this kind express the tragedies of slavery. The thought of Heaven winged his soul to flights of imagination, then he sang of 'Golden Slippers,' 'Starry Crown,' 'Long White Robe,' his soul was either with Satan in pain or with God in joy."[64]

The possibility for a potential musical hybridization remained a major concern for secondary teachers. J. Harold Brown, Crispus Attucks's first music teacher, frequently spoke out against this corruption of spirituals. After the school opened in 1927, the young educator worked to make his program a place to study "the best of music," a designation that did not extend to jazz. The young teacher was active in the Indianapolis music community, serving as head of the Indianapolis NANM affiliate, the

Indianapolis Music Club, and penning a weekly column in the city's black newspaper, the *Indianapolis Recorder*. A composer, Brown won the second NANM scholarship award while a student at Fisk University in 1923 for his "warmth and variety of tonal color, producing effect not often heard, carrying a distinction from those previously based on Negro Themes."[65]

Brown was an energetic music educator who sought to make the music program at Crispus Attucks High School a focus of the Indianapolis music community. Brown spearheaded a successful fund-raising program so the school could purchase its own organ, the first high school in the state to do so. He appealed for potential donors' sense of pride, pointing out Attucks would be the first high school in the state to have its own organ, and called for two thousand "civically-minded" people to donate one dollar each for the cause.[66] In 1931 Brown helped arrange for a regular fund-raising event at Attucks—a church choir competition with proceeds going back into church music programs. The various school choruses performed regularly at Indianapolis Baptist and AME churches.[67] This decision to use Attucks for such a competition was not incidental; Brown developed the Crispus Attucks music program around the themes of racial pride and religion. Like Henry Grant's music education program at Paul Laurence Dunbar High School in Washington, DC, Attucks music students studied and performed a combination of European classical music and black spirituals. At the school's inaugural commencement concert, student groups performed classical works by Haydn and Mendelssohn alongside spirituals such as "I Stood on the River of Jordon" (which Brown arranged for choir) and "Ev'ry Time I Feel the Spirit."[68] Brown also occasionally incorporated his own compositions into programs such as the 1934 commencement concert, his last as Crispus Attucks music educator, which included his cantata, "The African Chief."[69]

Brown also used his weekly *Indianapolis Recorder* column, "In the Music World," to speak out about the dangers jazz posed both musically and morally. At the heart of his criticisms was a palpable pride in the quality musical contributions of African Americans, and the need for universal recognition of those contributions. Like other NANM colleagues, Brown expressed deep fears over the influences jazz could have on young people and the possible musical consequences for the spiritual. For Brown, the possibility that those challenges would become habit and passed down through generations was a primary concern. Brown, like many of his colleagues, saw jazz as bringing an unwelcome secular influence on the spiritual, a practice he did not want young people to develop. He also understood the "jazz problem" on both religious and generational grounds and was reluctant to separate the two. The danger posed was not solely that jazz imposed secular influences on the religious spiritual or that young people approved the music considerably more than their parents. Instead, the danger existed in the combination of the two. Brown worried that if not kept in check, those jazz flourishes increasingly included in the spiritual would become standard practice as young people, with their jazz-favorable inclinations, grew and attained prominent positions in the church and in schools. Writing in his column, Brown rhetorically asked, "When the pianist in Sunday school adds certain flourishes and embellishments 'a la the jazz band variety,' does it add a certain air of sacredness to the occasion or is there an impulsive reaction to permit the feet to proceed unrestrained—or is there a feeling of disgust that such a secular strain has creeped into an otherwise sacred atmosphere?"[70] Regarding some of his colleague choir directors, who may feel some inclination to appeal to young people by including some jazz flourishes during the service music, Brown could be even harsher. In one *Indianapolis Recorder* piece he quipped, "Perhaps [they] are better fitted as a jazz band leader[s]." For Brown, jazz represented an unacceptable secular assault on the sacred spiritual, arguing, "The problem is whether the sacredness of the service is to be sacrificed."[71]

White music educators acknowledged the continuing relevance and importance of the spiritual. In contrast to jazz, the spiritual was acceptable black music and did not elicit pejorative terminology like "savage" and "wicked."[72] An article in *Music Supervisors' Journal* emphasized the positive reception conference-goers had given the Fisk Jubilee Singers at their performance during the 1922 national convention. That review noted, "The opportunity to hear that group of 300 colored men and women interpret, as no other group can, their own music, was once in a life-time."[73] White educators also praised the spiritual during a 1927 conference in Dallas held by the Department of Superintendence. One official commented, "No convention in the South is complete without Negro spirituals."[74]

Effusive (though perhaps tokenistic) white praise aside, NANM-associated educators were even more forthright in their criticisms of jazz and its potentially corrupting influence on their students. Lillian Lemon taught at the School of Music and Fine Arts in Indianapolis, a secondary music education institution that focused on young black musicians, similar to the Washington Conservatory of Music. Speaking in 1925, Lemon, the new NANM president who often collaborated with Brown on musical projects and events in Indianapolis, was even more adamant about the need to separate jazz and spirituals. In an interview with the *Chicago Defender*, she bluntly said, "Jazz is a desecration of the Negro Spiritual."[75] She would counter her disgust with jazz through effusive praise of other genres. In her NANM presidential address, she added, "It is happiness that we desire in this life, and music is happiness. And to everyone, no matter if you are a musicians or a music lover, cultivate a desire to sing, play or listen to great music, and especially to learn to appreciate our 'folk songs,' which are our richest inheritance, to know and recognize compositions by our Race Composers."[76] Other educators took a flippant approach. Olive Coleman Thomas, a teacher and music supervisor from Jackson, Mississippi, suggested that exposing young people to black folk songs would adequately serve to deter their interests in jazz. Thomas held that educators could counteract jazz's influence primarily by identifying the most effective ways to teach the spiritual and classical music in schools and continue their combined place in the curriculum. Suggesting a sense of racial pride would wash over students as they learn about the spiritual and other "good music," Thomas predicted, "Ragtime and Jazz will pass away as snow before the rays of the spring sun."[77] She also heartily endorsed classical music, praising it as "constructive, for it is the expression of beautiful thoughts." The Jackson teacher did, however, suggest actively involving parents in their children's education, partially to monitor whether young people were listening to jazz outside of school. And she was sure not mince words regarding the genre's general iniquity and its unavoidable physiological effects: "Music can be destructive. Jazz expresses the animal nature, and is compelling in its effects. Jazz works on the brain cells which in turn act on a certain nerve center in the spine, and set the whole body to rocking. It is sensuous instead of spiritual; it is, therefore, destructive. Jazz music is low vibrations; it scatters our energies and we become weak. . . . Real music is spiritual; it is the breath of God."[78]

Students were also well aware of the debate about the tension between the two genres. They understood that educators worried that jazz would corrupt performance practice of the spirituals, that jazz elements would increasingly find their way into that more revered genre. Writing in 1933—the year before Crispus Attucks principal Russell Lane suspended Jimmy Coe for playing "that kind of music"—another student at that school connected jazz to the spiritual and their mutual origin in the hands of black musicians. In a yearbook entry simply titled "This Jazz Age," Mildred Christian wrote, "Negro folk music may be considered from two points of view—Biblical themes from which the spirituals are made, and themes of work and play and love from which grow the work-a-day songs, the 'blues,' ragtime, and jazz.' " Her argument was not performance based; she may well have conceded that jazz riffs were increasingly heard in religious music. Instead, the Attucks student suggested the jazz was an organic outgrowth of the spiritual—simply stated that "our first and present blues and jazz music originated from the spirituals."[79] For Christian, this suggestion that jazz's origins were in the universally revered spiritual meant that secular genre necessarily embodied the themes of struggle, community, and faith so clearly evident in the spiritual. Though the musical delivery was certainly different, the message was the same. As late as 1936, one Attucks student gently chided another student for his interest in jazz by writing in the "Class Will" section of the yearbook, "I, Roberta Pope, bequeath my piano musicianship to Willis Dyer as an inspiration for him to further his study beyond the jazz status."[80] Students at Spelman High School pointed to the importance of spirituals in their education, without mentioning jazz by name. One student wrote in the *Spelman Messenger*, "There is a particular pathos about the old slave songs that invariably touches the hearts of those who hear them. . . . For this reason, if for no other, they will always remain a sacred heritage of the Negro race."[81]

Some students believed strongly enough that jazz belonged in the black musical canon that they developed their own professional groups. Following their graduation, one group of Crispus Attucks graduates formed their own jazz band, the Brown Buddies. The group was ambitious, dressed in matching brown uniforms and with matching music stands to present a professional image. The group drew inspiration for their name from their Attucks music teacher J. Harold Brown, despite his opposition to the genre. After local success, in 1932 the group moved out of Indianapolis to become the house band at Cincinnati's Cotton Club. Yet, despite their motivations, the group disbanded shortly after hearing another band with high school origins, the Jimmie Lunceford Orchestra. As Brown Buddies band member said, "We thought we were the greatest thing that ever hit Cincinnati. One morning we decided to go over from our job and catch this band we heard was going to play a breakfast dance . . . name of Jimmie Lunceford. Well, you can guess what happened. Lunceford gave them the downbeat, and a wall of sound came off that stand that nearly laid us on our backs! I think after that first number we forgot about trying to show those guys up!"[82]

Jimmie Lunceford had not begun his music career as a performer. Fresh out of Fisk University and one year of graduate study in business at New York City College, Lunceford accepted a position at Manassas High School in Memphis, in 1927. Lunceford had been a popular student at Fisk, serving as Athletic Council president, playing on the basketball team, and organizing student jazz bands for various student social events on campus.[83] At Manassas, Lunceford taught physical education, English, Spanish, coached the football team, and organized a school symphony orchestra, all while also keeping an eye on possible music ventures. Later in his life, Lunceford would recall he had a relatively liberal supervisor at Manassas High School, saying, "Jazz was very big in Memphis, and I included jazz in my teaching to cover all phases of music. At Manassas we had a very modern and broad-minded principal, who was in full accord with everything constructive. In short order my students were picking up jazz in great fashion, so well, in fact, that we organized a jazz band at the school."[84] Lunceford's matter-of-fact statement, or perhaps his humility, ignores the reality that he led what was likely the first school-sponsored jazz band in the country.[85] The novelty of jazz in schools also brought with it skepticism. Lunceford recognized the lingering unease many people, likely many of his students' parents, had about jazz. Regarding Memphis's famed Beale Street, Lunceford recounted, "I can't say very much about Beale Street and its jazz places because I had little opportunity to visit them. Being a school teacher, it wasn't considered dignified for me to visit such spots, much to my regret, except on very rare occasions."[86] Two years after the jazz band formed, the group turned professional and started playing shows around Memphis. The next year the group made its first recording on RCA. In 1929, Lunceford took a leave of absence from Manassas from which he never returned. He renamed the group the Chickasaw Syncopators and the group—which consisted of his high school students with some additional Fisk colleagues—began regularly touring. The group would prove quite successful, playing Harlem's famed Cotton Club, touring the United States and Europe and even being compared to the Ellington and Count Basie bands for a period in the 1930s. Although it was short lived, what was likely the country's first jazz program became one of the country's most popular jazz orchestras.

Though many of Lunceford's music education colleagues would have scoffed at including jazz in school music programs, African American music educators did slowly begin allowing jazz at their social gatherings in the late 1920s and early 1930s. Events explicitly devoid of sacred music, and with only adults present, were less contentious occasions to include jazz's syncopated rhythms. At least by the 1930 NANM conference in Chicago, there were enough jazz sympathizers in attendance to hire a jazz band, Roberts Society Syncopators, to perform at the postconference "frolic."[87] J. Harold Brown even had a role selecting music for early 1930s Indianapolis Alpha Phi Alpha dance fundraisers, which often included the "latest jazz" in their programs.[88] Still, including jazz in various social events remained major steps away from casting the genre as worthy of inclusion in the school music program. The NANM did not feature jazz in any of its convention pedagogy sessions until 1953, and did not follow that up with another session until six years later.[89] And while jazz had not yet penetrated the school curriculum, it slowly became a part of school-related social events.

Why Excluding Jazz Mattered to the NANM

Doris Evans McGinty argues in her edited collection of NANM primary sources that the organization came as an "island of opportunity for the African American musician."[90] Certainly, never before had a national organization been assembled for the sole purpose of advocating for African American music and performers. Conference attendees, music critics, and black musicians in general certainly recognized the significance of founding the country's first professional organization devoted to the propagation of black musicians and music. Reviewing the concert at the first NANM convention, *Chicago Defender* music critic Nora Douglas Holt similarly claimed the performance had "no precedent in the history of Negro musicians."[91] An article appearing in *New York Age* about the group's first conference stated, "Little organized effort has previously been made toward stimulating the undoubted racial talent of the Negro in music."[92]

Still, the organization developed a reputation as musically exclusive. For the early NANM members, jazz provided little evidence of musical integrity. As the earliest discussions about NANM membership suggest, the ideal of musician-as-artist was widespread among members, a philosophy that did not welcome the supposedly less refined genre. Calls for unity and a sense of music-based racial pride provided the context around which African Americans pushed for increased recognition and preservation of the spiritual. Jazz posed a specific danger to the spiritual, the musical embodiment of black identity. While white critics spoke of the encroaching blackness they feared jazz embodied, African American critics did not see the genre as any sort of external malicious influence. The danger was, in a sense, internal—a secular genre created by black musicians.

Chapter 4

The "Jazz Problem" in Higher Education
Attitudes of College Students and Faculty

During a speech to the 1925 graduating class at the University of Colorado, secretary of the Interior Hubert Work expressed palpable concern about how the "jazz spirit of the present day" could have disastrous effects on the country's future social mores. Work argued that college students were increasingly becoming "criminals," because of a combination of "meager mentality" and "moral stamina." Pleading with students for some change in behavior, he continued, "College neither makes nor mars boys, it only speeds them on the way they have already started. . . . Preparation for life's responsibilities is not made at 4 o'clock teas, jazz parties at night, or unrestricted social congregation of the immature."[1] As earnest as Secretary Work was in his plea, his speech came too late. By the late 1910s, higher-education students, especially those attending predominantly white institutions like University of Colorado, were quickly learning to love jazz. More than other cultural development of the 1920s, the music and its associated practices of dress and dancing emerged as the single most identifiable marker of the emergent youth culture taking shape on campuses with largely white student populations. However, such acceptance often stopped at the color line. For students at historically black institutions, jazz was more complicated. While many students were willing to criticize jazz, they were not willing to extend that criticism to some larger black aesthetic. Put another way, white critics on campus saw jazz's original sin as its blackness; black critics saw jazz's original sin as its secularization.

Widespread enthusiasm for the genre existed among white students. Most saw jazz as an indispensable component of their collegiate experience—the degree of enthusiasm for it was so high that many student jazz critics feared they may be socially ostracized if they spoke out against it. Yet this widespread interest in jazz at predominately white institutions was not synonymous with some wider project for black civil rights. White college students in the 1920s recognized jazz's origins among black musicians, and while many of them held prejudicial views that did not stop them from enjoying the music. And, for some, this interest in jazz ratified a sense of white superiority. One University of Illinois student felt comfortable enough about campus discussions of race to brag in the student newspaper about one campus jazz band that played so well it "would make any Southern darkey weep tears of envy."[2] Still, pockets of jazz critics developed on such campuses, often around student-run literary societies and magazines. Greater student opposition existed at evangelical liberal arts schools as well as at historically black colleges. Still, such disapproval was the exception rather than the rule among college students in the 1920s. For most, jazz was the background to their higher education. Faculty and administrators generally disliked jazz as much as did their secondary school counterparts, seeing little redeeming value in the music. School officials were more willing than those secondary educators to give students discretion to develop their personal aesthetic tastes and shape the cultural life of their schools. And a minority of faculty, primarily working in the social sciences, saw jazz and the broader cultural shift, at its minimum, as a social phenomenon worthy of study.

Student Interest in Jazz

Secretary Work's description of a jazz-infused undergraduate university experience was, on the whole, accurate, at least for white higher-education students. By the late 1910s, jazz emerged as *the* popular music on college campuses. As Helen Lefkowitz Horowitz accurately noted, "jazz came to college in high style."[3] Indeed, students cheered on and bought records of their favorite performers, other white-tuxedoed band leaders who bore little physical or musical resemblance to the black musicians who first developed the music in New Orleans and other locations. It was neither niche nor was it enjoyed by a minority of students. Students listened to it on their phonographs, on the radio, and at on-campus and off-campus concerts. The minority of student jazz critics firmly stood as outsiders, and often understood themselves as such. Those students spoke out about jazz as a form of social degradation, while simultaneously noting its enormous popularity.

Large universities, the sites of many such descriptions about jazz and college life, had more than their share of jazz enthusiasts. In 1918, the editorial board of University of Iowa's student newspaper, the *Daily Iowan*, critically editorialized about the "craze" and seeming senselessness of student interest in the music. Part of their criticism was University of Iowa students' level of indulgence. The editorial board wrote that " 'I Love You Honey,' 'Cleopatra Had a Jazz Band,' 'Oh, Those Big Blue Eyes,' and a hundred similar fixtures in the domain of the syncopated melody are all right for dessert occasionally, but for a steady diet, every meal and between meals, they work for a general run-down of the intellect." In a perhaps unfortunate editorial decision, the next page of the *Daily Iowan* contained an advertisement for a dance on campus the next day with music by Jinx's Jazz Hounds.[4]

Still, the *Daily Iowan* editorial board correctly represented student interest in the music. Jazz was undeniably a "craze" across many college campuses. One University of Illinois student listed the places one could hear jazz around campus: during meals at fraternity and boarding houses, on phonographs during "off hours," during silent films, in music shops, and, of course, in dance halls. The student went on to argue that curtailing students' ability to hear jazz would invalidate the college experience: "A college existence without jazz would be like a child's Christmas without Santa Claus. It would be empty, boresome [sic], unendurable, exasperating. We couldn't stand it."[5] Another University of Illinois student complained that his roommate listened to jazz so much, he began reciting jazz lyrics in his sleep. Lyrics like "Some girls do and some girls don't but I got more than my share" filled the dorm room even when the phonograph was off.[6] And another student wrote to his University of Illinois girlfriend that he played jazz on his saxophone whenever he missed her, but even that was not comfort enough.[7]

Students at non-state-sponsored institutions also took more than a passing interest in the music. Students at Loyola University, a Catholic institution in the unofficial jazz capital of Chicago, cited in school yearbooks how popular the genre had become among the study body. One student was reportedly never the same after hearing the "strains of the jazziest kind of jazz." Until the end of the 1924 academic year, he "marched to the strains of [the popular song] 'Margie.'" In other instances, the music's appeal extended beyond the physical. The yearbook editors, in a tongue-in-cheek manner, expressed hope that the angels would not play orchestral music, but jazz.[8] Student interest in the music also extended to normal schools, higher educational institutions designed specifically to educate future teachers.[9] In the considerably smaller city of Richmond, Kentucky, students at Eastern Kentucky Normal School expressed surprise and delight at the jazz band serenading the 1922 Halloween dance. Students enjoyed the music, though attempts to do the "Cake Walk" "had a peculiar effect on some."[10]

Students followed the recordings and tours of their favorite jazz musicians, some of whom regularly performed on some of the larger college campuses. The self-proclaimed "King of Jazz" Paul Whiteman regularly gave concerts at large state schools, much to the delight of students. Whiteman was the most popular jazz musician on white college campuses. Student jazz groups were critiqued on their ability to reproduce his ensemble's sounds, on whether they had "Paul Whiteman down." The University of Chicago student publication *The Phoenix* gushed, Whiteman "has made jazz an expression of art rather than a craze of the minute."[11] In 1925 Whiteman visited Indiana University to perform and socialize with students, a visit partially sponsored by the School of Music. To help publicize the event, the School of Music, along with the student newspaper, the *Indiana Daily Student*, organized a crossword puzzle contest, with the winner awarded free tickets to Whiteman's concert. Students were told to look for a combination of words in the puzzle that somehow referenced Whiteman and jazz.[12] While the School of Music may have planned such a promotion to help ensure high attendance at the concert they sponsored, the effort was not necessary; students were excited to see one of their musical idols in person. The *Indiana Daily Student* enthused, "The youths from the factories, mills and shops know Paul Whiteman and since they have seen cultured people coming to see him, these young music lovers begin to realize that he is something more than just the leader of a jazz band." Regarding the concert itself, the *Indiana Daily Student* music critic stated, "Of all the jazz, all one can say is it was perfect."[13]

Whiteman himself possessed the type of jocular personality that endeared him to many college students in the 1920s, though he was also occasionally tempered by his own ego. Regarding the popularity of his symphonic jazz among young people Whiteman once said, "Bring 'em on; the more the merrier and I'll prove to any music student that work is just play after all."¹⁴ The conductor was genuinely interested in college students, at least white college students, and enjoyed the campus atmosphere as a respite from the strain of touring. In an interview before the Indiana University concert, Whiteman regaled his student interviewer with stories of his college days at the University of Denver, his experiences playing on their football team, and provided tips on how to drink liquor in New York City. Whiteman even scheduled his visit to Indiana University a day early so he could spend time on campus and socialize with students, though on his own terms. The members of Beta Xi held a dinner in honor of "King of Jazz" Paul Whiteman during his visit to Indiana University. Never too concerned with social protocol, Whiteman opted not to attend, saying, "There are always so many conscientious folk who ask all manner of questions, which flatter one, but do not aid in the absorption of victuals."¹⁵

More charitably, Fred Waring, a Phi Kappa member at Penn State and one of the most prominent "sweet jazz" bandleaders, visited the University of Illinois chapter in 1930, much to the brothers' delight. In subsequent years, the bandleader went on to have a long and successful career: headlining at the Roxy in New York City, recording some 103 albums, reportedly becoming the country's highest-paid bandleader by 1933, and eventually receiving a Congressional Gold Medal.¹⁶ In 1930, his career was on the ascent; Waring was recording for the wildly popular Victor Talking Machine Company label and achieved his first hit with the song, "Collegiate." He brought with him to the University of Illinois a twenty-four-piece band, The Pennsylvanians. The visit centered on developing a relationship between the jazz enthusiasts and the musicians. The brothers welcomed Waring and his entourage by singing the Penn State fight song and then treating them to dinner in their dining hall. The musicians reciprocated by giving a standing-room-only hour-long concert in the living room. The Phi Kappa members joked afterward that Waring's pianist played their piano "as it has probably never been played before" and that some of the guests in attendance were so impressed that they "could not be dislodged from their front-row seats."¹⁷

Across the Midwest, Bix Beiderbecke similarly developed a reputation as one of the most popular jazz musicians on predominately white college campuses. Like Whiteman, Beiderbecke had the personality that endeared him to many college students. But whereas Whiteman dealt in bravura, Beiderbecke enjoyed the alcohol and social scene that associated with college life. In a 1971 interview, Louis Armstrong would recall, "Poor

Bix, he would never say 'no' [to a party].... It's a drag!"[18] Beiderbecke's alcoholism cost him his life in 1931 at the age of twenty-nine. The student newspaper at the University of Iowa—Biederbecke had attended the university for a month in 1925—carried a brief story on page three titled "Former University Man Dies in the East." Many student newspapers did not mention his death at all.[19]

In the early 1920s, however, Bix's career was very much on the assent. Beiderbecke, who had been expelled from his exclusive Chicago high school for spending too much time in dance halls, toured as a member of three bands in his career, though he was often the primary attraction. With his first group, the Wolverines, Biederbecke embarked on a touring schedule that combined performances at college campuses and public theaters and dance halls. In 1924, the Wolverines performed at Indianapolis's Rainbow Casino Gardens, the Cinderella Ballroom in New York City, as well as concerts at Midwestern colleges, including Butler College, Indiana University, and Miami University (Ohio). The student response at the Miami University concert was particularly positive. One attendee recalled, "Oxford at that time and Miami University had never had access to any *hot* music.... So when the Wolverines came on with this terrifically new, vitalized, energetic music, our horizons of dance music were expanded. The rest of the year, any fraternity dance committee chairman was begged to get a band that played like the Wolverines, and this was a near impossibility."[20] Meanwhile, Bix helped maintain popularity through regular touring. Beiderbecke and his ensembles toured on and off throughout the decade; they performed at both prominent dance halls as well as on college campuses. In April 1927, as part of Jean Goldkette's band, he performed at the University of Michigan, followed up with a performance at Detroit's Graystone Ballroom. The next month the group played for students at Penn State University before moving to the Ritz Ballroom in Bridgeport, Connecticut.[21]

The reality that popular jazz musicians like Whiteman and Beiderbecke were white was more than a coincidence on white-dominated campuses. As Richard Crawford observed in reference to Beiderbecke, "It was no accident that the first legendary jazz musician was white. In the 1920s, the general public would hardly have looked on a black figure as a positive symbol of anything."[22] Covering Whiteman's upcoming 1925 visit to Indiana University, an article in the *Indiana Daily Student* compared Whiteman's symphonic all-white ensembles to "negro orchestras."[23] Indeed, the most popular jazz musicians in overwhelmingly white universities were themselves white. Black musicians were found to be wanting, at least among a contingent of irony-deficient white college students. *The Columbia Evening Missourian* in 1921 praised one University of Missouri fraternity for regularly hiring a black pianist for their dances, thus assisting his "rise to local fame." After playing at the unnamed fraternity house while the members were entertaining guests, the "grinning darkey" (as the newspaper described him) acquired offers to play at campus sorority houses as well.[24] And such attitudes about equating jazz performance ability with race certainly continued well past the 1920s. During his 1939 visit to Indiana University, the *Indiana Daily Student* granted Duke Ellington faint praise for his "realistic interpretations of the Negro and jungle music he composes."[25]

The genre's popularity similarly impacted concert programming for campus concerts among nonjazz musicians. In the early 1920s the famed Navy Band conductor and composer John Philip Sousa had spoken out against jazz, at one point derisively calling it "music you listen to with your feet."[26] Though such a purist critique was common among musicians, it seemed increasingly dated as the genre's popularity did not diminish as so many critics had hoped. Perhaps aware that jazz was taking over the mantel of popular music that marches once held in the late nineteenth and early twentieth centuries, Sousa softened his position by the middle of the decade. He used his 1925 concert at the University of Illinois to showcase this different attitude, that the "pep" of jazz was just as enjoyable and similar to the march. Sousa composed two new marches, which were complimented by the new overture, "Jazz America." Sousa had previously even composed what he called a "jazz fantasy." The piece, perhaps a nostalgic wish for a return to the march's earlier popularity, bore the title "Music of the Minute."[27]

Humor and Marketing to Students

Students looked at jazz and saw opportunities for humor. The popular magazine *College Humor* regularly included jokes and stories on various aspects of college life. The magazine, based in Chicago, began publication in 1920, and included submissions from various campus magazine and newspapers as well as original material. The reprinted material mostly came from larger state schools, as well as Ivy League schools and other well-known private research universities. The magazine adopted a plainly masculine chauvinistic tone, with frequent references to the benefits and exploits of fraternity membership. Editors also regularly included material that belittled women,[28] African Americans,[29] and, occasionally, other racial minorities.[30] Submissions open came from large predominately white state universities as well as liberal arts colleges, not women's colleges or historically black institutions. A joke reprinted from the *Notre Dame Juggler* told of a man diagnosed with "syncopated heart" before revealing "syncopated: moving quickly from bar to bar!"[31] A cartoon, originally from the *Cornell Widow* and simply titled "Lager Rhythms" showed two men in tuxedos drowsily engaged in some high-step dance as a winged angel pours beer down from above.[32] The magazine's original stories also spoke to the natural combination of jazz and alcohol. One story, titled "The Younger Set," simply stated, "jazz and liquor went hand in hand, the pocket flask and the banjo were boon companions. John Richardson, friend and fraternity brother, was slowly getting shot."[33] Other jokes dealt in darker humor. One such example that appeared in the *Cornell Widow*, though reprinted from the magazine *Iowa Frivol*, found humor in popular dances. It read, "Chief of Police: What! You mean to say this fellow choked a woman to death in a well-lighted cabaret in front of over a hundred and fifty people? Did no one interfere? Cop: No, cap, everybody thought they were dancing."[34] Another, titled "This Jazz Age" spoke to the priorities of college students: "She: Good evening, Jack. Damn it all, papa just died and we'll have to be at least an hour late for the dance!"[35] Stewart Howe, a student at the University of Illinois, wrote and distributed a short periodical filled with jokes and observations about various campus events. Writing under the pen name, "Professor Prehn," his *Prehn's Bonmots* often referenced social events of students involved in Greek life. One joke, "Shots Follow Dance," Prehn meant as a play on the possible double meaning of "shot"—liquor or gunshots.[36]

Much of the humor appearing in college newspapers and magazines focused on Greek life and alcohol. Jokes quite often revolved around fraternity members' interest in drinking and enjoying college. One poem appearing in the *Daily Illini* under the title "Jazz Jingles" read, "There is a young Delt called Lonny / Who is a bright little sonny / In the dimmy Arcade / He now drinks limeade / We all laugh, cause it's funny."[37] Humor about Greeks and drinking extended beyond the amusement of a fraternity member not wanting to drink. An extended joke appearing in *College Humor*, but originally appearing in the *Washington Dirge*, similarly placed drinking and social events as important to Greek life. It read as follows:

GRAND GUARDER: Eater Ora Ankle is still out $47.50 for the liquid sunshine purchased for the last party.

GRAND GAZUMP: Are you aware that this fraternity is opposed to the use of liquor in any form?

GRAND GUARDER: I am. I said liquid sunshine . . .

GRAND GAZUMP: I understand. Proceed.[38]

College Humor also included material that addressed the differing opinions about the genre between adults and college students. Much of the humor dealt with sexual conquest—or at least arousal—and how jazz dancing could help lead to that end, designed to appeal to a male audience. One submission from the *Hamilton Royal Gaboon* left little question of the motivation about dances: "The Him: What are the last steps in the latest dances? The Her: The front porch."[39] Another joke rhetorically asked how young women could avoid "petting parties." The answers included avoiding jazz dances by regularly mentioning the Greek god of moral beauty Adonis and, more directly, "Stay away from college men."[40] Similarly, *College Humor* editors included jokes about how jazz dancing created sexual arousal both among the dancers themselves and among those merely watching. One short poem evoked, "It was a jolly party / Not so many moon ago / That I saw her shake the shimmy / Like a dish of fresh Jell-O."[41]

The magazine also regularly carried advertisements touting lessons that promised to teach students how learn to play jazz themselves. Music instrument companies were particularly eager to improve their sales-based college students' "jazz craze." Such ads typically described the ease with which students could learn to play their favorite songs, claiming no musical experience or even practice were necessary to play the "latest songs." The King Instrument Company bragged in *College Humor*, "You can play this beautiful imported Jazzy Sax without practice. No difficult scales or keys."[42] The U.S. School of Music, an organization based in New York City that sold method books, advertised the "revelation" of their approach. By purchasing their texts, jazz fans could "become a musician so quickly as to astound everyone . . . No 'trick music'—but actual notes, learned quickly right in your own home."[43] The Buescher Company similarly pushed, "You can do it—easy. Even if you failed with some other instrument, you can learn the simplified Buescher saxophone." The company also offered to provide three free lessons with each instrument purchase to "give you a quick start."[44]

Companies also did not hesitate to play off the extramusical motivations in their advertisements. Buescher claimed, "It will make you popular, in demand, the center of attraction everywhere you go."[45] The U.S. School of Music countered that their method could make one "popular, practically overnight."[46] Extramusical motivations also extended beyond popularity as both Buescher and the U.S. School of Music referenced how jazz could increase one's number of dates after merely a few lessons. Buescher did not hesitate to make vaguely sexual references in promoting their products, for example, "tantalizing music that sets them going."[47] Their competitor bought a half-page ad in one issue, showing a college man playing the saxophone, while looking over his shoulder at two clearly impressed women with bobbed hair and bare arms.[48]

As early at 1917, campus newspapers began carrying advertisements from local record stores about the latest records they had in stock. That year the *Daily Illini* carried an advertisement for the Original New Orleans Creole Band, which was touted as "The act that introduced 'Jazz' music to vaudeville."[49] Yet the tone for that advertisement was tame compared to later examples. Record stores increasingly constructed their advertisements to play into the enormous popularity jazz enjoyed among college students and marketed newly released phonograph records as unquestionably necessary additions to any student's phonograph record collections. Students read about "THE SEASON'S BIGGEST SONG AND DANCE HITS" and "Dance Records You Can't Be Without."[50] In 1929, the *Ohio State Lantern* carried an advertisement from Columbia Records for the perennially popular Paul Whiteman, which strongly suggested students "Look into This Paul Whiteman Matter" and purchase his latest record.[51]

Businesses that sold various products to higher-education students saw the student interest in jazz as a marketing possibility. In his cultural history of advertising, Juliann Sivulka argued, "U.S. manufacturers also developed products for clearly defined groups of customers for the first time. This concept would later become known as *marketing strategy*."[52] Businesses that recognized the widespread popularity of jazz among college students began citing the genre in their advertisements. Merely referencing jazz became a strategy to help sell various products as many companies used the word *jazz* as various parts of speech—a noun, a verb, an adjective—to appeal to college students. In some instances, the connection between jazz, a music genre, and the products being sold seemed tenuous, at best. Students at Cornell read in their student newspaper, the *Cornell Daily Sun*, that the cereal Shredded Wheat was "Full of Jazz and Ginger."[53] The advertisement did not explain exactly how the Natural Food Company, which produced Shredded Wheat at the time, managed to insert jazz into their cereal, only the unintentionally anthropomorphizing claim that "A dish of SHREDDED WHEAT avoids many ailments that are common to youngsters." The Hite Brothers Shoe Store in Champaign, Illinois, similarly tied in their wares with the popular genre when they marketed to students. In 1919, they advertised to University of Illinois students that their business was the "jazz shoe shining parlor." In case that description was not enough to bring college students into the store, the Hite Brothers also told students they could also capably "jazz those shoes and clothes."[54] And students at the College of Puget Sound read in 1924 that Dundee Woolen Mills offered to "tailor suits and overcoats to your measure . . . in the leading styles from the extreme jazz to the very conservative."[55]

Student Opposition

Despite the genre's overwhelming popularity, such advertisements would not have swayed those white college students who saw little positive in jazz. Certainly a minority in the 1920s, such college students expressed their disinterest, and often disgust, in the genre. Gender was often the dividing line between jazz opponents and supporters. While a minority, these jazz critics pointed to the morally questionable acts of their classmates that typically coincided with or followed jazz dances. At the University of Minnesota, the dean of women gleefully reported in 1922 that female students had taken action against some jazz dances. The Women's Self-Government Association handed out cards at its sponsored dances to couples deemed dancing too closely. The card read, "We do not dance cheek to cheek, shimmy, or dance other extreme dances. You must not. A second notice will cause your public removal from the hall. Help keep up the Minnesota standard."[56] At the University of Chicago, the Federation of University Women spoke out about the domination jazz had on the campus social scene, with one student arguing, "We get enough jazz at dances." The women blamed university officials and the campus in general for not supporting glee clubs adequately, and that "it's a disgrace the way the campus fails to support the glee clubs. . . . No one on our campus seems interested." As a solution, they put forward a compromise for glee club concerts, that "the music be neither highbrow nor jazz. Old fashioned songs and college songs are the best."[57]

Nostalgic references to some earlier aesthetic formed the basis of students' academic critique of the genre as well. One male student at Hope College in Michigan took to his college newspaper to indict jazz as a prime example of what he saw as an era of social and aesthetical degradation—"an age of degeneracy." The male student wrote passionately for a more refined aesthetic, arguing, "For altho [sic] science has advanced tremendously in recent years who can say that the great and good things of human life have not declined? In music we have jazz, in the painting the insane jargon of the futurists' mind, in poetry and writing beautiful senseless nothingness." He then offered up literature as a solution, a sort of tonic for the modernist impulses attractive to higher-education students "to find sympathy for a knowledge that our inmost emotions are shared." Specifically, the Hope College student suggested his classmates turn to Plutarch, Emerson, and Tennyson to engage a deeper and more substantial interpersonal connection listening or dancing to jazz provides.[58] Some students at Harvard similarly looked at jazz as a denigration of the English language. Outraged by crooner Rudy Vallee singing a sentence ending in a preposition during one concert, the students reportedly threw grapefruits at him.[59]

Other students in both large state schools and liberal arts colleges alike focused their criticism more toward jazz dancing. One University of Illinois pupil wrote to his student newspaper in 1924, asking for advice about how to behave at the upcoming prom since he did not know any jazz dances. His argument drew simultaneously on what he saw as immoral dancing as well as the social pressure among undergraduates to participate in them. He wrote to the *Daily Illini* editor, "I think that you should do something about the kind, quality and method of the public dancing at the best function this year. I went to the Freshman Frolic; I am going to the Prom; and I am worried." He went on to lament that he and his date, neither of whom had "much experience in matters Terpsichore," in fact, "couldn't dance in the good old-fashioned aimless sort of way that we were accustomed to." While the "good old-fashioned" dances certainly were important, the unnamed student's larger concern focused more on social implications as he revealed his trepidation that he and his girlfriend would become socially ostracized for neither wanting nor being able to dance as their peers did.⁶⁰ Similarly, one student at Denison University, writing under the pen name "Et Tu," complained in 1923 of the ulterior motive behind dancing. Dancing, in her argument—and not necessarily incorrectly—acted for many college students as a means to an end. She wrote, "I believe that 96% of those who dance do so because they like to pet. The other 4% are business men who need the exercise." The author held as firmly believed that "English professors are not as blasé as they appear" and, "I believe putting a fraternity freshman under orders is merely an excuse to allow the brothers to exercise the brute within them." However, such an assertion did not mean the anonymous author disliked jazz, since "I believe there is more music in 'Sweet Lady' rendered by Paul Whiteman et al. than there is in a dozen student recitals."⁶¹ One Ohio State University student spoke out even more forcefully about the effects jazz was having on the recreational habits of young people, that jazz parlors dominated college life. The article, also reprinted in the University of Illinois *Daily Illini*, had no name attached to it. Such anonymity may well have been the motivation to speak out forcefully against the music. She lamented how "Jazz is so prevalent that its influence on college life cannot fail to be marked." She continued,

> Jazz has deprived the modern girl of the majority of her abilities to entertain a man. She only waits until he asks, "where shall we go?" Then away to the haunts of syncopations or unessential trimmings . . . No longer does one hear of parties that seek to enjoy what nature offers, such as sleighing, coasting or skating. The modern couple can only seek the jazz parlors. When will this seemingly irresistible force—jazz—cease to hold domination over the so-called good times that college students have today? When the man puts his foot down and says, "No!"⁶²

Campus literary magazines became one of the few venues where jazz critics at large state and research universities could express their displeasure with the genre. At Indiana University, *The Vagabond* was a student-run bimonthly publication between 1923 and 1930 that offered "a medium of expression for the literary life on campus, and it hopes to hasten a rebirth of interest in science, art, and life at Indiana."⁶³ The magazine operated on the assumption that Indiana University was both too provincial and too immoral—and sorely in need of literary revival. Contributors to the periodical expressed a sort of combined disgust as well as resigned acceptance of jazz's popularity among the student body. Many described the music as if it were alcoholic beverages, acceptable in moderation, though dangerous if over consumed. For the *Vagabond's* editors, students interested in jazz necessarily had little interest in their formal education and instead were blights on the university, and lived in, "combined brothel and gin palace[s]."[64] One article specifically about Greek life described fraternities as campus institutions filled with such undergraduates. The anonymous author wrote, "There has come, happily—and coincident with the discovery of Jazz—the dawn of a new era: the rise of the younger ignorencia."[65] Other articles similarly continued the theme of jazz-fueled degradation. One alumnus contributed an article equating the music with female students willing to "neck" or "pet" without discretion. He wrote, "The young men searched the sorority houses and Memorial Hall to discover one of the osculatory daughters of jazz." Still, such students were the exception to the rule on campuses with overwhelmingly white students.[66]

Greater student opposition existed at historically black colleges. Students at these institutions spoke and wrote openly about concerns with the music. In both Midwestern and southern colleges, students cautioned about the moral lapses jazz often engendered. In 1927, one student at Atlanta University equated jazz with a sort of moral degradation, the categorical opposite of liberal education. Liberal education provided a means for "the Negro . . . to claim his place. . . . If given liberal education, he CANNOT be kept behind." However, "if he allows jazz, sex, and tawdry pleasures to call him too far from the knowledge he seeks, he will continue to remain shackled to white America who mistreats him for being her draw-back."[67] One year prior, a Fisk University student had expressed disgust at the physicality of jazz dancing. Like the Atlanta University undergraduate, he evoked jazz as a sort of artistic debasement across various expressive forms when he wrote, "[Young black artists] must 'jazz' away the charm and the beauty, the richness and grace of his literary creations, his music, his art in every cultural field in order to make a sale."[68] And one Morehouse student similarly spoke out against jazz as a regressive force in 1924, going so far as to argue that the music was "holding Negroes back musically."[69]

Other students opted to conspicuously avoid discussing the music. In his "Farewell" article as editor of the Atlanta University student publication the *Scroll*, Thomas Flanagan boasted the magazine had not indulged in "jazz stuff" with their "vulgar suggestive attitudes which they assume" similar publications had.[70] In separate pieces written five years apart on the efforts and compositions of black musicians, two female students both avoided any mention of jazz. In the essay "Negro Music and Composers," another Atlanta University student focused her analysis on music as a form of religious worship, at one point arguing, "It is ours to bear aloft the torch and plant it high." She cited contemporary black classical composers including Carl Diton, Harry T. Burleigh, and R. Nathaniel Dett as indicators of a "peculiar gift of the music on the level with brilliant musical figures of other races."[71] Five years later, Spelman College student Thelma Gilbert cited the same composers as evidence that "The colored American is finding himself" while also opting not to include jazz in such racial uplift.[72]

The major point of opposition to jazz in higher education was its possible influence on the musical genre of the spiritual. Similar to many black secondary music educators, students at historically black colleges preferred to discuss the importance of the spiritual rather than denigrate jazz. And like those teachers, black higher-education students pointed to the coexistence of struggle and aesthetic salvation the genre embodied. Unique to the spiritual, a historical performative element characterized the genre. As the Spelman student Gilbert described it, African Americans "felt the music. . . . Everywhere that it has been heard this music has awakened a responsive chord in the minds and hearts of those who hear it." She continued, "Nothing tells more truly what the Negro's life in slavery was than the song in which he succeeded, sometimes, in expressing his deepest thoughts and feelings."[73] Writing in 1930, another Spelman student echoed Gilbert's claim, arguing, "The Negro took complete refuge in Christianity and the spirituals were literally forged of sorrow in the heat of religious fervor."[74] And unlike white students and their overwhelming interest in jazz, this interest in the spiritual among students at Spelman and other colleges did not contrast with those of their teachers. In a talk to Spelman students in 1928, Rev. Howard B. Thurman spoke on "The Message of the Spirituals." His presentation was part musical performance, part lecture, as the priest extolled students to identify and consider the biblical teachings embedded in the music. Students appreciated Thurman's talk enough that the editor of the student publication *Spelman Messenger* reprinted it in its entirety.[75]

In his history of Fisk University, Joe M. Richardson noted how "Discipline in black schools was usually more strict than in the average American college."[76] Barbara Solomon has concurred that "black schools demanded the strictest behavior both on and off campus."[77] Indeed, throughout the

1920s, many historically black colleges did not have a campus atmosphere conducive to jazz and its associated trappings. Students often complained about how strictly controlled their lives were on campus, that they did not have adequate time off campus or away from university faculty and staff. In 1924, one Atlanta University student quipped that the most fun place on campus was the dining hall, while his classmate argued that the university had a "social problem."[78] Another equated students with marchers, as they followed a highly regimented schedule weekdays and weekends.[79] A Tuskegee student stuck a similar tone a decade earlier. Later in life she would reminisce, "Do you think we were free on this campus then to do what we wanted to do? Then you're wrong."[80] The music at the "Spelman Social"—dances between Spelman and Morehouse students—was performed by music department faculty, where jazz was the least likely music to be heard. Students at Fisk experienced similar restraints with strict prohibitions in place against leaving campus. Other students expressed approval at the limitations placed on students. One Morehouse freshman in 1926 applauded his school's ethos of "traditionalism."[81]

Even if students had been allowed greater off-campus privileges, jazz likely did not have made major inroads in students' lives since administrators and faculty remained opposed to the genre on campus and implemented restrictions to that end. Such critiques began appearing early in the twentieth century regarding ragtime, jazz's antecedent. In 1909, the white Atlanta University president hung up a sign in the school's music practice rooms outlining appropriate behaviors. Along with reminders about not deviating from the allotted schedule and not placing food or drink on the pianos, president Edward Twichell Ware indicated that "rag-time playing is prohibited."[82] Similar criticisms about the popular music continued into the 1920s, as jazz did not find any favor among music department faculty. Harvey Waugh, the head of the Fisk Music Department, cautioned his students in 1927 that they should avoid jazz because it was inherently antiintellectual. In contrast to classical music, Waugh told Fisk students, "Jazz takes no thinking on the listener's part."[83] One faculty member at Spelman warned parents not to allow "cheap vaudeville in the Victrola cabinet." Not mentioning jazz specifically, she clearly referenced it when writing in 1927, "All music is not good music. . . . Melodies may be gross and sensual or fine and spiritual."[84]

Despite the overwhelming general opposition, jazz was not wholly without its supporters on historically black campuses. At Fisk, an undercurrent of jazz quietly existed throughout the student body. Until 1926, administrators forbade student dancing as a preemptive solution to minimize immoral acts among the student body.[85] Before President Thomas Elsa Jones lifted that prohibition in 1926, students held "bootleg dances," which one Fisk student succinctly described as "inadequately chaperoned."[86] Jimmie Lunceford—the man who would go on to form one of the first high school jazz bands and then lead his own professional group—also looked for opportunities to get around the various proscriptions put in place on campus. Given the unwelcoming atmosphere to jazz at Fisk, Lunceford looked for opportunities to perform off campus and around greater Nashville. Lunceford had formed a student jazz ensemble, Jimmie's Boston Syncopators, and looked for performance opportunities. Taking advantage of the increasing popularity of radio, Lunceford and his ensemble first gave performances in 1926, at the recently founded radio station WDAD. Many Fisk students responded positively to hearing Lunceford's music and appreciated their popular classmate receiving such public recognition. One wrote, "Jimmie Lunceford, the leader, was a wizard on the saxophone, leaving everyone sending in messages, saying 'That's fine'—'That's All.' "[87]

Faculty Opinions

Like President Ware at Atlanta University and his order against playing ragtime, administrators at white institutions voiced their opposition to jazz. Yet unlike counterparts in secondary schools, college administrators rarely followed such public pronouncements with steps to minimize their students' interest in and contact with the genre. Though many university educators expressed a professional interest, generally critical, most did not instill the sort of policies designed to dissuade student interest. Much of the social responsibility for students rested on deans of students and other administrators, quite often the respective deans of men and women. These school officials attempted to regulate student exposure to the music, rather than convince students of the genre's immorality. The Penn State dean of men bemoaned in 1921 that "something of the nobility has gone out of the attitude of our young men toward young women."[88] Still, Dean Dan Warnock did recognize jazz's growing popularity, and the next year he approved one student's plan to forgo graduation to begin a career as a bandleader.[89] A half decade later, the male president of Smith College, an all-female school, sounded a similar warning to the Penn State administrator. Dr. William Neilson said in a Chicago speech, "The big problem we face is the tendency of the girls to run off [for] a weekend, only to exhaust themselves so completely they have to go to the infirmary on Monday. They dance more than they used to and they keep it up longer and later." Yet while such pronouncements do indicate a level of concern, they are more indicative of some general adherence to academic dialogue and debate than systematic attempts by campus officials to influence student behavior. For his part, Neilson concluded, "I blame it entirely on their parents."[90]

Such condemnations of jazz largely echoed similar attitudes among higher-education faculty. Jazz's "hot rhythms" found little support among those educators working in academia. Writing in the early 1990s, a decade itself known for its "culture war" discourse, Stanley Coben argued that "by the 1920s . . . most leading American intellectuals had announced their rebellions against [Victorianism]."[91] However, their opposition to jazz suggests those in the academy did not approve of a jazz-drenched world replacing some Victorian ethos. While faculty largely opposed the genre and many feared its implications for the future, they also stopped short of taking on the responsibility of changing student attitudes. Two general characterizations account for faculty attitudes to the music their students so enjoyed. First, this disfavor peaked in the early part of the decade. The interest white higher-education students quickly showed in the music was countered with an equal measure of disapproval among faculty. Second, attitudes among faculty to jazz were, to some degree, shaped by their academic disciplines. Scholars of English, philosophy, and other humanities found the music especially distasteful. Educators who studied and taught in the social sciences, while largely not willing to admit any personal interest in the music, saw it as an social phenomenon worthy of some academic inquiry.

Contrary to their colleagues in secondary schools, white professors preferred to ignore issues of race that swirled around jazz, at least initially. Why this avoidance? Many believed jazz was a passing fad, and any deeper discussion could potentially give it oxygen to survive. Particularly in the early 1920s, these faculty members made only brief references to jazz, as if doing more could somehow validate its existence. A pair of Harvard entomologists exemplified this attitude well in a 1920 paper on feeding habits of ants; they equated the increasingly chaotic life of food-deprived ants with a jazz concert.[92] The next year a classicist teaching at Wesleyan University attempted to horrify his colleagues in his characterization of a sort of disguised Hades in Ancient Greek literature when he wrote,

"Think of a heaven where the harps have been replaced by instruments of percussion and all the music is jazz!"[93] Historian J. P. Dunn declared himself poorly qualified to speak to the quality of musical transcriptions in a new collection transcribed by Francis Densmore in a 1921 review of three books on Native American history. Dunn quipped, "I have never been privileged to hear any Indian music that attained the midway standard, or even reviled jazz."[94] Similarly, Dunn's history colleague and Indiana University professor W. H. Morgan held that jazz was not any more melodious than a steam whistle.[95] And one Vassar College English professor located jazz as the primary source for the general superficial nature he believed young people exhibited in his class: "It is on top of real earnestness of outlook, I think, that superficial interest in jazz, in extravagant dancing, extravagant dressing, sensational films and books, froths and bubbles."[96]

As the decade progressed, however, more developed critiques of jazz slowly appeared. Like many other jazz critics, University of Chicago sociology professor William I. Thomas held that sex was the natural consequence of dancing, though could not bring himself to articulate it as such. In 1923 the prominent sociologist published an in-depth study on "The Unadjusted Girl," an early academic inquiry attempting to articulate how jazz dancing had impacted young people and their socialization skills. He argued the following:

> The modern dances are disgusting—the "toddle" and its variations and vibrations, the "shimmy" and its brazen pandering to the animal senses, and the worst offspring of jazz, the "camel-walk." There is but one idea predominant in these dances—one that we will leave unnamed. It is not only in dancing that this immorality appears. The modern social bud drinks, not too much often, but enough; smokes considerably, swears unguardedly, and tells "dirty" stories. All in all, she is a most frivolous, passionate, sensation-seeking little thing.[97]

Yet Thomas was no puritan. At the time he published *The Unadjusted Girl*, Thomas had attracted unwelcome and critical attention for his book *The Polish Peasant in Europe in America*. The book was one of the first studies to critically problematize causes of poverty on an international level. Critics opposed the "pragmatic" approach Thomas developed to the problem of Polish crime in Chicago, favoring instead a nonconsequentialist and universal moral condemnation of lawbreaking. Criticisms extended to his personal life. Thomas did not hide his attraction to multiple women, alienating him from many University of Chicago colleagues who did not find such behavior becoming for faculty at such a prominent and distinguished university. The university fired him in 1918, after the government brought charges against him under the Mann Act, a federal law passed in 1910, meant to stem the tide of prostitution involving women and girls. Thomas had been caught in a downtown Chicago hotel with a woman whose husband was serving overseas. In contrast to his progressiveness on some social issues, Thomas found jazz appalling and cited the music as the single factor responsible for the social degradation among girls.[98]

Like Thomas, other academics began writing more developed critiques of jazz in the second half of the 1920s. While most academics continued their general opposition to the music, their condemnations sounded less like brief asides and more as a central component of academic inquiry. University of Illinois English professor and Victorian literature specialist Joseph E. Baker, among others, represented this different approach of viewing jazz as less of a fad and more as a worthy opponent requiring a more expansive condemnation. Baker's criticism of the music may well have been the product of his disgust at the general diminishing Victorian ethos so evident by the mid-1920s. Regardless of his motivation, Baker's 1926 contribution to the *Classical Journal*, "Plato as a Contemporary Essayist," focused on how the ancient Greek philosopher would have responded to the music. The English professor held that Plato's psychology may have been "sounder" than what Baker saw as Jazz Age "all-inclusive acceptance of the new." As evidence, Baker quoted from *The Republic* on the necessity of censorship toward young people's more iniquitous dalliances: "For youngsters, as you may have observed, when they first get the taste in their mouths, argue for amusement, and are always contradicting and refuting others in imitation of those who refute them." More directly to the challenge jazz posed to the state, Baker quoted again from *The Republic*: "For any musical innovation is full of danger to the whole State, and ought to be prohibited. . . . When the modes of music change, the fundamental laws of the State always change with them." Of course, Baker did not discuss the implications about how—or if—such statements may have applied in an increasingly pluralistic society; his delight at an apparent Platonic condemnation of jazz may well have overruled such considerations.[99]

In contrast to such outright opposition, scholars working in the social sciences expressed some interest in jazz as an explanatory factor of social phenomena. By the middle of the decade, such academics problematized the music, often casting it as a worthy opponent in discussions involving ethics. Columbia University professor Leroy Bowman, whose research interests focused around questions of social organization, researched how the jazz-fueled dance hall craze had impacted the nature of relationships among young people and described his inquiry as "dispassionate study . . . without moralistic bias." Bowman tentatively concluded that dance halls created a sort of truncated relationship among participants, that the young people danced with multiple partners, but did not seek to develop relationships beyond that.[100] University of Iowa professor G. T. W. Patrick took a more critical approach when he argued that the "decadence of popular music to the jazz level"—along with a list of vices, including bank robbery, "automobile banditry," and general extravagance—all contributed to a widespread decline in what he called "social morale." Patrick believed that, as a result, patriotism was similarly in precipitous decline.[101]

For their part, music faculty, at least those at predominately white institutions, did not speak with a single voice on jazz's musical validity, though they were consistently quiet on issues of race. Edwin Stringham, a composer who taught at Columbia University's Teachers College, argued that jazz could be either "good or bad," and serious scholars should avoid wholesale indictments just as they should shun uncritical praise. He continued, "We need a little esthetical relaxation now and then. No form of music can do this as effectively as jazz. Jazz is the laughter, the fun, the 'sans souci' of the tone-world."[102] Stringham's colleague, Des Moines University dean and professor of Public School Music Raymond Carr, similarly refused to cast jazz as a necessary musical evil. Carr even suggested that secondary music educators might opt to begin music instruction with jazz, if only as a means to initiate student interest in music. In Carr's reasoning, educators could transition to other genres later.[103]

Other prominent faculty opted for more mainstream publications to voice their opinions. Not content to speak merely to his colleagues or students about jazz and its iniquities, John Erskine chose to speak out more publically about the social and aesthetic questions jazz precipitated. In 1926, while teaching English at Columbia University, Erskine wrote an article for the *New York Times Magazine* with the somewhat misleading title "Jazz Is Popular Revenge on Music," an article that was further discussed in the *Norwalk Hour*. Erskine took issue with how the English music critic Ernest Newman characterized jazz, generally, and Paul Whiteman's music, specifically. Newman's criticism emanated from a comment Whiteman made about the connection between classical music and jazz. The English critic responded, in Erskine's characterization, with the hope that "the jazz composers would 'keep their dirty paws' off the noble themes of real music." Erskine found such a response, at best, antiintellectual and prejudicial at worst, that it amounted to little more than name-calling. He wrote, "We should try . . . for an answer which would throw as much light as possible upon jazz. But if we start with a dislike of the thing, we may humor our prejudice by calling the audience hard names." Still, Erskine's was not a defense of jazz per se. He stopped short of attempting any qualitative judgments about the music and did not divulge his opinion. Instead, his criticism rested on the tenor and quality of the debate. He reasoned that jazz's widespread popularity merited serious inquiry: "The fact here is that jazz gives pleasure to an astounding number of persons in America." Referring to the music itself, Erskine would only write, "Whether good or bad, it is new."[104]

The Jazz Age, with its proliferation of popular music on a scale not previously seen, proved a tempting challenge for the Columbia faculty member and Erskine was ideally suited to level such critiques at the debates surrounding jazz. In biographer Katherine Chaddock's characterization, Erskine "was destined to be a Renaissance man without a Renaissance."[105] Yet Erskine's worldview occasionally blurred the lines between popular and high culture. He was a distinguished faculty member at one of the country's most distinguished universities, but he also wrote risqué stories for *Cosmopolitan*. A pianist, he soloed with the Philadelphia Symphony and New York Philharmonic, though he also contributed to *Harper's Bazaar* and the *New Republic*. Still, Erskine was most at home in dealing with matters of high culture. The Great Books course he first developed at Columbia in 1918, his attempt to solidify the canon of Western civilization, reflected his view that readers should "take the great masters first."[106] He also continued this criticism into the 1930s, and did not necessarily live up to his own standards of disinterested observer after being appointed head of a new institution, the Julliard School. In 1930, Erskine penned an article in *Music Supervisors Journal* in which he argued, "When you have great art incorporated in the life of the people, you needn't worry then about your calling on the faculty which undermines your work by telling the youngsters to play jazz."[107] The next year he similarly observed, "I have known very few college faculties in which one wouldn't hear criticism of the way the students danced."[108]

If Erskine's fundamental understanding of Western civilization rested on the shoulders of white writers and artists, Charles S. Johnson sought a framework to invigorate the imagination of black artists. The young Fisk sociology professor, and later president, saw jazz as a necessary ingredient in this epistemological mission. Johnson sought to develop a uniquely black aesthetic, a more all-encompassing canon of more experientially representative genres and works. He believed all music, regardless of genre, developed by black musicians should be seen as "the clue to the richest of Negro folk life to which the conscious racial artists have now turned frankly." For Johnson, jazz was a musical genre as well as "method," the psychological state that "marks the birth of a new consciousness and self-conception."[109]

In his Foreward to a Johnson biography, David Levering Lewis characterizes Johnson's scholarship as "never perceived as threatening to the status quo in the manner of a Du Bois, but rather as scholarship that encouraged greater understanding."[110] Like other black scholars, Johnson situated the spiritual as central to his analysis. Yet unlike many critics, Johnson did not see jazz as an artistic outlier to, or as a musical bastardization of, that more sacred genre. He saw such opposites as characteristic of the history of African Americans, writing, "The Blues always strike a note of despondency, and yet they provoke laughter." Quoting from Langston Hughes's poem, "The Negro Artist and the Racial Mountain," the young sociologist wrote, "*We younger Negro artists who create now intend to express our individual dark-skinned selves without fear or shame. . . .* We know we are beautiful and ugly too."[111] Blues and jazz worked in a particularly symbiotic manner, combining to contribute both the sorrowful and joyful in music. While Johnson's argument may well have been meant more as academic debate than a call for expanding the canon of acceptable genres in secondary music education, his vision for a "confident new generation" conspicuously included jazz.

Similarly, the prominent sociologist and scholar of black culture, Guy B. Johnson, while still a graduate student, speculated in the *Journal of Social Forces* about the connection between modernism and the revival of the Ku Klux Klan. Jazz, as the most accessible and recognizable manifestation of modernism, operated as a major enabler for the KKK's increasing influence in the 1920s. Johnson held that "the fad for jazz music and extreme forms of dancing" brought about a conservative backlash that helped the Ku Klux Klan increase its membership and that the KKK operated as a "reaction to Modernism."[112] Johnson's 1923 interpretation has held up to historical scrutiny. Or, more accurately, it was prescient in the ways scholars would interpret the KKK's cultural influence in the next century. Specific to Indiana, Richard B. Pierce also pointed to the rise in nativist sentiment following World War I as another factor for the KKK's increasing influence at the time.[113] Similarly, Stanley Coben argued that the organization acted as one of the "guardians" against modernity.[114] And, as Adam Laats has pointed out, they had more than a passing interest in schooling.[115]

Jazz and Morality in Higher Education

Regarding various iterations of moral education during the Jazz Age, B. Edward McClellan concluded that "administrators failed to capture campus life for the cause of moral education."[116] At predominately white institutions, faculty members were not successful in convincing students to avoid jazz and its associated vices. Part of this failure emanated from faculty not initially identifying the potential lasting significance of the cultural groundswell of the 1920s. Especially in the early part of the decade, many faculty members did little more than brush jazz aside as a crude and passing fad. Other scholars, primarily in the social sciences, looked at the cultural shifts taking place and saw an opportunity for serious and necessary inquiry. Yet for the overwhelming majority of higher-education students, little could have swayed their interest in jazz. The opinions and efforts of school personnel, many staunch jazz critics, had little impact on limiting the overwhelming popularity the music enjoyed among white college students. Still, this popularity was not universal. Greater opposition to the music and its associated trappings developed at many Evangelical Christian–affiliated institutions and historically black colleges. At both types of institutions, students critiqued the genre as musically unrefined and morally corrupting, and fought to counter what they saw as Jazz Age excesses taking hold at larger predominantly white schools. Even on campuses of state universities, pockets of opposition formed around literary societies. Many critiqued their fellow students' seemingly undying allegiance to the jazz lifestyle. Such critical appraisals were far from incorrect. As one University of Illinois student wrote, "Without the assurance of jazz from September to June, it would be folly to matriculate."[117]

Chapter 5

The Dance Craze on Campus
Negotiations and Public Perceptions

In the 1925 film, *The Plastic Age*, Hugh Carver enters fictional Prescott College as a nave freshman, ignorant about drinking, smoking, and petting.[1] Carver, a record-holder in the 440 meter sprint, rebuffs his roommate Carl Peters's initial offer of a cigarette and expresses little interest in the "harem" of attractive girls Carl has on his wall. Carver's primary interests of exercise and study do not change initially, though his college priorities do begin to when he joins a group of sophomores and sneaks into one of the women's dorms on campus. Cynthia Day, whom many men on campus desired, is attracted to the athletic freshman and insists they immediately dance together while another classmate plays the piano. Carver appears hesitant, and his initial attempt to dance the shimmy is timid and uncertain, though his reticence does not last long. Carver quickly begins to enjoy the fast-paced dance and the opportunity it provides to be close to the attractive female student. Carver returns to his room, reporting, "Fellows, I've been hazed and it was great!" Following that first late-night dance, Carver has increased difficulty maintaining his precollege lifestyle in the face of the corporeal pleasures that surround him on campus. It is through dancing that Carver begins embracing the jazz-fueled collegiate lifestyle, and the associated vices that surrounded it.

Though a work of fiction, *The Plastic Age* accurately represented many college students' interest in jazz dancing, at least at predominately white institutions. *The Plastic Age* became the second best-selling book of

1924, and the film remained in theaters three years after being released. Though it was a work of fiction, author Percy Mark's occupation as an English instructor at Brown University provided him the credentials to write about how young people spent their college years.[2] What made *The Plastic Age* unique among contemporary works was its vivid realistic take on college life, at least for predominately white universities, where jazz was something of a necessary social lubricant. It got students dancing, laughing, and petting.

When students wanted to enjoy themselves, when they wanted to have a good time, they wanted to dance. Students danced at proms, at fraternity dances, at house parties, and at off-campus hotels and country clubs. Dancing provided a way—a morally suspect way in the eyes of critics—to bring college men and women together for a good time. A sociologist studying undergraduate culture of the 1920s simply wrote, "Dancing is perhaps the most popular diversion of all."[3] Part of the allure for many students revolved around the provocative moves of the black bottom or the Charleston. To be sure, any criticism about the sexualized nature of jazz dancing was not inaccurate; the aphrodisiac-related qualities jazz dancing engendered only made it more appealing. As Helen Lefkowitz Horowitz noted, "Hedonism, always one of college life's distinct features, incorporated the new elements of each era. Men had always smoked and drank and enjoyed their kinds of music. Now they did so in the company of women, and the music shifted to jazz."[4]

Beyond university campuses, recreational dancing reached new heights of popularity in the 1920s. Across the nation, roughly 14 percent of men and 10 percent of women visited a dance hall at least once a week.[5] Dance hall proprietors responded by building halls that could house upward of 5,000 dancers. Demand for dance instruction was also high. Dancing pedagogue Arthur Murray's first advertisement in the *New York Times* produced over 37,000 responses.[6] Yet the dances Murray and other dancing instructors taught seemed tame in comparison to jazz's hot rhythms. Though the waltz, tango, and quickstep still enjoyed a not insignificant number of legacy aficionados, they were visibly different from jazz. Dress, particularly among women, had been notably more conservative, careful to not leave legs and arms bare. The shift toward less attire came, in part, out of necessity. Dancing to the more fast-paced shimmy, black bottom, and the Charleston was difficult when wearing long sleeves and corsets. Of course, jazz critics did not consider dancing ability when they saw exposed legs. Such changes in dress, coupled with the increased pace and body contact of jazz dancing, cast the emergent genre as "filthy" in critics' minds.[7]

This chapter looks at how faculty and student attitudes impacted the most popular form of recreation on campus: dance. Jazz dancing was central to the increasingly identifiable youth culture that was taking shape, especially on predominately white college campuses.[8] Yet for critics, jazz dancing embodied the most visible expression of the anxiety that surrounded student sexuality. This chapter explores that tension—how faculty and student attitudes impacted the most popular form of recreation on campus. And while any jazz dancing was banned in high schools, administrators at predominately white higher-education institutions grudgingly allowed students to dance as they wished at school-sponsored proms and other on-campus dances. In the Midwest, both Indiana University and the University of Illinois had relatively public debates about what type of dancing should be allowed on campus. Administrators at both schools worried how such decisions may impact their school's image, though ultimately acceded to student wishes. This was especially the case at large state schools, where fraternities and sororities dominated the social scene. At these institutions, students enjoyed considerable agency in shaping campus cultural life as they saw fit. Particularly for fraternities, a successful dance heightened the house's standing, wealth, and a codification of their cultural dominance on campus. Greater institutionalized opposition to jazz dancing among students existed in historically black, all female, and religiously conservative institutions. Despite their differences in student demographics and institutional missions, those schools often prohibited jazz dancing on moral grounds, a policy position many students at those institutions supported. Still, a certain irony undergirds any discussion around dancing on campus in the 1920s. Jazz, a recognizably black genre, found little welcome at historically black colleges, while also serving as the centerpiece of cultural life at the predominantly white colleges of the day.

University-Sponsored Dances

Inspired by the evening's drinking and dancing, a University of Chicago student penned a 1925 poem in praise of the prom. Appearing in the student magazine the *Phoenix*, it read in part, "Here's to the Prom! May it be glad and gay / Here's to the Prom / the one night to play (and lay) / And dance and play, and pay / Here's to the Prom, college life's last rebuttal / Here's to the Prom, may it dull care befuddle / And muddle, dull care befuddle."[9] That University of Chicago student was not alone in his gleeful anticipation of the annual dance. In the 1920s students and administrators alike at large universities viewed campus proms as the high point of the spring social season. The dances were often based around some exotic theme. At the University of Illinois in the 1920s, undergraduate students danced under tropical skies and winter wonderlands. They danced around desert scenes and "Oriental" sets.[10] Ultimately, proms' success rested on creating an atmosphere that would sell as many tickets as possible to avoid running a deficit.

The dances were expensive, and prom committees had to meet their financial obligations to a plethora of businesses to put on the events. Yet for their part, students were gladly willing to pay for the events. In the mid-1920s, students at the University of Michigan spent roughly $80,000 yearly on dances, roughly $921,000 in today's dollars.[11] Of the school's 9,000 students, 1,500 students also visited one of the city's two main dance halls at least once a week.[12] At the University of Wisconsin, students spent $100,000 ($1.1 million today) to go to proms, dances following football games, and other excuses to dance the "varsity drag."[13] The most costly disbursements often went to decorations, programs, catering, the musicians and, as late as 1922, the "war tax." At Ohio State University, the debt incurred at the 1921 Junior Prom took over a year to pay off. Officials opted to hold additional dances—cast as fundraisers—to raise the funds.[14] And despite the possible poor financial acumen of such a measure, or perhaps because of it, ticket prices could be too expensive for some students to afford. The University of Massachusetts student newspaper lamented in 1926 that "Those who are unfortunate enough not to be able to take it in, can only stand and look in from the outside at the glittering lights."[15] Jazz dancing, despite its popularity, had its financial limits.

The 1926 Indiana University Junior Prom, like other sanctioned campus dances, was carefully planned. The six-person student-run prom committee, four men and two women, all Caucasian, planned and carried out the evening's theme, a Japanese garden. The Men's Gymnasium housed the event; the makeshift ballroom, otherwise the basketball courts, was decorated with recognizably Japanese tropes. From the ceiling, twelve Japanese umbrellas hung down. Over the entranceway arches with latticework were ornamented with cherry blossoms.[16] Each fraternity—the most ardent jazz fans on campus—was assigned its own booth, cordoned off by a bamboo fence.[17] In the natatorium, tulips of assorted colors lined the walk on each side of the pool for students who wanted a break from dancing. Students not involved in Greek life could rest their feet by sitting at one of the twenty-five tables set up there. A "floating island," complete with electric fountain, lazily bounced around the pool as a small chamber orchestra provided less "syncopated" works.[18] The university hired the St. Louis–based Frank Trumbauer Orchestra to provide music for this, the "zenith social event" of the year. Easily one of the most popular bands in the country, the group had developed a reputation as "The Kings of Charleston Music." "The Voice of St. Louis," as the group was also nicknamed, was an eleven-piece band led by Trumbauer on alto saxophone and featured Bix Biederbecke on trumpet. Known for his "dirty" trumpet playing, Biederbecke was a particular favorite among Indiana University students since he had performed on campus three years earlier as part of The Wolverines.[19]

Dancing began at nine and lasted for an hour. At ten, junior prom queen June Bolinger and Jerry Tobin, president of the junior class, began their solo dance. Following that, they led all students in attendance in the Grand March. That procession began at the north end of the floor and ran the full course, eight couples abreast. The march was one of the highlights of the prom, and Bolinger and Tobin led dancers around the ballroom an unprecedented three times. After a short break, students continued dancing until two in the morning. A small army of chaperones observed the evening's festivities. Led by President William Lowe Bryan, nearly sixty faculty, administrators, and their spouses were on hand to make sure the students' behavior remained acceptable.[20]

Despite this careful organizing, one unavoidable controversy surrounding the 1925 junior prom forced the Indiana University Board of Trustees to make a decision they likely hoped to avoid. On the one hand, the board could bow to student pressure and change its policies about acceptable student behavior at dances. On the other, they could maintain their policy of forbidding one especially popular dance at the primary university-sanctioned dance of the academic year. In 1926, the dance in question was the Charleston, a jazz dance quickly gaining popularity on college campuses. Despite this 1926 concern about the Charleston, jazz dancing *writ large* had increasingly established a place at earlier proms. To students' delight, the popular jazz orchestra from Champaign, Illinois, Bill Donahue's Twelve, performed for the 1921 prom; in 1925, the yearbook, the *Arbutus*, similarly cited the "extraordinary leniency of the authorities in allowing the 'bacchanalian orgies' to continue till two in the morning."[21] That year, the *Indiana Daily Student* similarly referred to the "phantasmagoria of harmonies," the "mad worshipers of rhythm," and "rainbow-clad ladies" dancing to the syncopated tunes in that year's prom.[22] Such tongue-in-cheek humor aside, campus administrators likely may have looked at such behavior with concern for the 1925 junior prom. Still this public endorsement of dancing the Charleston in 1926 seemed a bridge too far. The prom, Indiana University's most prominent and widely covered dance of the year, would reflect poorly on the university if students could freely engage in "bacchanalian orgies." At the same time, the Board of Trustees must have recognized that such dances had become a major part of campus life and completely eliminating them could help dissuade students from attending.

Instead of publically allowing the dance, administrators shifted the focus to the building itself. The board ultimately opted to sidestep the morality associated with the Charleston. Instead, the group responsible for the university's overall budget and operation framed their decision to allow the dance in terms of public safety. The board's concern—or at least their stated concern—was that the Men's Gymnasium would collapse under the pressure of 600 undergraduate students dancing the Charleston.[23] That is, the board publically stated that the limestone Men's Gymnasium where the prom took place was not able to stand up to the Charleston. The university then paid an engineer to inspect the building, deciding whether it was structurally sound enough for the dance. In what must have been one of the engineer's stranger professional requests, he gladly obliged and inspected the building's integrity to survive the energetic dance. The Men's Gymnasium was quickly deemed structurally sound to withstand the dancing. The Board of Trustees avoided further implication by having a student, not board president or other school officials, announce the change, thus ensuring that the optics of the announcement cast the new policy primarily as a result of student demand, not administrator weakness. Prom committee chair Fred Hunt announced that the gym passed inspection and the university's ban on dancing the Charleston would be lifted for the 1926 prom.[24]

The decision to hire an engineer to inspect the building allowed an additional measure of face-saving for the board. Board members could point to their concerns about student safety while also having an easy rebuttal to accusations that they had abdicated their responsibilities in loco parentis by permitting the dance. University authorities were careful to specify that the decision to allow the dance at the prom applied to that event only. Registrar John W. Cravens made clear how the changed policy did not apply to future public dances; as noted in the yearbook, *Arbutus*, "For one night the university authorities allowed this form of dance to dominate."[25] The board and school administrators could claim that their decision to allow the dance was in fact an ethical decision—student safety—even if it required manufacturing the crisis.[26]

Two hundred and fifty miles to the south of Indiana University, a similar debate was taking place, though on very different terms, at Fisk University, Nashville's only all-black higher-education institution. In the fall of 1926, the campus community was discussing the merits of lifting the decades-long campus ban on dancing. For years, the rationale for the ban had not changed: dancing in any form was "a violation of the traditions of the university."[27] Yet by the mid-1920s, this complete ban on any form of dancing was increasingly being seen as arcane, an unnecessarily heavy-handed solution to a problem that did not exist. But unlike Indiana University, a vocal portion of the student body at Fisk voiced support for continuing to enforce the ban. Fisk students pointed to the various pernicious behaviors that swirled around jazz, not criticizing the dancing itself, but its extramusical consequences. Yet unlike predominately white institutions, Fisk students avoided mentioning sex and alcohol, in favor of less iniquitous concerns. One Fisk senior wrote, "In the hasty exchange of partners, one girl confides to another that she is 'dead' on her feet, but the urge of the Syncopators is as relentless as a ringmaster's whip. She is a stenographer and has worked at her desk overtime in order to secure this night's pleasure. . . . The moon, a mere wraith, mocks the folly of men."[28] Others were careful not to mention the word *jazz* or any closely associated terms—as if doing so would lend the genre an air of validity. Another Fisk student held that "[the dancer] must have the appropriate music, stage setting, and costuming. . . . The dancer who attains real skill has a good investment which brings her happiness, good health, and a means of satisfying her cravings for self-expression."[29] The dances between Morehouse and Spelman also ended considerably earlier than at colleges with a predominately white student body. One 1929 Morehouse-Spelman dance ended at 9:30, while the prom at the University of Illinois lasted until 2:00 in the morning.[30]

A larger percentage of Fisk student voices stopped short of saying that jazz was free of corruptive influences, while suggesting the campus dancing ban was simply too broad. As the reasoning went, not all types of dancing were equally nefarious, so by banning all forms of dance, the administration excluded those with the potential to benefit students. In a carefully worded argument—one that went out of its way to praise the benevolent administration—a junior warned, "A restriction that denies unto a group of individuals that which is wholesomely good and inherently desired has a tendency to destroy the character of that group of individuals."[31] Students ultimately greeted the end of dancing prohibition with a sense of cautious optimism after President Thomas Jones unilaterally lifted the ban in December 1926. That change came, in part, to pacify growing student unrest on campus. The previous year, then-President Fayette A. McKenzie resigned following an unprecedented student strike over his policies about control over student life. Students criticized him for being tyrannical; W. E. B. Du Bois penned critical pieces about McKenzie in *The Crisis*, as well as in *American Mercury*. Yet McKenzie was unrelenting in his discipline and uneven in his punishments, at one point writing, "Fidelity to school and college youth requires unfailing and constant supervision, constant insistence on regularity, reliability and fidelity."[32] Lifting the dancing ban, in addition to agreeing to eventual university recognition of fraternities and sororities, was an appeasement gesture by the new president to students. Following the end of the dancing ban, one anonymous *Greater Fisk Herald* student writer warned, "We must not give occasion for regret."[33] Faculty could be more pointed in their critiques. One complained the change in presidential leadership amounted to converting "the noble Fisk into a place of jazz."[34]

Dances at Atlanta-area historically black colleges similarly featured close oversight and little jazz as faculty and administrators sought to minimize the heightened physical arousal associated with jazz. Part of this motivation focused on countering stereotypes of African Americans, attempts to push back against what Stephanie Evans has termed "battle myths about 'wild' or 'uneducable'" black students.[35] One of the social highlights of the 1927 academic year at Atlanta University was the "Barn Social."[36] The event, which the junior and senior classes jointly organized, was built on the theme of a country dance. Students ate ice cream and peanuts, rested on haystacks, and danced a country reel. Including dancing, even one as innocuous as the country reel, was not a foregone conclusion. No dancing took place during first social between all-male Morehouse College and all-female Spelman College in 1926, when the Morehouse students and their chaperones made the short trip to the nearby campus. The gathering featured a "musical and literary program" by Spelman faculty and time for the students from each school to meet before the closing bell rang and the Morehouse students returned to their campus.[37] By 1929, dancing was allowed at Morehouse-Spelman events, though not jazz. However, outside of mixed-sex settings, students at some Atlanta schools were allowed more leniency to enjoy popular jazz dances. Female students at Atlanta University regularly held "Charleston contests" in their dormitories. One argued that such competitions disproved the popular belief that "girls can't have a good time without the fellows."[38]

The dynamics of the college dating atmosphere similarly motivated students to be skilled dancers who could also hold an interesting conversation with their dancing partner. This was particularly true for white students, who enjoyed relatively more agency around dancing than students at historically black colleges and universities. For both these men and women, the object of courtship at the time was rarely to obtain a steady partner. Instead, students sought to maintain casual relationships with multiple partners. In her history of shifts in dating practices across the twentieth century, Beth Bailey observed, though likely referring solely white young people, "You had to rate in order to date, to date in order to rate. By successfully maintaining this cycle, you became popular."[39] The dance floor, as the most public site of courtship, crucially shaped public perceptions and popularity. However, those who could not maintain, to some degree, various relationships were often stereotyped as boring and unattractive. A joke appearing in the *Trintonian*, the student newspaper at Trinity College in Texas, mocked this emphasis on dating and the centrality of dancing in that rite. It read as follows:

Papa—Have you heard from Mary lately?

Mama—Yes. She said that she almost flunked in her [exams] but has received three bids to the Junior Prom.

Papa—At last! My investment is bearing fruit.[40]

As perhaps one of the most perceptive writers of the decade—and Princeton alumnus—F. Scott Fitzgerald often wrote about the evolving social dynamics of young people. In his story, "Bernice Bobs Her Hair," Fitzgerald observed, "The idea of fox-trotting more than one full fox-trot with the same girl is distasteful, not to say odious." The story profiles one student, Bernice, whose more socially adroit, although jealous, cousin Marjorie intercedes when Bernice can only manage one continuous partner at a dance. After convincing one of her male friends to dance with her cousin, Marjorie complains to her mother later that evening how

Bernice is too socially awkward. Her mother counters, "What's a little cheap popularity?" Marjorie fervently replies, "It's everything when you're eighteen. I've done my best. I've been polite and I've made men dance with her, but they just won't stand being bored." Marjorie eventually agrees to tutor her cousin about how to carry herself and how to attract men. Her lessons work *too well*, and Bernice begins to overshadow her previously more socially adept cousin. To regain the focus of her peers, and one Yale student in particular, Marjorie convinces Bernice to bob her hair in the quintessential popular flapper style. Bernice agrees and the haircut is politely, though universally, condemned by her peers.[41]

Given such an environment, fictionalized by Fitzgerald though also widely accurate, students had an incentive to maintain as attractive an appearance as possible in the eyes of future suitors. College men in particular looked at their female classmates' dancing abilities as a crucial criterion for dating. One University of Chicago student wrote an ode to an imaginary "Sophisticated Blonde" who was "the only girl who could dance the Charleston to the music of Stravinski."[42] Many college women often sought to maintain this allure, especially in light of the sexually charged jazz dances. Asked whether she and her classmates were actually as "bad as they were painted," one Ohio State student replied, "We are."[43] She elaborated, "We are 'playing the game,' and flattering ourselves that we are 'doing it well' in all these things—smoking, dancing like Voodoo devotees, dressing décolleté, 'petting,' and drinking. There is no air of ultra-smartness surrounding us when we dance the collegiate, smoke cigarettes, and drink something stronger than a claret lemonade. . . . College girls thrive on thrills." Indeed, as Barbara Solomon has pointed out, on campus the flapper was "strong as well as self-centered."[44]

This public discussion of college students' sexual lives, one manifested through jazz dancing, also revealed a burgeoning area for research. In pair of mid-decade studies, two sociologists found that roughly 35 percent of white college men had intercourse before marriage, albeit not exclusively with white college women. The authors strongly suggested that many were having sex with prostitutes.[45] Despite that likelihood, college men certainly *sought* to sleep with college women, particularly to enhance their reputations. In his study of fraternity men, Nicholas Syrett argued, "The ability to seduce a girl was explicitly linked to a man's skill in so doing—sex as sport. Those who were most skillful at getting as much possible from girls—girls who were themselves trained to withhold—were the most lauded."[46] For their part, college women often felt more torn between the abstinence espoused by their parents and the appeal of increasingly visibly sexualized woman, the flapper, of the 1920s. As Kelly Schrum has correctly pointed out, "Girls in the 1920s struggled with sexuality. They were taught at home to refrain from sexual activity until marriage, but they enjoyed sexual images in movies, print media, and on the radio and admired the freedom of the idealized flapper."[47]

Still, anything approaching possible or perceived adult approval of college-age female sexuality remained taboo. In 1929, University of Missouri female students found a questionnaire in their mailboxes. It asked questions such as, "If you were engaged to marry a man and suddenly learned that he had at some point indulged in illicit sexual relations, would you break the engagement?" and, "Since sexual maturity, have you ever engaged in specific sexual relations?" The survey was a project of students in the sociology class of Harmon O. DeGraff, and further signed off by distinguished psychology professor Max F. Meyer. And while the survey itself may have been purely academic, the condemnation extended into the state's powers that be. Public outcry, up to and including the Missouri State Legislature, was swift and harsh. One failed resolution from a state representative sought increased state oversight by calling on University of Missouri President Stratton D. Brooks to take prompt action beyond calling the survey "sewer psychology." Among other consequences, the student survey authors left the university, and Brooks resigned over his ineffective handling of the crisis.[48]

In his study of interwar youth culture, Joseph Hawes also pointed to this generational tension; "the discussion of youthful sexuality, especially the celebration of female sexuality, was in large part a reaction against the ideology of Victorian repression."[49] Parents and university officials alike widely sought to instill in the younger generation the Victorian sentiments of modesty and restraint that they had been brought up with. Nowhere was this more apparent than in the policing of female students. University officials responsible for students' behavior, especially deans of women, pushed back against a generation of young women that believed they deserved greater autonomy than even "prewar" students. Yet any potential for postdance carnal acts led universities to minimize postdance activities for college women. The 1929 Indiana University social regulations specified, "Women students shall not be out driving after 10:30 except to return immediately from an entertainment or a dance."[50] One female student who returned to her dorm late after a dance was "bawled out" by the house mother.[51] Many students found ways around such regulations. One 1922 Wellesley graduate recalled, "We were not supposed to drive after dark, but that was nonsense. . . . We used to dazzle the college with stories about spark plugs, radiator cracks and blowouts. . . . We got away with everything and never used the same excuse twice."[52]

The responsibility for preventing this behavior on campus fell to deans of women. The Illinois Deans of Women, a statewide consortium of officials at universities and some high schools headed by the dean of women at Northwestern University, passed a resolution in 1921 that aimed "to endeavor in the coming year to abolish from dancing parties jazz music of the objectionable type and to provide at parties such adult companionship as shall be helpful and agreeable to young people."[53] Officials identified female dress, dancing, and the necessity of chaperones (called "adult companions") as the three most pressing problems needing to be addressed. They also cited the widespread opinions of dance teachers—"dancing masters"—that jazz dancing was inappropriate and morally debasing. Certainly, voicing such concerns was not unique and existed before the 1920s. As early as 1910, Dean Marion Talbot of the University of Chicago expressed concern that an increasing number of students "go to college openly and avowedly for a 'good time.'"[54] Dean Talbot belied her Victorian leanings as she complained of students then growing less interested in homemaking as their vocation. And, for Talbot, major consequences lay ahead without significant reform, including, but not limited to, divorce and "race suicide."[55]

Talbot's language added maintaining a sense of racial hierarchy to the wider antijazz mission. "Race suicide" was a popular Progressive Era concept that viewed the increase in immigration, coupled with the hesitancy among some women to have children, as accounting for alarming demographic changes. Edward Ross, a sociologist then at the University of Wisconsin, is credited with conceiving the term. Writing in a 1917 edition of *Scientific Monthly*, University of Michigan professor Warren S. Thompson wrote, "Professor Ross originally used the term—race suicide—to characterize what he believed to be the a movement in the growth of our population leading to the extinction of the older native stock and its replacement with the newer immigrant stocks—the Slavic, the Latin, and the Hebrew. According to this view our vital population questions are not questions of mere numbers but rather questions of quality."[56] Still, how was "race suicide" a relevant concern at predominantly white institutions? As

Talbot was undeniably aware, Big Ten institutions had a notable minority, though a minority nonetheless, of nonwhite students at the time. It seems highly unlikely that she would have been concerned about any upcoming sudden demographic shifts at the University of Chicago or other Big Ten universities. Her concern, instead, was more of a dance aesthetic one, highlighting jazz's origins among black musicians as further evidence of its dangerous moral inferiority.

For their part, college men enjoyed a greater degree of general discretion on campus. Talbot's counterpart, University of Illinois Dean of Men Thomas Arkle Clark, took a decidedly different tone on the question of college students and dancing. Speaking at a 1926 forum on the question of chaperones—a stance University of Chicago Dean Marion Talbot fervently supported—he said, "I believe the chaperone idea, even when it passes from many situations, will have left modern young people with a set of principles to which you will find they will adhere."[57] Such token praise aside, Clark did not express any concern about eliminating the chaperone from university-sponsored dances, even arguing that doing so could teach young people a lesson in responsibility to themselves and their peers. To this end, the dean characterized "modern youth," and young men in particular, as dreadfully afraid of not being viewed as "wise." This difference in emphasis, highlighting how campus policies could make students feel, was not a grace as widely extended to college women. He also offered domestic flattery to the female students in attendance at the forum, telling them, "I venture to say that if any of you were suddenly invited to a dance at midnight this evening, you could excuse yourself now and by midnight have made a new gown. It wouldn't look homemade, either."

Religion and Jazz Dancing on Campus

The approaches espoused at the University of Illinois and Penn State University appear generous compared to those universities that forbade dancing altogether; religiously affiliated colleges stood firm to maintain dancing bans throughout the 1920s. Wheaton College, a liberal arts college in the Chicago suburbs, was unrelenting in its student dancing prohibition, a ban which remained in place until 2003. Referencing the popular haircut among women jazz dancers, one faculty member's wife complained, "I disapprove of our coeds bobbing their hair because it is against the teaching of the Bible."[58] Specifically, Wheaton banned any dance that "may be immodest, sinfully erotic, or harmfully violent."[59] Baylor University, a Baptist institution in Waco, Texas, forbade dancing on campus and sought to minimize any opportunities students may have to dance off campus as well. To that end, in 1924 Baylor's President S. P. Brooks chose not to allow students to attend the Dallas Fair. He explained that their time would be better spent studying while also expressing concern the number of Baylor students wishing to attend could potentially turn the fair into the "Baylor Ball."[60]

DePauw University, a Methodist school in Greencastle, Indiana, similarly maintained a dancing ban until the late 1920s. The dancing issue among the larger Methodist community had been a hotly discussed topic since the early 1910s. A 1912 vote among the Methodist Episcopal General Conference whether to maintain its long-standing dancing ban passed 446 to 305.[61] Yet by the early 1920s, the supporters of dropping the prohibition were gaining greater numbers. The prominent New York Methodist Bishop Chester C. Marshall called on lifting the dancing ban and suggested that "the whole matter should be placed on the higher plane of individual decision and discrimination." Marshall argued that such reasoning was consistent with John Wesley's call to "do only such things as one can do in the name of Jesus Christ." Dancing opponents countered that maintaining the ban protected vulnerable women. In his 1921 text *Five Reasons Why Methodists Don't Dance*, Rev. Franklin F. Lewis argued, "The dance we are talking about is that social function where women's person is desecrated, cheapened and made public property."[62] Despite such criticisms, the church bishops did vote in 1924 to lift the ban.[63] That decision was, in part, a loosening of doctrinal definitions and decline of fundamentalist influence.[64]

Despite the change on the national level, DePauw University did not immediately follow suit and lift its prohibition on dancing. Thus, DePauw students had to find subversive ways to take part in the dance craze. On campus this meant sneaking around the faculty and staff chaperones at dinners and other social events. One relatively young English department faculty member took on the responsibility of chaperoning a 1924 Phi Delta Theta dinner. He later recalled, "The prevailing form for a fraternity party was a dinner lasting nearly all evening, with or without entertainment between courses, and sometimes with a hired orchestra that made toes tap under the table—but alas, wasted." For that 1924 dinner, the fraternity had hired a jazz band, which they positioned next to the chaperones. Over the course of the evening, the young faculty chaperone noticed some of the student couples retiring to another room. He asked the students why they were leaving and was told the students wanted to view the fraternity's poster collection. Following the students into the next room, the young English professor indeed found posters, but also students dancing to the jazz music being played in the other room. Perhaps, as a young faculty member not much older than the students he was supervising, Jerome Hixson was sympathetic to the college students and their wishes to dance. In any case, he did not report the students and may well have convinced other chaperones to do the same. He later wrote, "We made no scene. There was no time for more dancing. The Phi Delts thanked us profusely for being their chaperones."[65]

DePauw students also regularly drove to nearby towns such as Terre Haute and Brazil to fill their dances needs. Such activities—sneaking off campus without the necessary authorization—had become an open enough secret by 1928 that it was referred to the Student Affairs Committee meeting for review. During that gathering, a more liberal faculty member opined that on-campus chaperoned dances were actually safer for students since staying on campus prevented them from crowding into small cars to visit nearby towns. The new president, G. Bromley Oxnam, replied, "On a university campus there ought to be fifty-seven things to do at a party besides dance." One of the student members of the committee asked the president to suggest some. Oxnam replied, "Well, one could discuss the peace movement, slum clearance, scientific developments . . ." Faced with his inability to provide recreational activities other than dance, the DePauw president agreed to relax the university's rules. Parties could henceforth have a *limited* amount of dancing, though Oxnam specified that the events could not be advertised as "dances" so as not to upset the alumni. However, he shortly let go of that regulation as well and allowed a "dance" in the Bowman Gymnasium. Thomas Bowman, after whom the gymnasium was named, had been a Methodist Bishop and staunch dance opponent. Students and faculty joked that Bowman was turning over in his grave.

Catholic institutions did not impose the limitations that conservative Protestant schools like Concordia did. A variety of events at Catholic universities featured some amount of jazz dancing. At St. Catherine's University, also in Minnesota, the "famous Freshman Jazz Orchestra" provided the music for members of that class's first dance of their college careers. The school newspaper editorialized, "That was the first party to be given by the Class of '24, but we hope that it will not be the last."[66] Students at Loyola University in Chicago similarly were allowed to dance as they wished, both on and off campus. In 1924, the Pi Alpha Lamba fraternity included a Charleston dancing exhibition at their pre-Christmas "informal." Despite the title, considerable planning went into the event, held at the Auerton Hotel, under a "myriad of colorful draperies," with music provided by the Jinx Bryan's Syncopators.[67] Dances at the University of Notre Dame featured some of the most well-known jazz performers of the decade, including Isham Jones and the New Orleans Rhythm Kings. Student interest in dancing was so high that one undergraduate musician rented a floor of a downtown South Bend building to hold dances each Wednesday afternoon. A five-dollar investment to rent the space typically returned fifteen dollars for each band member.[68]

Why were Catholic institutions relatively welcoming for jazz dancing in the 1920s? Lynn Dumenil suggested in her cultural history that, for Catholics, the issue was best explained through the church's demographics and cultural aspirations. She wrote, "In the 1920s, the church was still an immigrant, primarily working-class institution and Catholic leaders occupied themselves with issues linked to their minority status vis-à-vis American society. Within the church, they pursued Americanization measures."[69] Dumenil's observation could well explain why jazz dancing was more welcome at Catholic colleges than other religiously affiliated institutions. Certainly, Catholic education leaders recognized jazz as a uniquely American. In their efforts to emphasize "Americanization measures," jazz appeared as unlikely, though not unwelcome, ally. While not necessarily an aesthetic endorsement, Catholic leaders may well have seen a sort of common cause in allowing jazz dancing on campus.

The combination of religiously based ethics and the jazz-based ethical challenges extended to state schools as well. In 1926 a former University of Illinois student, William O. Cross, published an article in the Episcopal weekly the *Witness*. Cross, at the time a student for the ministry, charged that "Drinking is now a minor vice for dating, a comprehensive diversion which includes dancing, drinking, and petting." In one example, he told of a trip by train the University of Illinois football team made, which included a "drunk . . . pajama dance" aboard the train. University officials responded, "There was a dance in one of the coaches, but it was orderly, chaperoned, and everybody was fully clothed." Cross did not single out the University of Illinois, but criticized schools across the wider Big Ten Conference for allowing similar indiscretions. Dr. George Craig Stewart, an Episcopal rector at St. Luke's Episcopal Church in Evanston, Illinois, and Northwestern University alumnus, issued the most detailed rebuttal to Cross's challenges. In a letter to the editor of *The Witness*, Stewart offered the somewhat dubious defense that "There was petting at college in my days; then it was called spooning, but it was not necessarily immoral, nor is bobbed hair, nor short skirts, nor dancing to the syncopated strains of jazz." Others offered more cogent defenses. The University of Chicago president argued, "No sweeping indictment of the undergraduate is warranted." The dean of Student Affairs at the University of Minnesota conceded that students in the Jazz Age had a "vicious nature," but countered, "I feel certain that the morals of our students, both men and women, are better, not worse [than in previous generations]."[70] To be certain, while Cross's article was written in an Episcopalian periodical, not everyone who responded to it belonged to that denomination. Still, for Big Ten administrators, any faith-based appraisal of jazz culture on campus that did not seek to wholly indict the genre made for an uncomfortable public relations campaign.[71]

Fraternities and Sororities

Looking at students' indulgences for jazz on campus, many critics singled out fraternities and sororities as the members of campus communities most responsible for helping spread the gospel of jazz at predominately white institutions. At a 1928 speech in Buffalo, Carnegie Institute of Technology chairman John L. Porter criticized what he saw as the decline in academic standards among fraternities. Speaking to the Grand Arch Council of Phi Kappa Psi, Porter said, "Fraternity years ago meant a linking of idea, ideals, ambitions, dreams, pride in achievement and comradeship." In contrast, Porter argued that "Several things have entered into collegiate life . . . which have had a tendency to break down scholastic standing and fraternity life. Jazz and girls are among these items."[72] Others lamented what they saw as a general jazz-filled fraternity life of the 1920s. Speaking at the 1922 New Jersey Methodist Episcopal Conference, Rev. John Handley of Ocean City criticized the music as a "virus" plaguing young people. Handley looked to the clergy to provide the solution for the "jazz problem" enveloping the nation. He intoned, "The time has come for the preachers to place themselves on record against this dance madness and other amusements, particularly in . . . fraternities."[73]

Jazz fit comfortably in such an atmosphere of celebration and amusement. The combination of jazz and Greek life in the 1920s was an ideal match; one early history of jazz refers to white fraternity members as "typical non-playing jazz zealots."[74] Indeed, jazz was funneled onto college campuses in large part due to the interest among sororities and especially fraternities. As early as 1916—when "jazz" was first being used in reference to music—student newspapers began referring to fraternity members' interest in jazz dancing. Fraternity- and sorority-sponsored dances provided a popular and enjoyable way of bringing university men and women together. Greek organizations held dances for various reasons and organized around various themes ranging from the local to the exotic to the historic. At the University of Illinois, the sorority Chi Omega celebrated the 1918 Peace Day with a Monday morning dance. The event featured confetti and streamers as Jordan's Jazz Band performed until the noon lunch ended the festivities.[75] In 1924 the Indiana University chapter of Alpha Tau Omega held a "fodder fest dance" with dance cards shaped like ears of corn.[76]

Some administrators voiced more pointed complaints to specific fraternities and their jazz-fueled parties. Just outside the jazz mecca of Chicago, the Northwestern University dean of men shuttered the chapter of Phi Epsilon Pi in 1926, after neighbors' complaints of "excessive noise" and "wild parties." The *Chicago Tribune* reported that one neighbor "refused to state whether he had or had not heard the clink of glasses or the strains of jazz," though he held that the fraternity had been a major disturbance to the neighborhood. University president Walter Dill Scott expressed his own disgust with the fraternity when he thundered, "The door to that house had not been locked in two years."[77] Some concerned citizens even sought some restraints to quiet Greek houses. In the nation's other jazz capital, New York City, one resident went so far as to take the Columbia University chapter of Theta Delta Chi to court over noise complaints and late night parties. According to the *New York Times*, the plaintiff complained, "It was nothing unusual . . . to be kept awake till 3 a.m. by the wailing of a saxophone or by the concentrated attack of an entire jazz band." In his guilty verdict, Judge William McAdoo ordered a probation officer to temporarily monitor the fraternity.[78]

"Dinner dances" were especially common and, like the Chi Omega dance, often built around a theme or idea. The Phi Kappa chapter house at the University of Illinois was converted into an "enchanting Spanish garden" for a 1930 dinner dance. Chapter members did not hesitate to praise their organizing abilities and alerted their alumni that the event was "called [by others] the best yet."[79] At least in terms of organizing, few events could match the university's Delta Chi 1921 dinner dance, a gathering held "in honor of King Solomon." The dance card for the evening included a brief comic story about the king—with references to fraternity members—as a sort of "justification" for the celebration. It explained, "The fields had produced the largest crop of potato chips and chipmunk ever known to the people of King Solomon's tribe."[80] Explaining how jazz dancing fit into such celebration, the last page indicated, "After the last of the Royal victuals had disappeared and the revelers had come out of their stupor, King Solomon bade the Jews-harp Jazzsters . . . to strum their melodies to fox-trot time that the people might dance ten times."

Greek organizations enjoyed a disproportionate impact on campus culture. Indeed, as Nicholas Syrett points out, "fraternities and sororities reigned social supreme on most college campuses."[81] Many fraternity and sorority members had little problem with the privileged positions they held in organizing campuswide events. At Syracuse University in the late 1920s, nearly half of students in fraternities or sororities claimed they *should* have a disproportionate amount of influence on the campus's social life.[82] This influence often extended to campuswide dances. Fraternities and sororities regularly had booths and special areas cordoned off for them at university-organized dances, a pleasure rarely extended to non-Greek students. And Greeks often organized campus-wide events. Fraternity members served as organizing chairs for both the 1919 and 1929 University of Illinois Junior Proms, as well as many in between. Greek and non-Greek students wishing to attend had to go to the chapter houses to purchase tickets.[83] Yet this general social dominance bred resentment. One alumnus (himself a Psi Upsilon member) wrote the Dartmouth president Ernest Martin Hopkins in 1920, complaining that "of about 226 officers, and memberships of importance, in student-life organizations, about 200 are held by fraternity men. Of course these 200 positions are not secured to fraternities by open and free competition."[84]

Fraternity members pointed to their abilities to hold their own dances as a source of pride. To that end, Greek organizations regularly bought phonographs, especially the Victor Victrola, as a way to hold dances as economically as possible. A joke in *College Humor* suggested that the Victrola was one of the most essential elements of the fraternity house, an indispensable component of 1920s fraternity life.[85] Increasingly inexpensive and portable, Victrolas were a simple option for listening and dancing to jazz. At the University of California, Berkeley, Alpha Chi Sigma—a professional fraternity for students interested in chemistry that also had a chapter house—members opted for fundraising to afford their house Victrola. The students raffled off football season tickets (then called "subscription") to purchase a "new Orthophonic Victrola."[86] That Victrola acquisition was on par with other crucial purchases, including silverware and new downstairs curtains. On the other hand, the inability to hold enjoyable and popular dances was a major disappointment. The University of Illinois chapter of Theta Chi complained to their alumni that they only managed to have one "Victrola dance" during the spring 1927 semester, though providing no explanation why.[87]

As Nicholas Syrett has pointed out, fraternities often operated on the assumption that "quality" men came from wealthy white families. And hiring musicians—a more expensive alternative to the cheaper Victrola dance—provided a display of wealth.[88] Indeed, fraternities hired musicians to play for their dances as an indicator of both wealth and popularity. Hiring live performers delineated among those Greek organizations that could afford such luxuries and those which could not. The University of Illinois chapter of Alpha Alpha Omega held its 1923 dinner dance at a local country club. Members and their guests enjoyed a five-course meal before retiring to the hall for an evening of dancing. Gus Webber and his band, regular performers for campus dances, provided music for the evening.[89] F. Scott Fitzgerald also wrote about live jazz bands at dances as an indicator of wealth. His short story "May Day" chronicles the experiences of the Gamma Psi dance from various vantage points. The Princeton fraternity decided to hold the dance off campus and chose New York City. Apparently, the band members were less than pleased with having to provide music for the event. Fitzgerald wrote that the band members sat down "arrogantly" and endured the "burden of providing music for the Gamma Psi Fraternity."[90]

Universities imposed various regulations on chapter house dances in hopes of minimizing inappropriate behavior. At Indiana University, the deans of men and women, respectively, had to approve the respective chaperones at least a day in advance. One article of the university's 1929 "Social Regulations" advised, "At each dance there shall be a floor committee of not less than three students who shall assist the chaperones and shall assist them in every possible way."[91] More generally, Indiana University Greek life dances were required to end by midnight and could only be held on Fridays and Saturdays. Fraternities and sororities were allowed two dances per semester, a number that had increased over the previous decade: in 1919, fraternities and sororities could only hold one dance each semester. Of the four permitted through the full academic year, only one could be a formal dance, though organizations could apply for more. The university also loosened regulations on times fraternity students could play the phonograph. In 1919, students were given specific times they could play their favorite records; by 1929 no such rule existed.[92]

Pan-Hellenic students did not necessarily follow such regulations to the letter. Some decided to hold dances without proper vetting and oversight. In an environment that praised what one scholar wryly described as the "accomplishments in the realms of the extra curriculum," losing dancing rights could be socially damning.[93] Still, students took that risk. As early as 1918, university officials disciplined fraternities for hosting mixed-sex dances without acquiring the proper authorization. Such *dances*, if the word even applies, were not necessarily large or meticulously planned events. In one instance, two Indiana University members of Kappa Sigma came before the Committee on Student Affairs—the body tasked with creating and enforcing such regulations—to be reprimanded for sneaking two women into their house for dancing. Minutes of that meeting dryly note, "There was dancing with Victrola music."[94] In some cases, punishments included a complete withdrawal of dancing privileges, or, perhaps even worse, permission for only single-sex dances. Still, at least at Indiana University, few infractions brought administrators to take such draconian actions. More often, officials opted to either decrease the number of permitted dances or insist they be held in a communal campus location rather than the more private chapter houses.[95]

At the University of Illinois, sororities faced restrictions on organizing dances that fraternities did not. Though they could, and did, hold off-campus dances, those sororities were forbidden to hold mixed-sex dances at their chapter houses throughout the 1920s. Certainly less popular, more informal single-sex dances had previously been permitted. In the face of student demand, the change finally came in 1932, after a meeting of the Women's League on revisions to regulations governing chapter houses. Following a subcommittee advisory board recommendation, the larger Women's League voted to rescind the ban, with apparently little fanfare. Though the board maintained a prohibition on "mixed dancing" during study hours, the new policy immediately went into effect.[96]

Organizing dances at single-sex schools required different planning skills than at coeducational institutions. Students at all-female Smith and Mount Holyoke colleges saw the fraternity dances at nearby all-male Amherst College as the height of the schools' social season. The fraternities advertised their events as "tea dances," a nod to the Eighteenth Amendment. In reality, the tea was often mixed bootleg whiskey, with a slice of lemon for show.[97] Amherst fraternities typically opened their dances to paying male nonmembers and, as a result, could spend more on such events. Smith and Mount Holyoke students could attend for free. Still, men outnumbered women at the dances roughly three to one. Such an environment inevitably bred competition, with men regularly cutting in on each other's dances. For the women, the ratio meant they could dance all night if they wished, and many did. Members of the hosting fraternity often took advantage of the situation by sneaking upstairs for additional "refreshment." Administrators at Smith and Mount Holyoke did not look kindly on their students eagerly leaving campus each weekend and traveling to Amherst. At Smith, the dances became so popular that officials instituted a policy of only allowing students to attend one dance per fraternity per year.[98]

The question of sexuality, especially female sexuality, played a central role in Greek life dances. As one historian of youth culture has argued, "Fraternities and sororities made it possible for young people to explore their own sexuality."[99] If judging, comparing, and objectifying women was a common hobby for many fraternities, dances provided the opportunity for the most arousing display of the sexualized female body, a culture of drinking and dancing in which jazz fit comfortably. Between the "hot rhythms" and bare arms, fraternity members looked at jazz dancing and saw certain aphrodisiac qualities. A cartoon on the 1925 dance card from the Indiana University chapter of Delta Tau Delta epitomizes the physical attributes many fraternity men found attractive, what made one "a man."[100] Little remarkable exists about the male dance partner in the drawing. He is dressed in a boldly patterned blazer and has a hint of shine in his hair, identifying him as a "slicker." He smiles. The woman, however, is cast in a much more sexualized light, one replete with recognizably flapper tropes. Her arms are bare and her lips are puckered as she looks at up her dance partner longingly. Her dress seems to be almost falling off her as she leans in to her clearly content, though poorly drawn partner (see fig. 5.1).[101]

Fairly or not, fraternity members' penchant for merriment did bring them a reputation among some of their classmates as less than intellectually curious students and more focused on the social concerns of their education. A satirical article in the Indiana University student literary magazine, the *Vagabond*, did not cast a flattering light on the all-male organizations. The unnamed author faux-mocked the perception

Figure. 5.1. Delta Tau Delta dance card. Courtesy Indiana University Archives, 1925.

of chapter houses as "combined brothels and gin palaces" but then rose to the defense of the "excitement hungry *homines sapientes*, schooled in the noble art of wenching . . . and conversant with the esoteric sex lore of their generation." Jazz dancing played a central role to the author's argument of a party-happy Greek system with music that provided the conduit for fraternity members to drink and date. The unnamed author wrote, "There has come, happily—and coincident with the discovery of Jazz—the dawn of a new era: the rise of the younger ignorencia." The music helped fraternity members achieve "the seduction of supposedly virtuous women" as the "rhythmic caterwauling of the jazz orchestra," along with requisite drinks, provided the necessary assistance for that goal. Such an education well-prepared those in the Greek life to enter the business world after graduation, a community seemingly filled with like-minded professionals. To the *Vagabond* author, this seemed like a natural fit, since "a restless, excitement-hungry boob, he joins hands with other boobs who, like himself, are recent alumni of campus fraternal orders." Thus merged, they would "become supernumeraries in the comedy of modern business."[102] Perhaps a reality of different reading interests, such criticisms went unanswered.

Some fraternity members went beyond being jazz enthusiasts and to being jazz musicians. None were more successful while in college or after than Hoagy Carmichael, an Indiana University member of Kappa Sigma, who would go on to be one of the country's most successful entertainers in the 1940s and 1950s.[103] Carmichael grew up in Bloomington and nearby Indianapolis. He credited the core of his music education to a black Indianapolis pianist named Reggie DuValle whom he later described as "high brown, long fingered."[104] The two first connected in 1916, when a sixteen-year-old Carmichael walked by DuValle's Indianapolis house and stopped to listen to the sounds coming from inside. Carmichael thought DuValle played piano in a manner more advanced than ragtime, though not yet identifiable as jazz. DuValle invited Carmichael in after seeing him sitting on the porch listening. At the time, DuValle was playing professionally in downtown Indianapolis with his jazz ensemble, Reginald DuValle and the Blackbirds. According to Carmichael, their lessons, which lasted less than two years, consisted of Carmichael making such observations as "You bring your thumb down on the chord right after you've hit it with your right hand" and DuValle replying, "Yeah. I want that harmony to *holler*."[105] The young musician quickly became absorbed in music, later recalling, "I *felt* jazz."[106] DuValle's son remembered the instances Carmichael came to the house for piano lessons as the only times a white person entered the family's house, other than the occasional insurance salesman.[107] In 1918, Carmichael dropped out of Indianapolis's Manual High School, with "neither of [the school nor me] grieving," and devoted himself to practicing jazz piano, while mixing cement and working in a slaughterhouse.[108]

By the beginning of the 1919–1920 school year, Carmichael had managed to convince his parents to let him move back to Bloomington, where they had lived when he was a boy. He reentered high school, well aware he was older than his classmates, and gathered around him a group of jazz musicians. After hearing him play, one of Carmichael's high school friends offered him and a friend five dollars to play for a fraternity dance. The dance was organized in a somewhat suspicious location, a Bloomington dance hall above a hardware store. That 1919 performance became the first of many when Indiana University students danced to Carmichael's piano. Years later Carmichael reminisced about that night, writing, "There was applause, thunderous applause, and now thirty couples jammed the floor. College couples from the Student Building dance. We are stealing their crowd!" The students who showed up commented, "Who is the kid on the piano?" and, "Boy, he can really go!" Carmichael recounted he could hear the tools rattling in the hardware store below.[109]

After high school, Carmichael enrolled at Indiana University, pledged Kappa Sigma, and continued performing. An early version of his jazz band consisted of Carmichael at the piano, a French horn player, and a percussionist. Despite these humble beginnings, Carmichael would assemble a more complete group of student jazz musicians and perform under the title Carmichael's Collegians and easily found success on campus. Musically and socially, Carmichael was popular on campus. As longtime chancellor and president Herman B Wells later wrote that Carmichael "enlivened the local scene."[110] Carmichael's Collegians quickly became the go-to choice for jazz music at the university, growing so popular so quickly that one student publication felt it was necessary to remind its readers "there are students other than Hoagland Carmichael who have helped to meet the needs of this new-born era."[111] Another student summed up the frequency of Carmichael at such dances when she simply wrote in her diary, "Hoag played."[112] Under the name Carmichael and Company, the group also played for the first Jordan River Revue in 1922.[113] The revue was a student-written and -produced "opera," and its success led to it becoming an annual tradition at the university. The choice to include Carmichael and his ensemble must have been a foregone conclusion; the group's enormous popularity on campus likely eschewed any real competition.[114]

Carmichael and his musician friends epitomized the ideal Greek life of the era, at least for white students. And the group maintained its popularity, in part, through impromptu and entertaining performances. Following a 1926 dance at the Kappa Sigma house, the band packed their instruments into a large truck they had secured. Many of the typical jazz band instruments of the day—trumpet, saxophone, banjo, violin, and trombone—were easily moved. However, the piano, Carmichael's instrument, presented a challenge. As a solution, the group borrowed the relatively lightweight green colored piano from the Book Nook, a local hangout just off campus where the group often played. With the band all assembled on the truck, they took off to "serenade" the sororities by automobile. The next year, Carmichael and his associates "marched" down the street wearing pajamas in what they called the "Book Nook Commencement Parade." The group marched around campus and downtown Bloomington wearing an assortment of robes, pajamas, and pinstriped hats. Carmichael, this time on trumpet, led the procession.[115]

Fun and games aside, Carmichael eagerly embraced the business component of being the most popular student jazz band on campus. To promote his group, Carmichael sent out letters to on- and off-campus groups he believed would be willing to hire them. One 1922 letter—printed on letterhead that read "Carmichael's Collegians/Dances, Banquets, Entertainments/'That's Our Business'"—described the ensemble and outlined the music prepared for the Christmas season.[116] The letter intentionally sought to professionalize the ensemble, differentiating it in a town of one-off competitors. Carmichael also marketed his ensemble as especially versatile, playing something everyone in attendance at a given event would enjoy. He wrote, "We are playing high-classed music of a wide variety with Chicago 'dirt' thrown in, in view of pleasing everyone." Gently nudging any hesitancy to book the band quickly, the letter added, "We have several engagements now booked and hope that you will make arrangements early in order that you may be included in our schedule."[117]

Carmichael further demonstrated his business acumen by hiring his friend Bix Biederbecke, by then a popular performer and leader of the Wolverines, to play a handful of dances at and around Indiana University. The two had met in a marijuana smoke-filled Chicago jazz club in 1922, just before Biederbecke was expelled from the city's Lake Forest Academy. A mutual friend had introduced the two, and they had reconnected the next year when they both showed up to hear Louis Armstrong play in Chicago.[118] Carmichael helped arrange a handful of Bloomington concerts for Biederbecke's group, the Wolverines, in late April and early May 1924, in addition to providing them with lodging at the Kappa Sigma house.[119,120]

Jazz and Campus Privilege

A certain irony about Carmichael's music education and career as a campus musician seems undeniable. Carmichael embodied the space some students, particularly white fraternity men, were given to shape the cultural life of their schools. He and his fraternity colleagues performed for fraternities and sororities, at university-sponsored events, and various off-campus dances. To be sure, the acclaim that came with that popularity was certainly warranted. Carmichael's musical abilities were unmatched by other campus jazz musicians. Since he was a boy living in Indianapolis, he was disciplined and routinely practiced piano.[121] Yet in addition to his hard work, Carmichael himself acknowledged he owed much of his musical abilities to a black piano instructor in Indianapolis who was not afforded the same educational opportunities Carmichael enjoyed. Fraternity members like Carmichael were often the most vocal jazz enthusiasts on campus, often viewing dancing as a way to get close to "the coeds." Though proms and other university-sponsored dances marked the height of the social season on many predominately white campuses, students at those universities looked for any opportunity to dance.

Reminiscing decades later, President Herman B Wells noted, "Campus life was so informal and unstructured that students fashioned their own fun for the most part and turned their ideas into enterprises."[122] Wells was not incorrect, particularly for predominately white institutions. Jazz, a genre that had been developed by black musicians, had been sanctified for performance at predominately white universities, and commodified financially by student jazz ensembles. Such privilege was not universal in higher education. Students at evangelical and historically black institutions faced stricter limitations on campus dancing, though many willingly adhered to that moral code. From university-wide proms to fraternity dances, "modern" dancing persisted on many campuses due to its overwhelming popularity among white students.

Conclusion

In *The Republic*, itself an extended discussion on the nature of educating youth, Plato argued for the importance of the "right" music as parents and educators seek to turn wild youth into morally sound adults. Plato believed that "music can dispose a child toward virtue because it directly moves [youth] on an emotional level," while also cautioning those in power to "guard as carefully as they can against any innovation in music . . . that is counter to the established order."[1] Whether one considers battles over rock 'n' roll in the 1950s, or the more contemporary cultural controversies over hip-hop, each generation battles over the ears of children as much as they do over their hearts. Still, no period in American history, aside from the Jazz Age, is known for a musical genre. Jazz, in the 1920s, represented a "constellation of cultural concerns," one highlighting, but not limited to, concerns about a sense of infusion of blackness into popular culture, a blending of genders as flappers developed a masculine aesthetic, and evolution.[2]

As late as 1931, the *Etude* editor James Cooke continued to prophesize about jazz's imminent demise. Speaking at a music conference in Detroit, he said, "There is a thin line of melody in it, under which there is the bump, bump, bump of the African jungle. Because of this sickening lack of variety, the public is already beginning to turn away, not only here, but in Europe also."[3] As it turns out, Cooke was partly right and partly wrong. His forecasting of jazz's impending demise was no less true today than it was then, whether he was willing to see it or not. By 1931, jazz's permanence was well established. As Mark Katz has dryly noted, toward the end of the 1920s, "Opposition to jazz cooled."[4] Still, Cooke was very much writing as a man of his time by highlighting jazz's association with black musicians. For many who saw European classical music as the height of musical cultural, Cooke included, jazz was immediately musically disqualifying. This reality made for a musical conundrum among those black educators who sought to develop a jazz-free aesthetic. In her edited collection of NANM documents, Doris Evans McGinty suggested, "Because of this emphasis [on classical or, "high art" music] N.A.N.M. could not avoid being considered an elitist organization."[5] Though McGinty's assertion about elitism is accurate, the emphasis on classical music should not overshadow the role the spiritual genres members deemed acceptable. Spirituals spoke to the juxtaposition of joy and suffering, the necessity of religion, and of the importance of community, all ideas NANM members wanted to preserve and maintain for the next generation.

Educators at historically black institutions crafted distinct messages to convince their students of jazz's musical and extramusical dangers, arguing that jazz would lead to "immodest dress" and that it would "jazz up" the Negro spiritual. The reactions to jazz in both secondary and tertiary education illuminate continuities across both levels of schooling. Nowhere is this truer than the opposition among black educators—and many students—to jazz. The efforts of Crispus Attucks High School Principal Lane and others to separate students from jazz points to a major complicating factor for black jazz critics—both white and black critics and supporters saw jazz as an outgrowth of the black community. Yet the concern among black educators was more specific than among their white counterparts. At both the secondary and tertiary levels, these teachers worried that jazz could "corrupt" the spiritual, that jazz's "hot rhythms" could find their way into that sacred genre. Many also worried that students would become more interested in the secular genre and lose interest in the narratives of tragedy and perseverance the spiritual carried.

White secondary teachers sought to instill in their students a sense of musical values similar to the one they were raised with, in essence, a lingering Victorian ethic that minimized the ethic of pleasure jazz embodied. Such opposition reached its nadir in the first half of the decade. Then, the need to make sure the next generation would not adopt jazz's lack of musical and moral standards served as justification, or perhaps excuse for rhetoric that pointed to jazz's derivation among black musicians as its original sin. Yet toward the middle of the decade, as the music's permanency became increasingly evident, the rhetoric similarly cooled. A handful of more moderate educators among music teachers agreed with their nonmusician colleagues that jazz had a degree of usefulness within schools. Yet such voices were often drowned out, especially in the early 1920s, in the overwhelming opposition to the genre.

White higher-education faculty and administrators largely had the same personal feelings about jazz, but responded differently. While many disliked jazz, they did not feel the degree of responsibility to stop its spread that their secondary education colleagues did. Such duties often fell to deans of men and women and, on occasion, public comment by university presidents. Particularly in the first half of the decade, many higher-education faculty merely brushed the "jazz problem" aside as a passing fad, while university officials generally allowed students more discretion to shape the cultural life of their institutions than high school pupils had. Toward the middle of the decade, some social science faculty began looking at the undeniable popularity of jazz and saw a social phenomenon requiring study. While not synonymous with any endorsement of musical or moral quality, such scholars recognized the unprecedented cultural shift taking place and sought to inquire into and problematize its causes and meaning.

The lives and experiences of university "coeds" and fraternity members, at least at predominately white universities, were characterized in print and on screen as championing a certain bon vivant frivolity that eschewed the Victorian ethos of social control. Bestsellers like *This Side of Paradise* by F. Scott Fitzgerald and *Unforbidden Fruit* by Samuel Hopkins Adams (under the pseudonym Warner Fabian) served both to glorify and satirize the jazz-drenched and gin-fueled white college lifestyle. Films such as *The Plastic Age* and *The Collegians* brought such stories into popular culture, creating a standardized visual example of a glorified college experience. Though caricatured, such depictions were not wholly incorrect. Jazz dancing was enormously popular on campus, particularly on large Midwestern state schools. Discussions on the merits of jazz typically involved the possible immorality of the Shimmy and other dances. Dances, particularly prominent ones like proms, were instances in which students and faculty negotiated what was and what was not appropriate. Such discussions occurred less often in evangelical colleges, where students saw few redeeming qualities in the music.

Writing in 1921, Will Earhart, the prominent music supervisor in Pittsburgh, vehemently rejected any assertion that public school instrumental programs were not capable of producing "fine music." Earhart's refutation rested on two basic points. First, he believed that instrumental programs could, indeed, teach the best music, and second, instrumental music programs were "one of the greatest safeguards against the ragtime and jazz that disgrace our age."[6] In the ninety years since he wrote, Earhart's first claim has proved correct. Throughout the twentieth century, band programs grew at an astonishing pace, both in enrollment and quality, and today remain the center of school music programs nationwide. However, Earhart's assertion about instrumental music as a "safeguard" against jazz has proven to be quite the opposite. As the folk dance movement waned during the 1920s, the school music program began to take a different shape. Band programs especially grew in popularity, due in no small part to the growth of bands during and following World War I. A consequence of this increase in school band programs was that all students, including those interested in jazz, received an increasingly sophisticated instrumental music education. Even without official jazz classes, these programs provided the next generation of musicians with the necessary technical skills that could adapt to learning various genres. Among others, early prominent jazz musicians Earl Carruthers and Charles Kynard both benefited from their music education in Kansas City public schools, years before jazz was introduced into the curriculum.[7] Earhart's formula—an approach copied many times over—backfired. Not only did excluding jazz from schools make it more attractive in many students' mind, the increase in school instrumental programs gave the next generation the basic technical skills to develop their jazz aptitude. Instead, students would have to seek out other places to learn those how to play the genre. What schools would not provide, students willingly sought out. This meant going to jazz clubs and dance halls to listen or even "sit in" on a performance, a considerably worse consequence than introducing students to the genre in the more friendly confines of the school. For Bix Biederbecke, this meant sneaking onto riverboats such as the SS *Capitol* and jazz clubs in downtown Chicago. Those were his schools.

Ronald Cohen's wonderfully sarcastic characterization of some generations of twentieth-century young people as "delinquents," at least in the eyes of more conservative adult critics, aptly sums up the general attitude among many educators about the influence jazz would have on their students.[8] Adults have long feared the corrupting influence of the next generation's music and the surrounding culture. A similar generational gap exists today regarding hip-hop much as it did in the late 1950s and 1960s about rock 'n' roll. In each case, the emergent genre is dismissed, particularly by white critics, as a musical degradation and morally corrupting influence. And in each case, the emergent genre has proved remarkably durable, despite, or perhaps because of, a combination of that criticism and youth-driven popularity. Still, the emphasis on school as antidote speaks to the widespread faith in public schooling that still had currency in the early twentieth century. Schools were the primary and logical institution to keep the spread of jazz contained. A cultural dividing line, jazz represented more than any other phenomenon the shift away from a Victorian ethos of restraint to a modern ethos of pleasure. Jazz embodied a combination of instinct and impulse, while the debate about it involved much more than musical aesthetics. The "jazz problem" meant changes in dress and dance. It involved the possibility of alcohol, drugs, and "petting." It was reprehensible enough when adults danced the Charleston; the possibility of young people doing so was unacceptable. Yet, by the end of the decade, the "delinquents" won.

Notes

Introduction

1. William Kenney, *Jazz on the River* (Chicago: University of Chicago Press, 2005), 115–40.

2. Jean Pierre Lion, *Bix: The Definitive Biography of a Jazz Legend*, trans. Gabriella Page-Fort (New York: Continuum, 2005), 25–26.

3. Lion, *Bix*, 33.

4. Lion, *Bix*, 43.

5. William Kenney, *Chicago Jazz: A Cultural History* (New York and Oxford: Oxford University Press, 1993), 114.

6. "Former University Man Dies in East," *Daily Iowan*, August 8, 1931.

7. Biographies of Bix include: Brendan Wolfe, *Finding Bix: The Life and Afterlife of a Jazz Legend* (Iowa City: University of Iowa Press, 2017); Richard M. Sudhalter and Philip R. Evans, *Bix: Man & Legend* (New Rochelle: Arlington House, 1974); Ralph Burton, *Remembering Bix: A Memoir of the Jazz Age* (Cambridge: Da Capo, 1974; repr., 2000).

8. "Heaven Protect Jazz!," *Daily Illini*, January 22, 1921.

9. "Work Assails Spirit of Jazz," *Los Angeles Times*, June 16, 1925.

10. Like other Jazz Age historians, I am less concerned about defining precisely when the Jazz Age began but more of what it looked like. Pointing simply to Willa Cather's famous quip that the "world broke in two in 1922" or even the end of World War I are entertaining but reductive signposts. One thing was for sure, the Jazz Age was not synonymous with the decade of the 1920s. It did not suddenly begin on January 1, 1920. See Jason Scott Smith, "The Strange History of the Decade: Modernity, Nostalgia, and the Perils of Periodization," *Journal of Social History* 32, no. 2 (1998).

11. James F. Cooke, "Where the Etude Stands on Jazz," *Etude*, August, 1924, 515.

12. The temptation to simply interpret this tension as a left/right divide proves incorrect. Among other examples, progressive Judge Ben B. Lindsey criticized jazz as being morally unhealthy. In his appropriately titled *The Revolt of Modern Youth*, Lindsey criticized "jazz music and the dancing that went with it . . . 'pelvic dancing.'" Judge Ben B. Lindsey and Wainwright Evans, *The Revolt of Modern Youth* (New York: Boni and Liveright, 1925), 94. For historical significance, see: Lynn Dumenil, *The Modern Temper: American Culture and Society in the 1920s* (New York: Hill and Wang, 1995).

13. Gary Day, *Varieties of Victorianism: The Uses of a Past* (New York: Palgrave Macmillan 1998); Thomas J. Schlereth, *Victorian America: Transformations in Everyday Life* (New York: Harper Collins, 1991); Mary E. Odom, *Delinquent Daughters: Protecting and Policing Adolescent Female Sexuality in the United States, 1885–1920* (Chapel Hill: University of North Carolina Press, 1995); Peter G. Filene, *Him/Her/Self: Gender Identities in Modern America*, 3rd ed. (Baltimore: Johns Hopkins University Press, 1998).

14. Susan Curtis, "Black Creativity and Black Stereotype: Rethinking Twentieth-Century Popular Music in America," in *Beyond Blackface: African American and the Creation of American Popular Culture, 1890–1930*, ed. W. Fitzhugh Brundage (Chapel Hill: University of North Carolina Press, 2011), 125.

15. Court Carney, *Cuttin' Up: How Early Jazz Got America's Ear* (Lawrence: University of Kansas Press, 2009), 129.

16. National Center for Education Statistics, *Digest of Education Statistics* (Washington, DC: U.S. Department of Education, 1998), 50.

17. Carney, *Cuttin' Up*, 129.

18. I borrow the title from a 1924 issue of *The Etude Music Magazine*. The full title was "The Jazz Problem: Opinions of Prominent Men and Musicians."

19. Mary Herron Dupree, "'Jazz,' the Critics, and American Art Music in the 1920s," *American Music* 4, no. 3 (1986); Alan Merriam and Fradley Garner, "Jazz: The Word," *Ethnomusicology* 12, no. 3 (1968).

20. I borrow the phrase from the subtitle of Adam Laats, *Fundamentalism and Education in the Scopes Era: God, Darwin, and the Roots of America's Culture Wars* (New York: Palgrave Macmillan, 2012). Other examples of this interpretation include: Alan Brinkley, *The End of Reform: New Deal Liberalism in Recession and War* (New York: Knopf Doubleday, 1996); Michael McGerr, *A Fierce Discontent: The Rise and Fall of the Progressive Movement in America* (Oxford and New York: Oxford University Press, 2003); Charles Postel, *The Populist Vision* (Oxford and New York: Oxford University Press, 2007); Gary Gerstle, *American Crucible: Race and Nation in the Twentieth Century* (Princeton and Oxford: Princeton University Press, 2002); Carl Smith, *Urban Disorder and the Shape of Belief: The Great Chicago Fire, the Haymarket Bomb, and the Model Town of Pullman* (Chicago and London: University of Chicago Press, 2007); Lizabeth Cohen, *Making a New Deal: Industrial Workers in Chicago, 1919–1939* (Cambridge: Cambridge University Press, 2008);

Alan Brinkley, *The End Of Reform: New Deal Liberalism in Recession and War* (New York: Knopf Doubleday, 2011); Erica Ryan, *When the World Broke in Two: The Roaring Twenties and the Dawn of America's Culture Wars* (Santa Barbara: Praegar, 2018); Constance Areson Clark, *God—or Gorilla: Images of Evolution in the Jazz Age* (Baltimore, MD: Johns Hopkins University Press, 2008); Linda Gordon, *The Second Coming of the KKK: The Ku Klux Klan of the 1920s and the American Political Tradition* (New York and London: Liveright, 2017); Felix Harcourt, *Ku Klux Kulture: America and the Klan in the 1920s* (Chicago and London: University of Chicago Press, 2017); Daniel E. Bender, *American Abyss: Savagery and Civilization in the Age of Industry* (Ithaca and London: Cornell University Press, 2011).

21. The racialized phrase "voodoo orgy" comes from: "Folk Dancing versus Jazz," *Oregonia*, June 28, 1920. Foundational works of this more comprehensive view of the decade include: Henry F. May, "Shifting Perspectives on the 1920s," *Mississippi Valley Historical Review* 43, no. 3 (December 1956); Roderick Nash, *The Nervous Generation: American Thought, 1917-1930* (Chicago: Rand McNally, 1970); Paula S. Fass, *The Damned and the Beautiful: American Youth in the 1920's* (New York: Oxford University Press, 1977); Gunther Schuller, *Early Jazz: Its Roots and Musical Development* (New York and Oxford: Oxford University Press, 1968). For works designed for a wider and popular audience, see: Sarah B. Churchwell, *Careless People: Murder, Mayhem and the Invention of the Great Gatsby* (New York: Penguin Books, 2013); Nathan Miller, *New World Coming: The 1920s and the Making of Modern America* (New York: Scribner, 2003).

22. The phrase "soul of America" is from the title of: Andrew Hartman, *A War for the Soul of America: A History of the Culture Wars*, 2nd ed. (Chicago and London: University of Chicago Press, 2019). Lisa McGirr, *The War on Alcohol: Prohibition and the Rise of the American State* (New York and London: W. W. Norton, 2016); Barry Hankins, *Jesus and Gin: Evangelicalism, the Roaring Twenties and Today's Culture Wars* (New York: Palgrave Macmillan, 2010); Carney, *Cuttin' Up*; Derek Vaillant, *Sounds of Reform: Progressivism and Music in Chicago, 1873-1935* (Chapel Hill and London: University of North Carolina Press, 2004); Warren Susman, *Culture as History: The Transformation of American Society in the Twentieth Century*, 2nd ed. (Washington and London: Smithsonian, 2003); Kenney, *Chicago Jazz*; Burton W. Peretti, *The Creation of Jazz: Music, Race, and Culture in Urban America* (Urbana: University of Illinois Press, 1992); Stanley Coben, *Rebellion against Victorianism: The Impetus for Cultural Change in 1920s America* (New York and Oxford: Oxford University Press, 1991); Kathy J. Ogren, *The Jazz Revolution: Twenties America and the Meaning of Jazz* (New York: Oxford University Press, 1989).

23. Dumenil, *The Modern Temper: American Culture and Society in the 1920s*, 8.

24. For example, Lara Putnam, *Radical Moves: Caribbean Migrants and the Politics of Race in the Jazz Age* (Chapel Hill: University of North Carolina Press,

2013); Cynthia M. Blair, *I've Got to Make My Livin': Black Women's Sex Work in Turn-of-the-Century Chicago* (Chicago and London: University of Chicago Press, 2010); Charles Hersch, *Subversive Sounds: Race and the Birth of Jazz in New Orleans* (Chicago and London: University of Chicago Press, 2008); Paul McCann, "Performing Primitivism: Disarming the Social Threat of Jazz in Narrative Fiction of the Early Twenties," *Journal of Popular Culture* 41, no. 4 (2008); Adrienne D. Dixson, "The Fire This Time: Jazz, Research, and Critical Race Theory," in *Critical Race Theory in Education: All God's Children Got a Song*, ed. Adrienne D. Dixon and Celia K. Rousseau (New York: Routledge, 2006); George Chauncey, *Gay New York: Gender, Urban Culture, and the Making of the Gay Male World, 1890–1940* (New York: Basic Books, 1995); Lawrence Schenbeck, *Racial Uplift and American Music, 1878–1943* (Jackson: University Press of Mississippi, 2012); W. Fitzhugh Brundage, ed., *Beyond Blackface: African Americans and the Creation of American Popular Culture, 1890–1930* (Chapel Hill: University of North Carolina Press, 2011).

25. A small number of observers attributed the music to other groups. Perhaps most prominently, the music journalist and one-time *Harvard Music Review* editor Gilbert Elliot, believed jazz had Spanish origins. He wrote, "In looking over some of this modern Spanish music one would be inclined to think that its authors were intimately acquainted with the intricacies of our rhythms . . . of which more . . . have also in some unknown fashion strongly influenced our jazz." Still, such views existed very much in the minority. Gilbert Elliot, "Our Musical Kinship with the Spaniards," *Musical Quarterly* 8, no. 3 (1922): 414.

26. In his famous music theory-rich history of early jazz, Gunther Schuller acknowledged, "the African and European lineages will become somewhat entangled." Schuller, *Early Jazz: Its Roots and Musical Development*, 4.

27. Not incidentally, 1920 was the first year a majority of Americans lived in cities, at that time defined as containing 40,000 inhabitants. Nash, *The Nervous Generation: American Thought, 1917–1930*, 78.

28. Larry Rue, "Trieste Has Guaranteed Cure for Jazz Habit," *Chicago Daily Tribune*, April 9, 1922; Edward Moore, "Fashion Turns Its Thumb Down on Jazz Rhythm," *Chicago Daily Tribune*, November 25, 1921.

29. Gerald Early, "Three Notes toward a Cultural Definition of the Harlem Renaissance," *Callaloo* 14, no. 1 (1991): 142.

30. "Ad—'Colored People Don't Want Classic Music!,'" *The Crisis*, January 1922.

31. Changes in technology helped account for jazz's greater popularity than its musical predecessor, ragtime. Listening to ragtime required either being able to perform it oneself or access to live performance, since it was primarily disseminated through sheet music. The phonograph, a predecessor of the current-day record player, fundamentally altered how people consumed music. The musical listening experience shifted from a necessarily public one to an increasingly private one. Prior to the phonograph's invention—and, more importantly, its mass

distribution—live performance had a sort of monopoly on music listening. From Vaudeville to opera, listening to music had a requisite social dimension, since live performance had been the only viable way to consume music. For many, the shift away from community-oriented musical listing was a truly regrettable loss as the phonograph moved performances away from quasi-ritualized social contexts to more private ones. Mark Katz has further pointed out that the phonograph had three positive distinct features over live performances: portability, affordability, and repeatability. Mark Katz, *Capturing Sound: How Technology Has Changed Music* (Berkeley: University of California Press, 2004), 10.

32. Radio's early history reflects extant Jim Crow dominance as much as any changing musical tastes. Due to a set of union and legal restrictions—especially the 1922 dispute between the American Society of Composers, Authors, and Publishers (ASCAP) and radio stations over licensing fees—radio listeners often heard white performers over the airwaves. As a result, the music programmed was more often the "sweet" or "orchestral" jazz of white performers like Vincent Lopez and Paul Whiteman rather than "hot" jazz of black performers such as Sidney Bichet, Jelly Roll Morton, or Louis Armstrong. See: William Barlow, *Voice Over: The Making of Black Radio* (Philadelphia: Temple University Press, 1998), 21–22.

33. William T. Ellis, "Children Test for Jazz Civilization," *Dallas Morning News*, January 1, 1921.

34. Kelly Schrum, *Some Wore Bobby Sox: The Emergence of Teenage Girls' Culture, 1920–1945* (New York: Palgrave Macmillan, 2004), 103–4; For statistics on record sales, see Carney, *Cuttin' Up*, 91; For statistics on radio sales and radio stations, see Ralph G. Giordano, *Social Dancing in America: A History and Reference* (Westport: Greenwood, 2007), 49.

35. Edward A. Krug, *The Shaping of the American High School: Volume 2, 1920–1941* (Madison: University of Wisconsin Press, 1972), 117.

36. Krug, *The Shaping of the American High School: Volume 2, 1920–1941*, 126.

37. Oscar and Mary Handlin, *The American College and American Culture: Socialization as a Function of Higher Education* (Berkeley: The Carnegie Commission on Higher Education, 1970), 43.

38. Nicholas L. Syrett, *The Company He Keeps: A History of White College Fraternities* (Chapel Hill: University of North Carolina Press, 2009), 186; David Levine, *The American College and Culture of Aspiration 1915–1940* (Ithaca: Cornell University Press, 1986), 139. In her seminal study of youth in the 1920s, *The Damned and the Beautiful*, Paula Fass summarizes such changes by noting "the school and the peer group—came to define the social world of middle-class youth." Fass, *The Damned and the Beautiful: American Youth in the 1920's*, 120.

39. National Center for Education Statistics, *The Traditionally Black Institutions of Higher Education, 1860 to 1982* (Washington, DC: U.S. Department of Education, 1994), 26, 29.

40. Daniel A. Clark, *Creating the College Man: American Mass Magazines and Middle-Class Manhood, 1890–1915* (Madison: University of Wisconsin Press, 2010), 5.

41. George Oscar Bowen, "First Things First," *Music Supervisors' Journal* 14, no. 5 (1928): 21.

42. Ironically, educators involved in the Americanization project ultimately wished to deny the importance of a true American art form like jazz to students. Adam Laats, *The Other School Reformers: Conservative Activism in American Education* (Cambridge: Harvard University Press, 2015); Zoe Burkholder, *Color in the Classroom: How American Schools Taught Race, 1900–1954* (New York: Oxford University Press, 2011); Jeffrey Mirel, *Patriotic Pluralism: Americanization, Education, and European Immigrants* (Cambridge and London: Harvard University Press, 2010); Paul Ramsey, *Bilingual Public Schooling in the United States: A History of America's "Polyglot Boardinghouse"* (New York: Palgrave Macmillan, 2010); Jonathan Zimmerman, "'Each "Race" Could Have Its Heroes Sung': Ethnicity and the History Wars in the 1920s," *Journal of American History* 87, no. 1 (2000); B. Edward McClellan, *Moral Education in America: Schools and the Shaping of Character since Colonial Times* (New York: Teachers College Press, 1999); Kate Rousmaniere, *City Teachers: Teaching and School Reform in Historical Perspective* (New York: Teachers College Press, 1997); Diana Selig, *Americans All: The Cultural Gifts Movement* (Cambridge and London: Harvard University Press, 2008); Lawrence J. Nelson, *Rumors of Indiscretion: The University of Missouri "Sex Questionnaire" Scandal in the Jazz Age* (Columbia and London: University of Missouri Press, 2003).

43. Robert L. Osgood, *The History of Special Education: A Struggle for Equality in American Public Schools* (Westport: Praeger, 2008); A. R. Ruis, *Eating to Learn, Learning to Eat: The Origins of School Lunch in the United States* (New Brunswick and London: Rutgers University Press, 2017); Thomas Hine, *The Rise and Fall of the American Teenager* (New York: HarperCollins, 2000); Barry Franklin and Gary McCulloch, eds., *The Death of the Comprehensive High School?: Historical, Contemporary, and Comparative Perspectives* (New York: Palgrave Macmillan, 2007); David Tyack, *The One Best System: A History of American Urban Education* (Cambridge and London: Harvard University Press, 1974).

44. Often cited synoptic histories of higher education include: John R. Thelin, *A History of American Higher Education*, 3rd ed. (Baltimore: Johns Hopkins University Press, 2019); Philo Hutcheson, *A People's History of American Higher Education* (New York and London: Taylor & Francis, 2019); Christopher J. Lucas, *American Higher Education: A History* (New York: Palgrave Macmillan, 2016). Recently published and more specialized studies in higher education history include: Christine A. Ogren and Mark A. VanOverbeke, *Rethinking Campus Life: New Perspectives on the History of College Students in the United States* (Cham: Springer International Publishing, 2018); Christopher P. Loss, *Between Citizens and*

the State: The Politics of American Higher Education in the 20th Century (Princeton and Oxford: Princeton University Press, 2012); Andrea Turpin, *A New Moral Vision: Gender, Religion, and the Changing Purposes of American Higher Education, 1837–1917* (Ithaca: Cornell University Press, 2016); Syrett, *The Company He Keeps: A History of White College Fraternities*; Stephanie Y. Evans, *Black Women in the Ivory Tower, 1850–1954: An Intellectual History* (GainesvilleFL: University Press of Florida, 2007); William Wright, *Harvard's Secret Court: The Savage 1920 Purge of Campus Homosexuals* (New York: St. Martin's, 2005); David A. Hoekema, *Campus Rules and Moral Community: In Place of In Loco Parentis* (Lanham: Rowman & Littlefield, 1994); Helen Lefkowitz Horowitz, *Campus Life: Undergraduate Cultures from the End of the Eighteenth Century to the Present* (New York: Knopf Doubleday Publishing Group, 1987). Finally, the 1970s and 1980s saw an increase in books highlighting the college experiences of female and nonwhite students. See: Barbara Solomon, *In the Company of Educated Women* (New Haven: Yale University Press, 1985); Helen Lefkowitz Horowitz, *Alma Mater: Design and Experience in the Women's Colleges from Their Nineteenth-Century Beginnings to the 1930s*, 2nd ed. (Amherst: University of Massachusetts Press, 1993); Lynn D. Gordon, *Gender and Higher Education in the Progressive Era* (New Haven and London: Yale University Press, 1990); Elaine Kendall, *"Peculiar Institutions": An Informal History of the Seven Sister Colleges* (New York: G. P. Putnam and Sons, 1976).

45. Fass, *The Damned and the Beautiful: American Youth in the 1920's*, 47.

46. John R. McMahon, "Our Jazz-Spotted Middle West," *Ladies Home Journal*, February, 1922, 38.

47. Hoagy Carmichael, *The Stardust Road and Sometimes I Wonder: The Autobiography of Hoagy Carmichael* (New York: Da Capo Press, 1999), 85.

48. Charles A. Sengstock, *That Toddlin Town: Chicago's White Dance Bands and Orchestras, 1900–1950* (Urbana and Chicago: University of Chicago Press, 2004).

49. Aldon Morris, *The Scholar Denied: W. E. B. Du Bois and the Birth of Modern Sociology* (Berkeley and Los Angeles: University of California Press, 2017); Julie Reuben, *The Making of the Modern University: Intellectual Transformation and the Marginalization of Morality* (Chicago and London: University of Chicago Press, 1996).

50. A seminal analysis of the influence of pedagogical hegemony of European classical music, at least in higher education, is Bruno Nettl, *Heartland Excursions: Ethnomusicological Reflections on Schools of Music* (Urbana and Chicago: University of Illinois Press, 1995).

Chapter 1

1. John R. McMahon, "Our Jazz-Spotted Middle West," *Ladies Home Journal*, February, 1922, 38.

2. "Get 'em Young, Teach 'em Grace, Urges Pavlova," *Chicago Daily Tribune*, March 27, 1922.

3. Nat Shapiro and Nat Hentoff, ed., *Hear Me Talkin' to Ya: The Story of Jazz as Told by the Men Who Made It* (New York: Dover Publications, 1955), 78.

4. Hentoff, *Hear Me Talkin' to Ya*, 85.

5. Hentoff, *Hear Me Talkin' to Ya*, 93.

6. Eileen Southern, *The Music of Black Americans: A History* (New York: W. W. Norton, [1983] 1997), 365, 78.

7. James R. Grossman, *Land of Hope: Chicago: Black Southerners, and the Great Migration* (Chicago: University of Chicago Press, 1991), 252.

8. Grossman, *Land of Hope*, 4.

9. Dominic A. Pacyga and Ellen Skerrett, *Chicago, City of Neighborhoods: Histories & Tours* (Chicago: Loyola University Press, 1986).

10. Amy Absher, *The Black Musician and the White City: Race and Music in Chicago, 1900–1967* (Ann Arbor: University of Michigan Press, 2014), 17, 20.

11. Absher, *The Black Musician and the White City: Race and Music in Chicago, 1900–1967*, 22.

12. "Educator Says Movies and Jazz Retard Student," *Chicago Daily Tribune*, April 8,1922.

13. Edith Hilderbrant, "Music Memory Contests," *School Review*, April 1922, 300.

14. Hilderbrant, "Music Memory Contests," 300.

15. Donald H. Berglund, "A Study of the Life and Work of Frederick Stock during the Time He Served as Musical Director of the Chicago Symphony Orchestra, with Particular Reference to His Influence on Music Education" (PhD, Northwestern University, 1955), 65.

16. "Stock's Aids Move to Ruin Craze for Jazz," *Chicago Daily Tribune*, 1922.

17. Chicago Board of Education, September 22 Board Meeting Minutes, 1920, Chicago Board of Education Archives, Unboxed Meeting Transcription.

18. "Stock's Aids Move to Ruin Craze for Jazz."

19. "Stock's Aids Move to Ruin Craze for Jazz."

20. Chicago Symphony Orchestra, Children's Concert Program—Fifth Season, Fourth Program, 1924, Artistic Series—Education Concert Programs, Chicago Symphony Orchestra Archives, Box 1.

21. Music memory contests were listening competitions that were popular from the mid-1910s through early 1930s. Students would be given a list of works and "practice" listening to them. During the competition, students would have to recognize which works were being played. See James A. Keene, *A History of Music Education in the United States*, 2nd ed. (Centennial: Glenbridge, 2009), 280–86.

22. Berglund, "A Study of the Life and Work of Frederick Stock," 126.

23. Chicago Symphony Orchestra, Children's Concert Program—Sixth Season, Fifth Program, 1925, Artistic Series—Education Concert Programs, Chicago Symphony Orchestra Archives, Box 1. Stock's concern in music education became increasingly common in the 1920s among conductors who led major orchestras. New York Philharmonic Walter Damrosch used radio to lecture on various topics of music and music history. These lectures, designed primarily for middle and high school students, ran from 1928 to 1942 under the title "Music Appreciation Hour" on the National Broadcasting Corporation (NBC) stations. Damrosch was especially outspoken in his view of jazz as a sort of musical monstrosity. Speaking at a Chicago music education conference in the year his radio project started, Damrosch told attendees at the opening session, "Jazz is a monotony of rhythm. . . . It is rhythm without music and without soul. Personally, it annoys me. Undoubtedly it stifles the true musical instinct, turning away many of our talented young people from the persistent continued study and execution of good music." "Damrosch Assails Jazz," *New York Times*, April 17, 1928.

24. Glenn Dillard Gunn, "Stock Stirs Spark of Harmony in Souls of Rising Generation," *Chicago Herald and Examiner*, January 28, 1923.

25. William Barlow, *Voice Over: The Making of Black Radio* (Philadelphia: Temple University Press, 1998), 21–22.

26. Genevieve Forbes, "Copyright Bar Stirs Radio Fans' Static," *Chicago Daily Tribune*, April 15, 1923.

27. Radio stations in Chicago and elsewhere responded to the uncertainty by featuring more live and in studio performances to circumvent the new ASCAP fees. However, because musicians unions were overwhelmingly white, one result was considerably more white jazz groups received air time than their black counterparts. In the end, the ASCAP tax had little effect on the amount of jazz on the radio." Barlow, *Voice Over*, 21–22.

28. For a breakdown of the geographic breakdown of the city's dance halls, see Absher, *The Black Musician and the White City: Race and Music in Chicago, 1900–1967*, 24–28.

29. Saul Alinsky and Constance Weinberger, "The Public Dance Hall," 1928, University of Chicago Special Collections, Ernest W. Burgess Papers, Box 126, Folder 10.

30. William Kenney, *Chicago Jazz: A Cultural History* (New York and Oxford: Oxford University Press, 1993), 31–32.

31. Alinsky and Weinberger, "The Public Dance Hall," 9, 15, 22.

32. Kenney, *Chicago Jazz*, 161.

33. Alinsky and Weinberger, "The Public Dance Hall," 2.

34. Alinsky and Weinberger, "The Public Dance Hall," 3.

35. Alinsky and Weinberger, "The Public Dance Hall," 9.

36. Alinsky and Weinberger, "The Public Dance Hall," 31.

37. "Coonskin Coat Comes in for College Censure," *Chicago Daily Tribune*, March 18, 1927.

38. "A Look into the Lurid Limelight of Our Most Syncopated Cities," *College Humor*, Winter [January] 1925, 58.

39. Herman B Wells, *Being Lucky: Reminiscences and Reflections* (Bloomington: Indiana University Press, 1980), 41.

40. Park, "The Natural History of the Newspaper."

41. Chicago College of Dental Surgery, *Dentos* (Chicago, 1926), 116.

42. Paul Cressey, Letter to Ernest W. Burgess, November 6, 1928, Ernest W. Burgess Papers Box 130, Folder 5, University of Chicago Special Collections.

43. Paul Goalby Cressey, *The Taxi-Dance Hall: A Sociological Study in Commercialized Recreation and City Life* (Chicago: University of Chicago Press, [1932] 2008), 15.

44. The term *taxi dancer* refers to the similar pay structure with taxi drivers. In each case, the employee's pay is proportional to the amount of time spent with the customer.

45. Cressey, *The Taxi-Dance Hall*, 4.

46. Cressey, *The Taxi-Dance Hall*, xii.

47. Though not referenced in Cressey's work, many of the male dancers were also Filipino men. Rhacel Salazar Parrenas, " 'White Trash' Meets the 'Little Brown Monkeys': The Taxi Dance Hall as a Site of Interracial and Gender Alliances between White Working Class Women and Filipino Immigrant Men in the 1920s and 30s," *Amerasia Journal* 24, no. 2 (1998).

48. Paul Cressey, "A Study of Gaelic Park—Draft," Ernest W. Burgess Papers, Box 130 Folder 7, University of Chicago Special Collections, 14–15.

49. Cressey, "A Study of Gaelic Park—Draft," 12, 16.

50. "A Study of Gaelic Park—Draft," 14.

51. "A Study of Gaelic Park—Draft," 14.

52. Historians have argued adults vastly overestimated the amount of sexual activities taking place among young people in the 1920s. Beth L. Bailey, *From Front Porch to Back Seat: Courtship in Twentieth-Century America* (Baltimore: Johns Hopkins University Press, 1989), 80–81.

53. Louise James Bargelt, "Doctor Evolves Rest Cure for Jazz Age Child," *Chicago Daily Tribune*, December 9, 1923.

54. Bargelt, "Doctor Evolves Rest Cure for Jazz Age Child." As questionable as such diagnoses may seem, even more debatable ones existed. One Austrian doctor believed jazz gave one of his clients a goiter. "Jazz Gives Woman Goiter, Physican Finds," *Chicago Daily Tribune*, June 26, 1927.

55. "Kissing Is O.K. for Young Folks, Physician Says," *Chicago Daily Tribune*, March 16, 1922.

56. "Edward Moore, Noted Critic and Musician, Dies," *Chicago Daily Tribune*, October 7, 1935.

57. Edward Moore, "In Which the Music Critic Is Instructed as to His Plain Duty," *Chicago Daily Tribune*, December 18, 1921.

58. Edward Moore, "Fashion Turns Its Thumb Down on Jazz Rhythm," *Chicago Daily Tribune*, November 25, 1921; Edward Moore, "Where Are the Popular Tunes of Yesteryear?," *Chicago Daily Tribune*, October 23, 1921.

59. Moore, "Where Are the Popular Tunes of Yesteryear?"

60. I discuss in chapter 2 how some educators emphasized European folk dancing as a recognizably white, and therefore natural antidote to jazz.

61. Court Carney, *Cuttin' Up: How Early Jazz Got America's Ear* (Lawrence: University of Kansas Press, 2009), 64.

62. Carney, *Cuttin' Up*, 67.

63. In his study of the *Defender*, music and racial uplift, Lawrence Schenbeck argued, "Jazz, as part of the entertainment world, was seen in a positive light insofar as it had potential for material 'uplift' but could be considered negative to the extent that it reinforced stereotypes about blacks. As a signifier in the black discourse on man-hood, it appears to have been associated with economic opportunity rather than with narratives about cultural authenticity." Lawrence Schenbeck, "Music, Gender and 'Uplift' in the Chicago Defender," *The Musical Quarterly* 81, no. 3 (Autumn 1997): 349.

64. Dave Peyton, "The Musical Bunch—Interested Music Teachers," *Chicago Defender*, July 17, 1926.

65. "School Board Bans Teaching Language of Hun: Favors Superintendent's Idea Regarding German in Elementary Work," *Chicago Daily Tribune*, September 7, 1918.

66. Chicago Board of Education, January 25 Board Meeting Minutes, 1922, Chicago Board of Education Archives, Unboxed Meeting Transcription, 502.

67. Genevieve Forbes, "Mortenson Asks Parents to Curb Student Revels," *Chicago Daily Tribune*, January 26, 1922.

68. "Parents Back Mortenson in Fight on 'Petting,'" *Chicago Daily Tribune*, March 21, 1922.

69. "Parents Back Mortenson in Fight on 'Petting,'"

70. "Parents Back Mortenson in Jazz Crusade," *Chicago Daily Tribune*, January 29, 1922.

71. "For More but Smaller High Schools," *Chicago Daily Tribune*, February 2, 1922.

72. "News of the Day through the Eye of the Camera," *Chicago Daily Tribune*, January 27, 1922.

73. Other superintendents lent their voices to the cause of altering the public to such morally reprehensible music, though not to the degree that Mortenson did. B. B. Cobb, the superintendent of schools in Waco, Texas, framed his argument against jazz as a challenge to democratic ideals. Speaking to the state teachers' convention in 1922, Cobb began by arguing, if done well, the effects of music

education should be felt outside the music classroom, indeed, outside the school. In his view, music should act as a crucial ingredient in students' understanding of democracy. Cobb pointed to chorus singing as one of the most democratic activities in which students can engage. Each student had an individual part to perform, but must also be aware of what was taking place in other sections of the ensemble. The whole group, in turn, was held together and led by a conductor, who succeeded when the larger group did. Cobb then identified the challenge of keeping students interested in such beautiful music, not the desire for personal pleasure that came from the "uncontrollable craze for speed" of jazz. He went on to argue that jazz—here a major challenge to future democracy—was "unspeakable," while calling for more courses in "wholesome, restful music." In Cobb's view, one similarly held by other educators, jazz leads students away from friends and family toward a life devoted to seeking personal pleasures. Fortunately, the solution was equally clear, since "it is only through the schools that we can reach the masses of our people and implement early in their lives the best in musical art."

Likewise W. F. Webster, the Superintendent of Minneapolis public schools, used his 1927 address at the National Education Association Department of Superintendence meeting to speak out about the necessity of music education and, simultaneously, the dangers of jazz. Webster explicitly sought to put music on par with other subjects by listing all the advantages he believed came with music education. Webster, who did not hide his personal interest in music and other performing arts, lamented how the "good New England stock" that took the first steps to develop a public system of education, did not include music alongside the "honored trilogy"—Reading, Writing, and 'Rithmetic. The superintendent challenged that pedagogical hierarchy partially on scholastic terms, pointing out that students studying music in Minneapolis high schools had a disproportionately high number of "A's," while also recording a similarly low number of "F's." Webster also argued that beautiful music could do more than any other subject to instill in students a love of family and general exemplary deportment. He explained, "Mother at the piano and, beside her, brother or sister with a violin or saxaphone [sic], is the surest protection against a wasted life I know." Webster even compared the often unappealing sounds of a young student practicing scales as a welcome alternative to the police siren, which he saw as a constant refrain for wayward youth. Beauty, which Webster never precisely defined, acted as a major theme in his analysis. Beautiful music (he cites Rossini, Sibelius, and Chopin, among others) instills in students a general sense of appropriate behavior, while jazz would create the opposite effect. Referring to the upstanding behavior of the student audience at one high school concert, Webster wrote, "The spell of beauty was over them, and the behavior was as lovely as the music." However, the opposite of musical beauty, jazz, threatened to disrupt any such behaviors among students, since "This [behavior] could not have been, had they been soused in jazz; but beauty begets refinement, and refinement is the mother of self-control." To guard against such conditions, the Superintendent noted, "Music for a short period each day is study, not recreation." B. B. Cobb, "Music as an Essential," *Music Supervisors' Journal* 9, no. 4 (1923): 19; W. F. Webster, "Music and the Sacred Seven," *Music Supervisors' Journal* 13, no. 5 (1927).

74. Education, January 25 Board Meeting Minutes, 503.

75. Kelly Schrum, *Some Wore Bobby Sox: The Emergence of Teenage Girls' Culture, 1920–1945* (New York: Palgrave Macmillan, 2004), 25.

76. Schrum, *Some Wore Bobby Sox*, 25. Similarly, Karen Graves has argued a contradiction undergirded girls' education at the time—while an increasing number of girls were attending secondary school, their choices about what their education may consist of was shrinking. That is, greater access did not necessarily mean greater opportunities. Karen Graves, *Girls' Schooling during the Progressive Era: From Female Scholar to Domesticated Citizen* (New York and London: Garland, 1998).

77. "98% of School Children Good, Mortenson Says," *Chicago Daily Tribune*, January 27, 1922.

78. "Mortenson to Quit Schools," *Chicago Daily Tribune*, August 29, 1923.

79. "School Official Says He Hears too Much Jazz," *Chicago Daily Tribune*, February 11, 1927.

80. Kenney, *Chicago Jazz*, 88.

81. "Plan 'Sings' as Jazz Antidote among Youth," *Chicago Daily Tribune*, June 9, 1924.

82. "City Wide Open, Youth Periled, Report Asserts," *Chicago Daily Tribune*, March 18, 1928.

83. "Opinions Vary on Meaning of Preston Creed: Leaders Ponder at Last Rites Are Held," *Chicago Daily Tribune*, April 16, 1925.

84. "Philip Yarrow, Vice Crusader, Is Dead at 82," *Chicago Daily Tribune*, June 16, 1954.

85. Rev. Phillip Yarrow, ed., *Fighting the Debauchery of Our Girls and Boys* (Chicago: Self-Published, 1923), ix.

86. "List Jazz Dance Halls of City as Morally Unfair," *Chicago Daily Tribune*, February 20, 1922.

87. Yarrow, *Fighting the Debauchery of Our Girls and Boys*, 89.

88. Yarrow, *Fighting the Debauchery of Our Girls and Boys*, 97.

89. "Both Jazz Music and Jazz Dancing Barred from All Louisville Episcopal Churches," *The New York Times*, September 19, 1921.

90. A clericus resolution is a formal church resolution passed, in this case, by the Kentucky Diocese. "Ban Jazz Dancing and Auto Spooning," *Washington Post*, November 19, 1921.

91. Robert H. Harper, ed., *Annual of Louisiana 76th Conference of the Methodist Episcopal Church, South* (1921).

92. "Kansas Federation Denounces Church Music," *Herald* (Hayti, MO), December 9, 1920.

93. "Vows He'll Mop Floor to Keep Yarrow in Jail," *Chicago Daily Tribune*, June 28, 1931.

94. Yarrow, *Fighting the Debauchery of Our Girls and Boys*, 189. See also, Jeffrey P. Moran, *Teaching Sex: The Shaping of Adolescence in the 20th Century* (Cambridge and London: Harvard University Press, 2000).

95. Yarrow, *Fighting the Debauchery of Our Girls and Boys*, unpaginated section of illustrations between 198 and 99.

96. Yarrow, *Fighting the Debauchery of Our Girls and Boys*, 207.

97. Yarrow, *Fighting the Debauchery of Our Girls and Boys*, 197.

98. Yarrow, *Fighting the Debauchery of Our Girls and Boys*, 209.

99. Yarrow, *Fighting the Debauchery of Our Girls and Boys*, unpaginated section of illustrations between 198 and 99.

100. Yarrow, *Fighting the Debauchery of Our Girls and Boys*, 285.

101. Yarrow, *Fighting the Debauchery of Our Girls and Boys*, unpaginated section of illustrations between 198 and 99.

102. "Opera Manager Urges Students to Hear 'Aida,'" *Marshall News*, December 9, 1924.

103. Austin City High School, *The Maroon and White* (Chicago, 1924).

104. Austin City High School, ed., *The Maroon and White* (Chicago: 1929).

105. "The Rhythm of the Age," *Chicago Daily Tribune*, October 23, 1927.

106. Dana Epstein, "Frederick Stock and American Music," *American Music* 10, no. 1 (1992): 32.

107. Epstein, "Frederick Stock and American Music," 32.

108. Chicago Symphony Orchestra, Children's Concert Program—Eighth Season, Fifth Program, 1927, Artistic Series—Education Concert Programs, Chicago Symphony Orchestra Archives, Box 1.

Chapter 2

1. Frederick Neil Innes, "The Musical Possibilities of the Wind Band," *Music Supervisors' Journal* 10, no. 5 (1924): 42.

2. J. C. Seegers, "Teaching Music Appreciation by Means of the Music-Memory Contest," *Elementary School Journal* 26, no. 3 (1925): 218.

3. Felix Harcourt, *Ku Klux Kulture: America and the Klan in the 1920s* (Chicago and London: University of Chicago Press, 2017).

4. Stanley Coben, *Rebellion against Victorianism: The Impetus for Cultural Change in 1920s America* (New York and Oxford: Oxford University Press, 1991), 75.

5. His speech was reprinted in: Carl Engel, *Discords Mingled: Essays on Music*, ed. Carl Engel (Freeport: Books for Libraries Free Press, 1967), 141.

6. "High Lights of the Convention," *Music Supervisors' Journal* 8, no. 5 (1922): 14.

7. Engel, *Discords Mingled: Essays on Music*, 143.

8. Engel, *Discords Mingled: Essays on Music*, 144. When Engel gave this 1922 speech, a small number of high school jazz bands had begun to appear, primarily in some schools to provide music for dances and other social events, albeit also with a civic purpose. In 1919, the jazz band at El Paso High School played for a Kiwanis Club meeting held at their school. The previous year, Columbia High School in Missouri began an annual fund-raiser dance, "Jazz Night." The school's jazz band provided music and proceeds benefited the school's year book. Still, such performances were very much the exception. And school official may well have been more interested in raising the funds than in entertaining any discussions of morality. "Kiwanis Will Visit High School," *El Paso Herald*, April 15, 1919; "Net $682 in Jazz Carnival," *Evening Missourian* (Columbia), April 2, 1920.

9. "High Lights of the Convention," 14.

10. Carl Engel, "Views and Reviews," *Musical Quarterly* 8, no. 4 (1922): 626.

11. Abe Martin/E. B. Birge, "A Postlude by Abe Martin," *Music Supervisors' Journal* 7, no. 4 (March 1921): 4.

12. Arthur L. Manchester, "Music Education, a Musical America, the American Composer, a Sequence," *Musical Quarterly* 10, no. 4 (1924): 595.

13. James Francis Cooke, "June [Editorial]," *Etude*, June, 1924, 369.

14. Michael L. Mark and Charles L. Gary, *A History of American Music Education* (Lanham: Rowman and Littlefield Education, 2007), 295, 99.

15. Will Earhart, "Is Instrumental Music in Public Schools Justified by the Actual Results? (Concluded)," *Music Supervisors' Journal* 8, no. 2 (1921): 39.

16. Will Earhart, "Factors of Musical Appeal and Responses of Pupils to Them," *Music Supervisors' Journal* 17, no. 2 (1930): 23.

17. Earhart, "Is Instrumental Music in Public Schools Justified by the Actual Results? (Concluded)," 39.

18. Earhart, "Is Instrumental Music in Public Schools Justified by the Actual Results? (Concluded)," 36.

19. "Ad—Are You Fighting Jazz and Cheap Popular Music?," *Music Supervisors' Journal* 9, no. 1 (1922): 28.

20. Will Earhart, "The Reveille by Alice W. Brockett [Review]," *Music Supervisors' Journal* 9, no. 2 (1922): 37.

21. Earhart, "The Reveille by Alice W. Brockett [Review]," 38.

22. Alice Brockett, *The Reveille* (Franklin, OH and Denver, CO: Eldridge Entertainment House, 1922), 2.

23. Brockett, *The Reveille*, 19.

24. Brockett, *The Reveille*, 22.

25. Brockett, *The Reveille*, 27.

26. Brockett, *The Reveille*, 23.

27. Brockett, *The Reveille*, 27.

28. E. B. Brockett, "Instrumental Music in the High School" (paper presented at the Proceedings of the High School Conference, University of Illinois Urbana, 1921), 335.

29. Edwin J. Stringham, "'Jazz'—An Educational Problem," *Musical Quarterly* 12, no. 2 (1926): 191.

30. Larry Rue, "Trieste Has Guaranteed Cure for Jazz Habit," *Chicago Daily Tribune*, April 9, 1922. The *Chicago Daily Tribune* author who wrote the article assured readers that "oscillatum Ethiopius" was not intended to be offensive. Instead, it was merely the term scientists used when discussing the genre.

31. Madge R. Cayton, "The Origin of Jazz," *Cayton's Monthly*, February 1, 1921, 10.

32. Mabel Bray, "The Correlation of the Singing Lesson and the Listening Lesson" (paper presented at the Sixteenth Annual Meeting of the Music Supervisors' National Conference, April 9-13, 1923), 117.

33. Manchester, "Music Education, a Musical America, the American Composer, a Sequence," 595.

34. Anne Shaw Faulkner, "We Need a Universal Language," *Ladies Home Journal*, November 1919, 37.

35. "Cartoon—Will Our Dance Orchestras Come to This?," *Etude*, May 1925, 322.

36. "Cartoon—Will Our Dance Orchestras Come to This?" See also: Werner Sollors, *Ethnic Modernism* (Cambridge and London: Harvard University Press, 2008).

37. Constance Areson Clark, *God—or Gorilla: Images of Evolution in the Jazz Age* (Baltimore: Johns Hopkins University Press, 2008), xi.

38. Clark, *God—or Gorilla: Images of Evolution in the Jazz Age*, 14-15.

39. Bauer and Peyser would remove such references for the 1939 edition of *How Music Grew*. Ruth Zinar, "Racial Bigotry and Stereotypes in Music Books Recommended for Use by Children," *Black Perspective in Music* 3, no. 1 (Spring 1975): 34, 35.

40. Anne Shaw Faulkner, *What We Hear in Music: A Course of Study* (Camden: Victor Talking Machine Company, 1924), 62.

41. Louis C. Elson, *The National Music of America and Its Sources* (Boston: L. C. Page, 1924), 241, 64.

42. Zoe Burkholder, *Color in the Classroom: How American Schools Taught Race, 1900-1954* (New York: Oxford University Press, 2011), 11, 15.

43. Faulkner, *What We Hear in Music: A Course of Study*, 55.

44. Burkholder, *Color in the Classroom: How American Schools Taught Race, 1900-1954*, 34.

45. Bray, "The Correlation of the Singing Lesson and the Listening Lesson," 117.

46. "Jazz Music in High School Class in Typewriting," *Ogden Standard* (Ogden, UT), November 18, 1919.

47. Louise Freer, "Modern Tendencies in Physical Education" (paper presented at the Proceedings of the High School Conference, University of Illinois Urbana, November 1921), 347.

48. Thelma Parker, "Shortridge Teachers Are Proud of 'Bobs,'" *Shortridge Daily Echo*, September 21, 1927.

49. "Teaches 'Jazz' in Newark High School," *New York Tribune*, March 21, 1919.

50. Frances Elliott Clark, "Music in Education (Concluded)," *Music Supervisors' Journal* 5, no. 2 (1918): 18.

51. Ralph G. Giordano, *Satan in the Dance Hall: Rev. John Roach Straton, Social Dancing, and Morality in 1920s New York City* (Lanham: Scarecrow Press, 2008), 76.

52. "Put Snuggle Dance All up to the Girls," *New York Times*, August 22, 1922.

53. Giordano, *Satan in the Dance Hall*, 76.

54. Elizabeth Burchenal, "Folk Dancing" (paper presented at the Music Supervisor's National Conference Meeting, 1918), 40.

55. Linda J. Tomko, "*Fete Accompli*: Gender, 'Folk-Dance,' and Progressive-Era Political Ideals in New York City," in *Corporealities*, ed. Susan Leigh Foster (London: Routledge, 1996), 62.

56. "Folk Dancing versus Jazz," *Oregonia*, June 28, 1920. Teaching young people folk dancing in schools also exemplified the increased effect formal education had on students' lives in the Progressive Era. Among other examples, David Churchill has studied how Chicago teachers used physical education, particularly for boys, as a way to instill in students a particularly masculine ideal of their gender. David Churchill, "Making Broad Shoulders: Body-Building and Physical Culture in Chicago, 1890–1920," *History of Education Quarterly* 48, no. 3 (2008).

57. Luther H. Gulick, "Preface," in *Folk-Dances and Singing Games: Twenty-six Folk-dances of Norway, Sweden, Denmark, Russia, Bohemia, Hungary, Italy, England, Scotland and Ireland, with the Music, Full Directions for Performance, and Numerous Illustrations, Volume 1*, ed. Elizabeth Burchenal (New York: G. Schirmer, 1909), xii. Gulick claimed Burchenal taught as many as two thousand New York City educators how to properly teach folk dancing in their own classes.

58. For example, Elizabeth Burchenal, *Folk-Dances and Singing Games* (New York: G. Schirmer, 1909), 3, 5, 7.

59. Burchenal, "Folk Dancing," 39.

60. Giordano, *Satan in the Dance Hall*, 89.

61. Indeed, by 1930 rural youth made up only one-third of the nationwide enrollment in high schools, despite having roughly half of the total high school-age population. Edward A. Krug, *The Shaping of the American High School: Volume 2, 1920–1941* (Madison: University of Wisconsin Press, 1972), 120.

62. Dessie Stephens, "To the Editor: Farmers and Music," *Etude*, January 1924, 59.

63. C. A. Fullerton, "Music in Rural Communities," *Music Supervisors' Journal* 14, no. 2 (1927): 39.

64. Carl Withers [James West], *Plainville, USA* (New York: Columbia University Press, 1971, 1st repr.), 16.

65. Elizabeth Burchenal, "Reviving the Folk Dance," *National Education Association Journal* 15 (1926): 241.

66. Brockett, "Instrumental Music in the High School," 336.

67. Mabelle Glenn, "The Symphony Orchestra in the Public School: The Kansas City (Mo.) Plan," *Music Supervisors' Journal* 10, no. 3 (1924): 24. Though all but impossible to verify, this claim seems quite unlikely given the hold jazz had on Kansas City at the time, where omnipresent jam sessions operated as "educational institutions." See Martin Williams, "Jazz: What Happened in Kansas City?," *American Music* 3, no. 2 (1985): 174.

68. "Current Topics," *Music Supervisors Journal* 9, no. 3 (1923): 40.

69. Margaret M. Sleezer, "Student Citizenship at the Senn High School," *The School Review* 32, no. 7 (1924): 518.

70. "'Old Question,' Says Symphony Director, Branding Jazz Music as Temporary Craze," *Indiana Daily Student*, February 6, 1925.

71. Otto Graham, "The Development of Instrumental Music" (paper presented at the The Proceedings of the High School Conference, 1922), 333.

72. "Is Music Related to School Life?," *Music Supervisors' Journal* 8, no. 2 (1921): 26.

73. "Music Contest Creates Interest," *Oregonian*, February 16, 1921.

74. Clara Ellen Starr, "Music Appreciation in the Junior High School of Detroit," *Music Supervisors' Journal* 12, no. 2 (1925): 53.

75. Keene, *A History of Music Education in the United States*, 280–82.

76. Hilderbrant, "Music Memory Contests," 303.

77. The decline of music memory contests itself deserves greater scholarly attention. Two good starting points that describe some of the characteristics of that decline are: Keene, *A History of Music Education in the United States*, 242–59 and Gary, *A History of American Music Education*, 319–23.

78. Percy Scholes, *Music: The Child and the Masterpiece* (Oxford: Oxford University Press, 1935), 178.

79. Clarence G. Hamilton, "The Teacher's Round Table," *Etude*, December 1927, 913.

80. Russell Gilbert, "Deportment at the Piano," *Etude*, March 1925, 116.

81. "A Message to Midwest Band and Orchestra Contest Participants," *Music Supervisors' Journal* 11, no. 5 (1925): 69.

82. C. C. Birchard, "What about the Saxophone?," *Music Supervisors' Journal* 12, no. 1 (1925): 57.

83. William Arms Fischer, "The Radio and Music," *Music Supervisors' Journal* 12, no. 3 (1926): 67.

84. Despite increasingly warm references, some educators continued to voice frustrations about their students' preferences for jazz before other genres. Will Earhart, the Pittsburgh music supervisor who had so fervently endorsed *The Reveille*, was one the few educators who continued full-throated attacks, which increasingly appeared worn out. Speaking in 1929, he complained how the "jazz phonograph records by the Saxy Six and radio broadcastings of the Nit-Wit Roadhouse Orchestra" provided little benefit to students compared to the Philadelphia Symphony Orchestra. Earhart's critiques were not, however, representative of how his colleagues were speaking about jazz. By the end of the decade, critical commentary increasingly revolved around the acknowledgment that young people's interest in jazz amounted to more than a passing fad. Will Earhart, "Art in Life and Musical Art for the Child" (paper presented at the Journal of the Proceedings of the Annual Meeting of the Music Supervisors' National Conference, Twenty-Second Year (May? 1929): 71.

85. Ralph G. Giordano, *Social Dancing in America: A History and Reference* (Westport: Greenwood, 2007), 135.

86. Nathan Miller, *New World Coming: The 1920s and the Making of Modern America* (New York: Scribner, 2003), 83.

Chapter 3

1. "Ad—'Colored People Don't Want Classic Music!,'" *Crisis*, January 1922, 139. The NANM lobbied the Victor Company beginning in the early 1920s, apparently unsuccessfully, about recording African American musicians who played music other than jazz and blues. NANM, Third Annual Meeting Minutes, 1922, National Association of Negro Musicians Collection, Center for Black Music Research, Columbia College, Box 2, Folder 59.

2. Though other synonyms were used at the time, I use the word *spiritual* here. I do so partly because the word continues to be used in this way and partly because *spiritual* implies a connection with the sacred, a point black music educators often emphasized when critiquing jazz. Other terms used during the Jazz Age included "Negro folk songs," "black folk songs," or simply, "our music."

3. J. Harold Brown, "In the Music World," *Indianapolis Recorder*, December 29, 1928.

4. Edward A. Krug, *The Shaping of the American High School: Volume 2, 1920–1941* (Madison: University of Wisconsin Press, 1973), 126.

5. Kyle P. Steele, *Making a Mass Institution: Indianapolis and the American High School* (New Brunswick, Camden, and Newark, and London: Rutgers University Press, 2020), 39, 44.

6. Richard B. Pierce, *Polite Protest: The Political Economy of Race in Indianapolis* (Bloomington: Indiana University Press, 2006), 11–12.

7. Zoe Burkholder, *An African American Dilemma: A History of School Integration and Civil Rights in the North* (New York: Oxford University Press, 2021), 75.

8. Steele, *Making a Mass Institution: Indianapolis and the American High School*, 71.

9. As cited in Burkholder, *An African American Dilemma: A History of School Integration and Civil Rights in the North*, 75.

10. "Church Notes," *Indianapolis Recorder*, May 28, 1932.

11. Eloise Keller Butler, "Mother's Day Program Was Great Success," *Indianapolis Recorder*, May 14, 1932.

12. "Over One-half Attucks Seniors Wish to Become Public School Teachers," *Indianapolis Recorder*, July 8, 1933.

13. Crispus Attucks High School, *The Attucks: Crispus Attucks High School Yearbook*, (1931), 6.

14. Eloise Butler, "Helen C. Laster and Cornell A. Talley in Joint Recital," *Indianapolis Recorder*, June 4, 1932. Lane served as principal at Crispus Attucks from 1930 until 1957. He then became Assistant Superintendent of Indianapolis Public Schools, a position he held until his retirement in 1968.

15. Lissa Felming May, "Early Musical Development of Selected African-American Jazz Musicians in Indianapolis in the 1930's and 1940's," *Journal of Historical Research in Music Education* 27, no. 1 (2005): 24.

16. Coe would go on to have a successful career, recording nineteen albums as a leader and a sideman over fifty years. In 1942 he replaced Charlie Parker in Jay McShann's band and, after serving in World War II, served as a sideman with Tiny Bradshaw. During the 1960s he played in bands backing Aretha Franklin and Gladys Knight, among others. After retiring from full-time touring, he worked a number of jobs in the Indianapolis area, including teaching jazz in the city's public schools beginning in the mid-1960s. In 1984, he served as Jazz Artist in Residence for the Indianapolis Public Schools. Workman Chuck, "Tribute to Jimmy Coe," *NUVO*, February 25, 2004.

17. May, "Early Musical Development of Selected African-American Jazz Musicians in Indianapolis in the 1930's and 1940's," 24.

18. E. Elliot Rawlins, "Keeping Fit—The Intoxication of Jazz," *New York Amsterdam News*, April 11, 1923.

19. E. Elliot Rawlins, "Keeping Fit: Jazz-A Drug," *New York Amsterdam News*, April 1, 1925.

20. William Nunn, "Has the Negro Church Been Weighed in the Balance and Found Wanting?," *Pittsburgh Courier*, October 2, 1926.

21. Sterling A. Brown, "Negro Character as Seen by White Authors," *Journal of Negro Education* 2, no. 2 (1933): 198.

22. Mannes was brother-in-law to the conductor and ardent jazz critic Walter Damrosch, the longtime conductor of the New York Symphony Orchestra.

Damrosch once described jazz as "rhythm without soul." Neil Leonard, *Jazz and the White Americans: The Acceptance of a New Art Form* (Chicago: University of Chicago Press, [1962] 1970), 32.

23. David Mannes, *Music Is My Faith: An Autobiography* (New York: W. W. Norton, 1938), 34.

24. Lester A. Walton et al., "Black-Music Concerts in Carnegie Hall, 1912-1915," *Black Perspective in Music* 6, no. 1 (1978): 71-72.

25. Walton et al., "Black-Music Concerts in Carnegie Hall, 1912-1915," 73.

26. Walton et al., "Black-Music Concerts in Carnegie Hall, 1912-1915," 71.

27. Walton et al., "Black-Music Concerts in Carnegie Hall, 1912-1915," 73.

28. Walton et al., "Black-Music Concerts in Carnegie Hall, 1912-1915," 72-74.

29. Lester A. Walton, "Concert at Carnegie Hall," *New York Age*, May 9, 1912.

30. R. Nathaniel Dett, Negro Music, 1920, National Association of Negro Musicians Collection, Center for Black Music Research, Columbia College, Box 7, Folder 25, 14.

31. Dett, Negro Music, 15-16.

32. Mannes, *Music Is My Faith: An Autobiography*, 211, 12.

33. Doris Evans McGinty, ed., *A Documentary History of the National Association of Negro Musicians* (Chicago: Center for Black Music Research, 2004), 15-16.

34. Clara E. Hutchison, National Association of Negro Musicians, 1929, National Association of Negro Musicians Collection, Center for Black Music Research, Columbia College, Box 5, Folder 10.

35. Henry Grant, Paul Laurence Dunbar High School 2nd Annual Music Festival Program, 1919, National Association of Negro Musicians Collection, Center for Black Music Research, Columbia College, Box 7, Folder 10.

36. NANM, Minutes of the First Annual Meeting, 1919, National Association of Negro Musicians Collection, Center for Black Music Research, Columbia College, Box 2, Folder 56, 3.

37. NANM, Minutes of the First Annual Meeting; Emmett J. Scott, "Initial Conference of Negro Musicians and Artists," *Tuskegee Student*, June 28, 1919. For discussion of the leadership opportunities for women in the NANM see Anita J. Mixon, "WOMEN SPEAKING IN AND FOR INSTITUTIONS: A RHETORICAL HISTORY OF THE POLITICS OF RESPECTABILITY IN BLACK CHICAGO, 1919-1939" (PhD University of Illinois at Urbana-Champaign, 2017), 80-91.

38. Wellington A. Adams, "Conference of Colored Musicians at Dunbar," *Washington Bee*, May 17, 1919.

39. Willis Charles Patterson, "A History of the National Association of Negro Musicians (N.A.N.M.): The First Quarter Century, 1919-1943" (PhD, Wayne State University, 1993), 24-25.

40. Mark Robert Schneider, *"We Return Fighting": The Civil Rights Movement in the Jazz Age* (Boston: Northeastern University Press, 2002), 27-29.

41. NANM, Minutes of the First Annual Meeting.

42. NANM, Minutes of the First Annual Meeting.

43. NANM, Minutes of the First Annual Meeting.

44. Clarence G. Allen, "Negro Musicians Urge against Perversion of Their Songs, at Second Convention," *Musical America*, August 7, 1920.

45. Henry L. Grant, "Individualism and Organization," *Negro Musician* 1, no. 3 (June 1921): 1.

46. NANM, Minutes of the First Annual Meeting.

47. NANM, Minutes of the Second Annual Meeting, 1920, National Association of Negro Musicians Collection, Center for Black Music Research, Columbia College, Box 2, Folder 58.

48. NANM, Minutes of the First Annual Meeting.

49. McGinty, *A Documentary History of the National Association of Negro Musicians*, 31; NANM, Minutes of the Fifth Annual Convention, 1923, National Association of Negro Musicians Collection, Center for Black Music Research, Columbia College, Box 2, Folder 61.

50. Scott, "Initial Conference of Negro Musicians and Artists."

51. NANM, Minutes of the Fifth Annual Convention.

52. For a discussion of Dett's approach to composition, particularly his embrace of romanticism and mistrust of modernism, see Lawrence Schenbeck, *Racial Uplift and American Music, 1878–1943* (Jackson: University Press of Mississippi, 2012), 108–70.

53. NANM, Minutes of the First Annual Meeting, 9.

54. Grant, "Individualism and Organization."

55. One exception came from a warning Dett leveled in 1920, The composer complained how "one sometimes hears in Negro concert choruses and in the playing of 'rags' and jass [sic] music, and other dance tunes by untutored or only partially educated Negro orchestras and pianists, effects which surpass in real characterization any of the results obtained by Dvorak." Despite this criticism, Dett vehemently disagreed with the suggestion that ragtime music was first developed by Jewish musicians. Seeming generally bewildered, Dett claimed, "[Jewish musicians'] assiduity in Negro music is one of the paradoxes of American civilization." Dett, Negro Music, 13, 21.

56. NANM, Minutes of the Second Annual Meeting, 11.

57. Grant, "Individualism and Organization."

58. NANM, Minutes of the Second Annual Meeting, 11.

59. NANM, Minutes of the First Annual Meeting.

60. Allen, "Negro Musicians Urge Against Perversion of Their Songs, at Second Convention."

61. NANM, Constitution and By-Laws, 1926, National Association of Negro Musicians Collection, Center for Black Music Research, Columbia College, Box 2, Folder 31.

62. Samuel A. Floyd Jr., "The Invisibility and Fame of Harry T. Burleigh: Retrospect and Prospect," *Black Music Research Journal* 24, no. 2 (2004): 190.

63. "Harry Burleigh Bewails Misuse of Folk Songs," *Chicago Defender*, November 18, 1922.

64. NANM, Third Annual Meeting Minutes, 15. Work would change his opinion about the connection between the spiritual and jazz. Writing in *The Fisk Herald* in 1930, he called jazz "an offspring of the Negro folk song," a claim he avoided in the early 1920s. John W. Work, "The Negro's Contribution to Music," *Fisk Herald*, May 1930.

65. NANM, Minutes of the Fifth Annual Convention, 17. The Crispus Attucks teacher at one point argued that African Americans were *not* naturally more musical than whites—and cited a University of North Carolina study he believed proved it—pointing out such claims had previously been used to discredit or downplay their musical contributions. J. Harold Brown, "In the Music World," *Indianapolis Recorder*, January 19, 1929; McGinty, *A Documentary History of the National Association of Negro Musicians*, 162.

66. "Attucks Organ Purchasing Plan Made," *Indianapolis Recorder*, May 28, 1932.

67. "To Launch New Attucks Organ Campaign," *Indianapolis Recorder*, May 21, 1932.

68. First Annual Commencement of the Crispus Attucks High School, 1928, Crispus Attucks Museum, IUPUI Digital Collection, https://cds.ulib.iupui.edu/collections/CAttucks.

69. Crispus Attucks Commencement Program, 1934, Crispus Attucks Museum, IUPUI Digital Collection, https://cds.ulib.iupui.edu/collections/CAttucks. Brown resigned his position at Crispus Attucks High School in 1934 to take a position at Florida Technical and Mechanical College. Brown had long hoped to obtain a position at Hampton (where he taught during the summers) or Fisk and believed the move would better position him the next time a teaching opportunity opened at either of those schools. "J. Harold Brown Resigns from Attucks," *The Indianapolis Recorder*, October 13, 1934.

70. Brown, "In the Music World."

71. Brown, "In the Music World."

72. A 1921 story in the *New York Tribune* described itself as a "scientific study" of jazz as having connections to "savage music." "That Wicked Jazz The Child of Old Peru?," *New York Tribune* (New York), May 8, 1921.

73. "High Lights of the Convention," 16.

74. Krug, *The Shaping of the American High School: Volume 2, 1920–1941*, 129.

75. Patterson, "A History of the National Association of Negro Musicians (N.A.N.M.): The First Quarter Century, 1919–1943," 188.

76. Patterson, "A History of the National Association of Negro Musicians (N.A.N.M.): The First Quarter Century, 1919–1943," 198.

77. Olive Coleman Thomas, "How to Create an Appreciation for Good Music in the Public Schools," *Mississippi Educational Journal for Teachers in Colored Schools* 3, no. 3 (January 1927): 59. Thomas's wording was not necessarily

uncommon. Critics frequently combined jazz and ragtime in their indictments. Some, like R. National Dett of Hampton, even included blues as well. Such lack of distinctions between musical genres was likely due to a general ignorance and stereotyped opinions that failed to recognize very real musical distinctions. Dett, Negro Music, 13.

78. Thomas, "How to Create an Appreciation for Good Music in the Public Schools," 59.

79. Crispus Attucks High School, *The Attucks: Crispus Attucks High School Yearbook* (Indianapolis, 1933), 38.

80. Crispus Attucks High School, *The Attucks: Crispus Attucks High School Yearbook* (Indianapolis, 1936), 32.

81. Thelma Gilbert, "The Negro in Music," *Spelman Messenger*, February, 1927, 16.

82. Duncan P. Schiedt, *The Jazz State of Indiana* (Pittsboro: [Self-Published], 1977), 183, 87.

83. James M. Lunceford, "Has the Athletic Council Succeeded," *Greater Fisk Herald*, June 1926; "Campus News," *Greater Fisk Herald*, January 1926. While a student at Fisk, Lunceford dated Nina Yolande Du Bois, W. E. B. Du Bois's daughter. The elder Du Bois did not care for Lunceford, a major reason she and Lunceford split up and did not marry when they were both still students. In one letter to his daughter, Du Bois wrote, "I am not taking Jimmie very seriously . . . Nothing is more disheartening and idiotic than to see two human beings without cultivated tastes, without trained abilities, and without power to earn a living locking themselves together and trying to live on love." Eddy Determeyer, *Rhythm Is Our Business: Jimmie Lunceford and the Harlem Express* (Ann Arbor: University of Michigan Press, 2009), 21–22.

84. Determeyer, *Rhythm Is Our Business: Jimmie Lunceford and the Harlem Express*, 29.

85. Determeyer, *Rhythm Is Our Business: Jimmie Lunceford and the Harlem Express*, 30.

86. Determeyer, *Rhythm Is Our Business: Jimmie Lunceford and the Harlem Express*, 28.

87. NANM, Official Souvenir Program of the Twelfth Annual Convention, 1930, National Association of Negro Musicians Collection, Center for Black Music Research, Columbia College, Box 2, Folder 68.

88. "Alpha Phi Alpha Has Pretty Dance," *The Indianapolis Recorder*, May 14, 1932.

89. Doris McGinty, Convention Notes, N.D. [2002?], National Association of Negro Musicians Collection, Center for Black Music Research, Columbia College, Box 2, Folder 18.

90. McGinty, *A Documentary History of the National Association of Negro Musicians*, 54.

91. Nora Douglas Holt, "Musicians Organize National Association," *Chicago Defender*, August 9, 1919.
92. "Musicians Organize," *New York Age*, May 17, 1919.

Chapter 4

1. "Work Assails Spirit of Jazz," *Los Angeles Times*, June 16, 1925.
2. "Jazz Band Hold Snappy Practice for Chicago Game," *Daily Illini*, February 28, 1919.
3. Helen Lefkowitz Horowitz, "The Organized," in *Campus Life: Undergraduate Cultures from the End of the Eighteenth Century to the Present* (Chicago: University of Chicago Press, 1987), 86.
4. "Editorial—The Ragtime Craze," *Daily Iowan*, May 9, 1918.
5. "Heaven Protect Jazz!," *Daily Illini*, January 22, 1921.
6. "Ex-Cited" "Advice" *Daily Illini*, February 25, 1917.
7. "Edwin," Letter to Nina Ruth Harding, November 21, 1922, Nina Ruth Harding Papers, 1899–1930, Student Life Archives, University of Illinois Archives, Box 1.
8. Loyola University, *Loyolan* (Chicago, 1924), 100, 208.
9. For a history of normal schools, see Christine A. Ogren, *The American State Normal School: An Instrument of Great Good* (New York: Palgrave Macmillan, 2005).
10 "Hallowe'en Party Big Event of Year," *Eastern Progress*, November 7, 1922.
11. "Musical Notes," *Phoenix*, November, 1928.
12. "Whiteman Orchestra to Be Advertised by Cross-Word Contest," *Indiana Daily Student*, March 28, 1925.
13. "Whiteman Program Traces Jazz through Stages of Development," *Indiana Daily Student*, April 18, 1925. Burton Peretti has argued white students found the "sweet jazz" of white artists such as Whiteman more palatable than jazz performed by black-led ensembles. Burton W. Peretti, *The Creation of Jazz: Music, Race, and Culture in Urban America* (Urbana: University of Illinois Press, 1992), 95.
14. "Whiteman Makes His Work Play and Keeps Jocularity Abounding," *Indiana Daily Student*, April 14, 1925.
15. "Whiteman to Arrive Early to Spend Day on Indiana Campus," *Indiana Daily Student*, April 11, 1925. Despite his appreciation for the university atmosphere, Whiteman did not hesitate to chastise students when he believed it to be appropriate. During a concert at University of Michigan, also in 1925, he berated the student audience who complained that the performance started later than scheduled. Sam Pepsus, "Diarist Awaits Whiteman at Stair Landing; Dines with Him on Frankfurters and Onions," *Indiana Daily Student*, April 18, 1925.

16. "Fred Waring's America: 1930's and 40's: Radio Days," updated 2021, https://libraries.psu.edu/about/collections/fred-warings-america/1930s-and-40s-radio-days.

17. "Fred Waring and Orchestra Pay Visit to House," *Phi Kappa News*, November 1930, 2.

18. Jean Pierre Lion, *Bix: The Definitive Biography of a Jazz Legend*, trans. Gabriella Page-Fort (New York: Continuum, 2005), 290.

19. "Former University Man Dies in East," *Daily Iowan*, August 8, 1931.

20. Lion, *Bix*, 61.

21. Lion, *Bix*, 140–41.

22. Richard Crawford, *America's Musical Life: A History* (New York: Norton, 2001), 638.

23. "Paul Whiteman, Carded for Program Here April 17, Is Uplifter of Present Day Jazz," *Indiana Daily Student*, April 10, 1925.

24. "Fraternity Men Aid Negro Jazz Artist's Rise to Local Fame," *Columbia Evening Missourian*, October 3 1921.

25. "Duke Ellington Calls Swing 'Emotional Bounce of Jazz,'" 6, *Indiana Daily Student*, October 13, 1939.

26. Evelyn Danovsky, "Melody in F," *Flower Echo*, October 31, 1933.

27. "Sousa and Band Give Campus Concert Tonight," *Daily Illini*, November 5, 1925. Not all visiting musicians giving campus concerts spoke so kindly of the genre. College students also attended performances by visiting musicians who went out of their way to criticize the genre. Such critiques often revolved around how age acted to shape perceptions of musical quality. Competitors in an "old fiddlers" competition at Cornell's Conservatory Hall in 1926 did not hide their disdain. Talking with student newspaper reporters, the participants spoke forcefully against jazz, emphasizing its bastardization of their cherished art. One such musician stated that jazz was "the homicide of harmony and the murder of melody." Another commented, "I don't think of it and I don't want to think of it." One positive comment came from a participant who merely stated that he had begun to enjoy it, largely because the music was "here to stay." "Jazz Recieves Censure by Old Fiddlers Who Contested in Ithaca Yesterday," *Cornell Daily Sun*, May 4, 1926.

28. One joke told of a female college student who, when asked about the "age of Elizabeth," responded with how old she believed her friend Elizabeth was. Hamilton Royal Gaboon, "Joke—Age of Elizabeth," *College Humor*, August 1925, 61.

29. One such joke, reprinted from the *Notre Dame Juggler*, told of a white farmer who rented some of his land to a black farmhand on the agreement the white farmer would receive one-third of the wheat grown. When asked why he did not raise any wheat, the black farmhand replied, "Yessa! boss. I sho' did, but it's funny, you was supposed to get a third of it but there was only two loads." *Notre Dame Juggler*, "Joke—Rented Land and Wheat," *College Humor*, October 1925, 74.

30. More liberally, the magazine also included pieces by Zelda Fitzgerald, Dawn Powell, and others that critiqued women's Jazz Age gender expectations. Ashley Lawson, "Making the Most of the Middle: Zelda Fitzgerald and Dawn Powell in College Humor," *Journal of Modern Periodical Studies* 9, no. 2 (2019).

31. Notre Dame Juggler, "Clairvoyant," *College Humor*, September 1925, 17.

32. Cornell Widow, "Lager Rhythms," *College Humor*, October 1925, 84.

33. Frank Rowsey, "The Younger Set," *College Humor*, March 1925, 69. John Thelin has pointed out how alcohol found its way into various campus activities in the 1920s: "Homecoming celebrations, commencement week reunions, proms, year-round fraternity gatherings–all were associated with alcohol." John R. Thelin, *A History of American Higher Education*, 3rd ed. (Baltimore: Johns Hopkins University Press, 2019), 211.

34. Iowa Frivol, "Very Little Difference," *College Humor*, July 1925, 93.

35. "Joke—This Jazz Age," *College Humor*, Winter (January), 1925, 25.

36. Professor Prehn, "Joke—'Shots Follow Dance,'" *Prehn's Bonmots*, February 12, 1930, 8.

37. Abe Martin, "The Campus Scout," *Daily Illini*, January 19, 1917.

38. Washington Dirge, "Fraternity Meeting," *College Humor*, August 1925, 64.

39. Hamilton Royal Gaboon, "Joke—Latest Dance Steps," *College Humor*, September 1925, 28.

40. Washington Columns, "How to Avoid Petting Parties," *College Humor*, March 1925, 84.

41. Notre Dame Juggler, "Joke—Jolly Party," *College Humor*, October 1925, 74.

42. "Ad—Play Right Away on This Jazzy Sax," *College Humor*, Holiday December 1924, 80.

43. "Play 'Jazz' on the Saxophone," *College Humor*, August 1925, 121.

44. "Ad—Play Jazz in a Week on Your Buescher Saxophone," *College Humor*, October 1925, 109.

45. "Ad—Who Else Wants to Play Jazz?," *College Humor*, July 1925, 123.

46. "Ad—Be Popular! Play Jazz on the 'Sax,'" *College Humor*, November 1925, 113.

47. "Ad—Test Your Talent Free on a Buescher Saxophone," *College Humor*, November 1925, 126.

48. "Ad—Be Popular! Play Jazz on the 'Sax,'" 113. Though not as common, college newspapers also carried advertisements for businesses offering some form of jazz education. Again here, such companies addressed the ease with which students could learn the genre. The *Cornell Daily Sun* carried such a promotion for a local music store, Hickey's Lyceum Music Store. It read, "Do you play the banjo? Do you play the saxophone? Do you play the drums? If so why not get in on the 'jazz' game. We will show you have to get in on the 'jazz' wagon without much training or time. Drop in and talk it over." "Ad—Hickey's Lyceum Music Store," *Cornell Daily Sun*, September 26, 1924.

49. "Ad—The Original New Orleans Creole Band," *Daily Illini*, November 16, 1917.

50. "Ad—Dance Records You Can't Be Without," *Daily Illini*, November 15, 1919; "Ad: Brunswick Records," *Ohio State Lantern*, January 18, 1923.

51. "Ad—You'd Better Look into This Paul Whiteman Matter!," *Ohio State Lantern*, December 6, 1929.

52. Juliann Sivulka, *Soap, Sex, and Cigarettes: A Cultural History of American Advertising*, 2nd ed. (Boston: Wadsworth Press, 2012), 132.

53. "Ad—Full of Jazz and Ginger," *Cornell Daily Sun*, April 18, 1921.

54. "Ad—Hite Brothers Shoe Shining Parlor," *Daily Illini*, December 10, 1919.

55. "Ad—Dundee Woolen Mills," *Puget Sound Trail*, February 27, 1924.

56. Krug, *The Shaping of the American High School: Volume 2, 1920–1941*, 23.

57. "Women Condemn Jazz Tunes on U. of C. Campus," *Chicago Daily Tribune*, March 8, 1922.

58. Ralph C. Meima, "Literature and Life," *Anchor*, January 24, 1921, 2.

59. James Hart, "Jazz Jargon," *American Speech* 7, no. 4 (1932): 242.

60. "Others' Opinions," *Daily Illini*, December 3, 1924.

61. "Et Tu," "Confessions of a College Cynic," *Flamingo*, January 1923, 10.

62. Ohio State Lantern, "Jazz Hounds," *Daily Illini*, January 17, 1920.

63. Vagabond Editorial Board, "Vagabond Editorial Board and Mission," *Vagabond*, October 1923, 33–34. In his memoirs, longtime Indiana University president and chancellor Herman B Wells described it as a "flourishing literary magazine . . . developed by the students themselves." Wells, *Being Lucky*, 33.

64. "Notes of Higher Culture at Indiana University: On Immorality," *Vagabond*, 1924, 2.

65. "On Fraternities," *Vagabond*, March, n.d., 22.

66. Williams M. Toner, "Halltree: A Parody," *Vagabond*, 1926, 4.

67. "Tomorrow's Freedom," *The Scroll*, April 1927, 11.

68. Maurice E. Newsome, "They Call It Dancing," *The Greater Fisk Herald*, December 1926.

69. O. E. Jackson, "Our Prospects in the Realm of Music," *Athenaeum*, November 1924, 54.

70. Thomas Jefferson Flanagan, "Farewell," *The Scroll*, April 1925, 3.

71. Ethelyn Holmes, "Negro Music and Composers," *The Scroll*, April 1925.

72. Gilbert, "The Negro in Music," 6. Evidence suggests Flanagan may have later changed his mind about jazz. Within a year of his "Farewell," he contributed an original poem into *The Scroll* the next year titled "Honey, Can You 'Charleston?'" It read, in part, "The light shine dim and the music's so sweet / Honey, can't you 'Charleston?' / Every heart's fired to the leap and the beat / O' the tune o' the 'Charleston.'" Thomas Jefferson Flanagan, "Honey, Can You 'Charleston'?," *The Scroll*, January 1926, 8.

73. Gilbert, "The Negro in Music," 16.

74. "Negro Spirituals of African Origin," *Spelman Messenger*, January 1930, 59.

75. Howard B. Thurman, "The Message of the Spirituals," *Spelman Messenger*, October 1928. Aside from than their critiques, students at historically black colleges saw opportunities for humor in the massive popularity jazz enjoyed throughout the decade. Yet while white college students joked of drunken debauchery on the dance floor and the varying musical preferences between them and adults, black college students teased each other about their abstinence from the genre. Clark Atlanta University's yearbook included submissions that similarly poked fun at students and their disinterest in the music. The "Can You Imagine?" section featured entries like "Erma Hamilton Doing the Charleston," "The girls of Warren Hall attending dances in the city," and "Sarah Neal singing jazz." Clark University, *Pasticcio* (Atlanta, 1926), unpaginated humor section.

76. Joe M. Richardson, *A History of Fisk University, 1865–1946* (Tuscaloosa: University of Alabama Press, 2002), 84.

77. Barbara Solomon, *In the Company of Educated Women* (New Haven: Yale University Press, 1985), 159.

78. Harry O. Schell, "The Social Problem of Atlanta University," *The Scroll*, November 1926, 11.

79. John Oakes, "Goose Stepping," *The Scroll*, January 1926, 9.

80. Stephanie Y. Evans, *Black Women in the Ivory Tower, 1850–1954: An Intellectual History* (Gainesville, FL: University Press of Florida, 2007), 111.

81. R. W. Riley, "The Attitude of a New Student," *Maroon Tiger*, November 1926, 5.

82. Edward T. Ware, Notice to Pupils in Music, 1909, Edward T. Ware Papers, Atlanta University Center Archives, Box 34.

83. "Music," *Greater Fisk Herald*, March 1927.

84. Mrs. Kemper Harreld, "Music in the Home," *Spelman Messenger*, January 1927, 14.

85. Richardson, *A History of Fisk University, 1865–1946*, 106–7.

86. "Dancing," *Greater Fisk Herald*, December 1926.

87. "Campus News," 29.

88. "Declares Jazz Lowers Tastes," *Los Angeles Times*, August 14, 1921.

89. "Fred Waring's America: 1920's—Rise to Fame," updated 2021, https://libraries.psu.edu/about/collections/fred-warings-america/1920s-rise-fame.

90. "Holds Jazz Upsets Life at College," *Los Angeles Times*, January 5, 1926.

91. Coben, *Rebellion against Victorianism: The Impetus for Cultural Change in 1920s America*, 36.

92. W. M. Wheeler and I. W. Bailey, "The Feeding Habits of Pseudomyrmine and Other Ants," *Transactions of the American Philosophical Society, New Series* 22, no. 4 (1920): 273.

93. Joseph William Hewitt, "The Humor of the Greek Anthology," *Classical Journal* 17, no. 2 (1921): 72.

94. J. P. Dunn, "Review," *Mississippi Valley Historical Review* 9, no. 3 (1922): 259.

95. "Jazz, Steam Whistle Equally Melodious, Prof. Morgan Asserts," 1, *Indiana Daily Student*, October 30, 1924. Morgan also applauded an article that had just appeared in the campus literary magazine the *Vagabond*, "The End of the Jazz Age." That satirical article considered the jazz interest from twenty years in the future. It began, "Except for a few poor wretches in insane asylums, I am the only survivor of the Jazz Age, and I should not be alive now were it not for the fact that from infancy I have been lame and tone-deaf." For the *Vagabond* article, see: Sir Polonius Panurge, "The End of the Jazz Age," *Vagabond*, Autumn 1924, 22.

96. Christabel F. Fiske, "Problems in the Teaching of Poetry," *English Journal* 12, no. 8 (1923): 539.

97. William I. Thomas, *The Unadjusted Girl: With Cases and Standpoint for Behavior Analysis*, vol. 4, Criminal Science Monographs (Boston: Little, Brown, 1923), 47.

98. Andrew Abbott and Rainer Egloff, "The Polish Peasant in Oberlin and Chicago: The Intellectual Trajectory of W. I. Thomas," *American Sociologist* 39, no. 4 (December 2008): 217.

99. Baker was not without a sense of humor. At one point he argued that Plato approved of lying to achieve state policy ends. Baker quipped, "He would be at home in Washington." Joseph E. Baker, "Plato as a Contemporary Essayist," *Classical Journal* 22, no. 3 (1926): 211, 13, 15.

100. Leroy E. Bowman and Maria Ward Lambin, "Evidences of Social Relations as Seen in Types of New York City Dance Halls," *Journal of Social Forces* 3, no. 2 (1925): 286.

101. G. T. W. Patrick, "Can the Sentiment of Patriotism Be Refunded?," *American Journal of Sociology* 30, no. 5 (1925): 569, 77.

102. Stringham, "'Jazz': An Educational Problem," 192.

103. Raymond Norman Carr, *Building the School Orchestra: A Guide for Leaders* (Elkhart: C. G. Conn, 1923), 98. Contrasting such moderate appraisals, studio performance educators were more critical, especially about jazz influences creeping into classical performance. Clarence G. Hamilton, a prominent Wellesley University piano professor, countered that "it is no wonder that a piano touch suffers from much jazz playing," while the American Conservatory of Music pianist Heniot Levy similarly complained that popular music created a "mania for speed" among his students. Heniot Levy, "Curbing the Music Student's Mania for Speed," *Etude*, March 1925, 161; Clarence G. Hamilton, "The Teacher's Round Table," *Etude*, August 1924, 561.

104. "Jazz Is Popular Revenge on Music," *Norwalk Hour*, November 8, 1926, 8. Erskine may have been influenced by his Columbia English colleague William Morrison Patterson, who had prominently defended the genre as early as 1917. James Lincoln Collier, *The Reception of Jazz in America: A New View* (Brooklyn: Institute for Studies in American Music, 1988), 31.

105. Katherine Elise Chaddock, *The Multi-Talented Mr. Erskine: Shaping Mass Culture through Great Books and Fine Music* (New York: Palgrave Macmillan, 2012), 9.

106. Chaddock, *The Multi-Talented Mr. Erskine: Shaping Mass Culture through Great Books and Fine Music*, 84; Warren Susman, *Culture as History: The Transformation of American Society in the Twentieth Century*, 2nd ed. (Washington and London: Smithsonian Institute Press, 2003), 118.

107. John Erskine, "De-Centralizing Our Music," *Music Supervisors Journal* 16, no. 5 (1930): 33.

108. John Erskine, "Give Music a Larger Place in Education," *Music Supervisors Journal* 17, no. 4 (March 1931): 17.

109. Charles S. Johnson, "Jazz Poetry and Blues," *Fisk Herald*, May 1930, 14, 15.

110. David Levering Lewis, Forward to Patrick Gilpin and Marybeth Gasman, *Charles S. Johnson: Leadership beyond the Veil in the Age of Jim Crow* (Albany: State University of New York Press, 2003), x.

111. Johnson, "Jazz Poetry and Blues," 116.

112. Guy B. Johnson, "A Sociological Interpretation of the New Ku Klux Movement," *Journal of Social Forces* 1, no. 4 (1923): 443.

113. Pierce, *Polite Protest*, 3.

114. Coben, *Rebellion against Victorianism: The Impetus for Cultural Change in 1920s America*, 145. More recent scholarship has suggested that, while the KKK was odiously regressive in their views, they smartly adopted thoroughly modern communication techniques: "Rather than a 'bulwark against modernism,' it is more profitable to consider the men and women of the Invisible Empire as thoroughly modern Americans." Harcourt, *Ku Klux Kulture: America and the Klan in the 1920s* (Chicago: University of Chicago Press, 2017), 9.

115. Adam Laats, *The Other School Reformers: Conservative Activism in American Education* (Cambridge: Harvard University Press, 2015).

116. B. Edward McClellan, *Moral Education in America: Schools and the Shaping of Character since Colonial Times* (New York: Teachers College Press, 1999), 68.

117. "Heaven Protect Jazz!"

Chapter 5

1. Wesley Ruggles, *The Plastic Age* (Los Angeles: B. P. Schulberg, 1925).

2. Unfortunately for Marks, administrators at Brown did not care for the image of student life he characterized in *The Plastic Age*. In the afterward of the book's 1980 reissue by Southern Illinois University Press, the latter day Brown English faculty member R. V. Cassill explained the circumstances of Marks's firing by writing, "He was let go from his teaching job at Brown—not, according

to the enduring consensus of those who survived his departure, because he *had* written a risqué and sensational book that tarnished Brown's reputation along with others, but because he was the sort of person who *would* do such a thing. (Such delicate distinctions are requisite in institutions cherishing a reputation for academic freedom.)" R. V. Cassill, "Afterword," in *The Plastic Age* (Carbondale: Southern Illinois University Press, 1980), 333–34.

3. Robert Cooley Angell, *The Campus: A Study of Contemporary Undergraduate Life in the American University* (New York and London: D. Appleton, 1928), 165.

4. Horowitz, "The Organized," 13.

5. Given the strict segregation of many dance halls, such estimates likely represent primarily the number of white dancers. Kenney, *Chicago Jazz*, 18–19.

6. Giordano, *Social Dancing in America*, 44.

7. The "filthy" quote comes from Yarrow, *Fighting the Debauchery of Our Girls and Boys*, 132. See also Anne Louise Wagner, *Adversaries of Dance: From the Puritans to the Present* (Urbana: University of Illinois Press, 1997); Marshall and Jean Stearns, *Jazz Dance: The Story of American Vernacular Dance* (New York: G. Schirmer, 1979).

8. Steven Mintz, *Huck's Raft: A History of American Childhood* (Cambridge and London: Harvard University Press, 2004), 213–32.

9. L.E.B., "Here's to the Prom," *Phoenix*, January 1925, 10.

10. Joe Ator, "Tropical Sky and Desert Sands Carry Prom Dancers to Orient," *Daily Illini*, December 9, 1922; Roy Dooley, "500 Prom Couples Celebrate amid Wintry Setting," *Daily Illini*, December 1, 1925.

11. Bailey, *From Front Porch to Back Seat*, 63.

12. Angell, *The Campus*, 165.

13. Bailey, *From Front Porch to Back Seat*, 63.

14. "Junior Prom Debt of Long Standing at Last Wiped Out," *Ohio State Lantern*, January 9, 1922.

15. Bailey, *From Front Porch to Back Seat*, 63.

16. "First Shipment of Decorations for Prom Arranged in Men's Gym," 2, *Indiana Daily Student*, April 15, 1926.

17. "Plans Are Completed for Indiana's Premier Social Activity," *Indiana Daily Student*, April 16, 1926.

18. "Prom With Inspiring Beauty Caps Social Season on Campus," *Indiana Daily Student*, April 17, 1926.

19. "Frank Trumbauer's Band: King of Charleston Music," *Indiana Daily Student*, April 10, 1926.

20. "Prom with Inspiring Beauty Caps Social Season on Campus."

21. Indiana University, *Arbutus* (Bloomington, 1925), 225.

22. Leon Wallace, "Dancers Will Revel in Starry Phantasmagoria of Harmonies, Colors at Fifth Prom Tonight," *Indiana Daily Student*, May 1, 1925.

23. Indiana University, *Arbutus* (Bloomington, 1926), 255.

24. "Trustees Will Permit Charlestoning at Prom," 4, *Indiana Daily Student*, March 17, 1926. Other schools similarly had concerns about how jazz dancing would reflect back on the university. The University of Michigan canceled the 1921 Junior Hop due to inappropriate dancing. John McMahon, editor of the conservative magazine *The Ladies' Home Journal* applauded the move. He wrote, "The students were very contrite and made all kinds of promises to be good, but in view of the fact that they had broken the same promises the year before the faculty was obdurate." Despite the actions of Michigan officials, canceling dances remained exceptionally rare. McMahon, "Our Jazz-Spotted Middle West."

25. University, *Arbutus*, 255.

26. "Trustees Will Permit Charlestoning at Prom." In 1925, the year before Indiana University officials lifted the Charleston dancing ban, a Boston dance club had collapsed under what officials called "overcrowding," eventually killing forty-four people. The Associated Press initially reported the Pickwick Dance Hall had been "weakened by a fire ten weeks ago and flanked by a lot in which a building had been removed to make way for new construction," though deeper inspection revealed the wood supporting the club on a pier was rotten. While that building stood in stark contrast to the limestone gym at Indiana University, the event may have weighed on university administrators given the publicity surrounding the tragedy. The Pickwick owner was later indicted for manslaughter. "Pickwick Pier Rotten, Asserts Gen. Goethals," *Washington Post*, August 3, 1925; "43RD Body Removed from Ruins of Club," *Washington Post*, July 7, 1925; "Bodies of 12 Found; 17 Injured in Ruins of Boston Building," *Washington Post*, July 5, 1925; "39 Bodies Taken from Club Debris; Looter Shot Down," *Washington Post*, July 6, 1925.

27. Herbert Shaw, "Dancing at Fisk," *The Greater Fisk Herald*, October 1926, 12–13.

28. Newsome, "They Call It Dancing," 16.

29. Anna L. Jones, "An Evaluation of the Art of Dancing," *The Greater Fisk Herald*, April/May 1926, 14.

30. Maenelle Dixon, "Spelman and Morehouse Get Acquainted," *Campus Mirror*, October 1929, 7.

31. "Dancing," 8.

32. Richardson, *A History of Fisk University, 1865–1946*, 85. For an overview of McKenzie's presidency, see James Anderson, *The Education of Blacks in the South, 1860–1935* (Chapel Hill and London: University of North Carolina Press, 1988), 264–70.

33. "Dancing."

34. Raymond Wolters, *The New Negro on Campus: Black College Rebellions of the 1920s* (Princeton: Princeton University Press, 1975), 65.

35. Evans, *Black Women in the Ivory Tower, 1850–1954*, 111–12. I fully acknowledge Evans was referring to only female students in her quote. Still, critics saw jazz as *so* nefarious, its influence so vile, no gender distinction would have seemed relevant.

36. "The 'Barn Social,'" *The Scroll*, March 1927, 8.
37. "The Spelman Social," *Maroon Tiger*, November 1926, 3.
38. "Hen Parties," *The Scroll*, November 1926, 12.
39. Bailey, *From Front Porch to Back Seat*, 30.
40. "Joke—Have You Heard from Mary?," *Trintonian*, June 8, 1920, 4.
41. F. Scott Fitzgerald, *Flappers and Philosophers*, ed. James L. W. West III (Cambridge: Cambridge University Press, 2012), 111, 14.
42. "To a Sophisticated Blonde," *The Phoenix*, October, 1925.This view of attractiveness was not universal among college men. A 1928 survey at the University of Missouri revealed roughly half of college men there desired an, "old fashioned girl," while the other half looked for a "modern girl." Lawrence J. Nelson, *Rumors of Indiscretion: The University of Missouri "Sex Questionnaire" Scandal in the Jazz Age* (Columbia and London: University of Missouri Press, 2003), 41.
43. "Girls Seek Risque, Thrive on Thrills but Believe Situation Unalarming," *Ohio State Lantern*, January 10, 1922.
44. Solomon, *In the Company of Educated Women*, 158.
45. The researchers did not inquire about the sexual patterns of white college women prior to marriage. Nicholas L. Syrett, *The Company He Keeps: A History of White College Fraternities* (Chapel Hill: University of North Carolina Press, 2009), 220–21.
46. Syrett, *The Company He Keeps*, 223.
47. Schrum, *Some Wore Bobby Sox*, 153.
48. The Mexico, Missouri *Ledger* responded to news of the questionnaire by wiring the University of Missouri President Brooks that "Sex minded teachers and students might better go to the red-light districts for laboratory experiments." The *Columbia Daily Tribune* called the survey "a filthy questionnaire," though it also published extended excerpts of the document. The university chapter of the sorority Alpha Chi Omega issued a critical statement, though it stopped short of calling for any resignations or expulsions. The American Association of University Professors also investigated and ultimately sided with academic freedom. Nelson, *Rumors of Indiscretion*, 1–12.
49. Joseph Hawes, *Children between the Wars: American Childhood, 1920–1940* (New York: Twayne, 1997), 26.
50. Campus Council and Student Affairs Committee, 1929, Students–Rules and Regulations, Indiana University Archives, Indiana University Social Rules 1916–1929.
51. Mildred Valeda Daum, Personal Diary, 1920–1924, Mildred Valeda Daum Diary and Scrapbooks, 1919–1924 (Collection C 448), Indiana University Archives, unpaginated entry for February 20, 1921.
52. Elaine Kendall, *"Peculiar Institutions": An Informal History of the Seven Sister Colleges* (New York: G. P. Putnam, 1976), 172–73. Similarly, at the University of Illinois, female students could neither visit fraternities without a chaperone

nor could they attend dances that did not have a chaperone. Dean of Women, Woman's League Rules, 1925, Student Life and Culture Archives, University of Illinois Archives, Dean of Students—Dean of Women, Box 6.

53. "Women Deans Open Fight on Jazz in Dancing," *Chicago Daily Tribune*, November 20, 1921.

54. "Fears Colleges' Moral Tone: Dean Marion Talbot Writes They, Promote Race Suicide," *Chicago Daily Tribune*, April 21, 1910.

55. Dean Talbot resigned her position in 1925, citing her age as the primary reason. At the time of her retirement, she told the *Chicago Tribune*, "The modern girl is more frivolous than the girl of my college days." "Dean Talbot of U. of C. to Quit Her Post," *Chicago Daily Tribune*, April 1, 1925. In their study of campus culture, Oscar and Mary Handlin briefly discuss, though do not identify, one Dean of Women who struck a similar tone to Talbot. They wrote, "She knew positively that they were not dancing six inches apart in obedience to the edict she had issued when the shimmy dances had come straight from the black and tan cabarets of Chicago to the hectic sex-swirl that was the state university." Oscar and Mary Handlin, *The American College and American Culture: Socialization as a Function of Higher Education* (Berkeley: The Carnegie Commission on Higher Education, 1970), 69.

56. Warren S. Thompson, "Race Suicide in the United States," *The Scientific Monthly* 5, no. 1 (1917): 22. See also Thomas MacNamara, *Birth Control and American Modernity: A History of Popular Ideas* (Cambridge: Cambridge University Press, 2018), 37–64.

57. "Finds Delusion of Wildness in Modern Youth," *Chicago Daily Tribune*, February 19, 1926.

58. Giordano, *Social Dancing in America*, 323.

59. Giordano, *Satan in the Dance Hall*, 29.

60. "Dance Not the Only Reason Baylor Women Can't Go to Fair Says Prexy," *Daily Lariat*, October 4, 1924.

61. "Dance Ban Stands," *Milwaukee Journal*, May 18, 1912.

62. Rev. Franklin F. Lewis, *Five Reasons Why Methodists Don't Dance* (Chicago: Glad Tidings, 1921), 36.

63. "Methodists Lift Amusements Ban," *Illinois Fiery Cross* 1924.

64. George M. Marsden, *Fundamentalism and American Culture*, 2nd ed. (Gary: Oxford University Press, 2006), 178.

65. Jerome Hixson, *Past Perfect: Recollections of Jerome Hixson* (Greencastle: DePauw University, 1982), 18–19.

66. "Class Notes."

67. Loyola University, The Loyolan, 1926, 250.

68. Schiedt, *The Jazz State of Indiana*, 28.

69. Lynn Dumenil, *The Modern Temper: American Culture and Society in the 1920s* (New York: Hill and Wang, 1995), 177.

70. Genevieve Forbes Herrick, "Rush to Defense of Co-Eds," *Chicago Daily Tribune*, September 15, 1926.

71. Conservative opposition to college student dancing extended beyond the clergy. One concerned Indiana citizen wrote Indiana University President William Lowe Bryan in 1922 to express his concern about jazz dancing and the associated questions of morality among the university's students. The critic, Clark Russell, initially framed his argument as a sort of civic concern, one Hoosier expressing some worry about the effects jazz dancing had on the well-being of students at that state university. He was merely stating his worry about possible physical and moral long-term consequences the seemingly frenetic dancing could have on the younger university students. Yet toward the end of the letter, the tone quickly shifted from concern to almost threatening. Russell pointed out to Bryan that, as a tax-paying citizen, he did not like the thought of his taxes funding such activities. The Hoosier tax payer dropped the persona of a concerned citizen to make sure President Bryan understood how hard he worked for his income and how strongly he disliked it going toward such "disgusting" ends. Russell to President Bryan, 1922, Indiana University President's Office Correspondence, 1913–1937, Indiana University Archives, Box 48.

72. "Holds Jazz and Girls Wreck Scholarship," *New York Times*, June 30, 1928.

73. "Jazz Country 'Jazz Mad,'" *Evening World*, March 14, 1922.

74. Leonard, *Jazz and the White Americans*, 68.

75. "Society Notes," *Daily Illini*, November 14, 1918.

76. Dance cards were small booklets women carried during dances to record the names of their dancing partners. Alpha Tau Omega, Dance Card, 1924, Indiana University Archives, Reference File—Dance Cards, Box 1.

77. "Lock N.U. 'Frat' for Wild Party," *Chicago Daily Tribune*, September 7, 1925.

78. "Irate at Fraternity Din," *New York Times*, November 19, 1926.

79. "Social Festivities End with Formal: Called Best Yet," *Phi Kappa News*, June 1930, 2.

80. Dance Card: Delta Chi Dinner Dance, 1921, University of Illinois Student Life Archives, Student Affairs—Student Organizations—Dance Programs, Box 1.

81. Syrett, *The Company He Keeps*, 185.

82. Syrett, *The Company He Keeps*, 197.

83. "Plans Are Completed for Indiana's Premier Social Activity"; "Junior Prom Tickets Go on Sale Today—Prize Poster Is Picked," *Daily Illini*, March 5, 1919; "Junior Prom Date Set for December 6," *Daily Illini*, November 13, 1929.

84. Syrett, *The Company He Keeps*, 196–97.

85. Boston Beanpot, "Essential Parts of a Fraternity," *College Humor*, October 1925, 75.

86. "New Victrola," *Sigmagram*, April 1926, 2.

87. "Active Chapter," *Tau Topics*, May 1927, 1.

88. Syrett, *The Company He Keeps*, 214.

89. Alpha Alpha Omega, Dance Card—Dinner Dance, 1923, University of Illinois Student Life Archives, Student Affairs—Student Organizations—Dance Programs, Box 1.

90. F. Scott Fitzgerald, *Tales of the Jazz Age* (New York: Charles Scribner's Sons, 1922). The Fitzgerald story is also discussed in Kathy J. Ogren, *The Jazz Revolution: Twenties America and the Meaning of Jazz* (New York: Oxford University Press, 1989), 149–50.

91. Campus Council and the Student Affairs Committee, Social Regulations, 1929, Students–Rules and Regulations.

92. Committee on Student Affairs, Committee Social Rule Recommendations, 1919, Students–Rules and Regulations, Indiana University Archives, Indiana University Social Rules 1916–1929; Campus Council and the Student Affairs Committee, Social Regulations, 1929, Students–Rules and Regulations.

93. Syrett, *The Company He Keeps*, 207.

94. Campus Council and Student Affairs Committee, Meeting Minutes, 1919, Students–Rules and Regulations.

95. Campus Council and Student Affairs Committee, Meeting Minutes, 1918, Students–Rules and Regulations.

96. "W. L. Lifts Old Dancing Ban in Sororities," *Daily Illini*, March 17, 1932.

97. Kendall, "*Peculiar Institutions*," 176.

98. By the late 1920s, each of the seven "Sister Schools" had constructed a multipurpose building that held dances, plays, banquets, and other social activities. Bryn Mawr was the last of those institutions to allow on campus dancing. In 1929, administrators agreed to hold the first recognized dance—a "tea dance" with Princeton men. Syrett, *The Company He Keeps*, 225.

99. Hawes, *Children between the Wars*, 27. See also Syrett, *The Company He Keeps*, 183–228.

100. Syrett, *The Company He Keeps*, 225.

101. Delta Tau Delta, Dance Card, 1925, Indiana University Archives, Reference File—Dance Cards, Box 1.

102. "On Fraternities," 22.

103. Richard M. Sudhalter, *Stardust Melody: The Life and Music of Hoagy Carmichael* (New York: Oxford University Press, 2003).

104. Hoagy Carmichael, *The Stardust Road and Sometimes I Wonder: The Autobiography of Hoagy Carmichael* (New York: Da Capo Press, 1999), 16.

105. Carmichael, *The Stardust Road and Sometimes I Wonder*, 17.

106. Carmichael, *The Stardust Road and Sometimes I Wonder*, 22.

107. "Indiana Avenue and Beyond: A History and Heritage Reflecting a Community of Jazz in Indiana," 2011, http://jazzindianaavenue.wordpress.com/. At the time, Indianapolis was roughly 10 percent black, with three recognizably black neighborhoods. Pierce, *Polite Protest*, 11–12.

108. Carmichael, *The Stardust Road and Sometimes I Wonder*, 17. Carmichael later acknowledged his debt to his black piano teacher back in Indianapolis. Reminiscing about his first performance in Bloomington above the hardware store, he wrote, "There was the steady beat of my left hand and the slight accent of the upbeat—Reggie's trick." Carmichael, *The Stardust Road and Sometimes I Wonder*, 22. In a 2011 interview, DuValle's son, himself a jazz musician, said, "[Carmichael's] very indebted to my father for the things my father helped him do." Taborn, "Indiana Avenue and Beyond: A History and Heritage Reflecting a Community of Jazz in Indiana."

109. Carmichael, *The Stardust Road and Sometimes I Wonder*, 21–23.

110. Wells, *Being Lucky*, 33.

111. Tempo, "The Era of Sock," *Vagabond* 1, no. 3 (1924): 22.

112. Daum, Personal Diary.

113. Jordan River Revue Program, 1922, Jordan River Revue Records, Indiana University Archives, Box 1.

114. Other student-run jazz bands existed on campus. The "Crimson Serenaders," played a relatively "sweeter" or less, "hot" jazz. Amos Ostot, also a member of Kappa Sigma, led the rival group. Among other on-campus performances, the Serenaders played the 1926 postprom dance and by 1929 had taken the task of providing music for the Jordan River Revue. Jordan River Revue Board, Orchestra Contract, 1929, Jordan River Revue Records, Indiana University Archives, Box 1; "Ad—Post Prom Dance," *Indiana Daily Student*, April 16, 1926.

115. Schiedt, *The Jazz State of Indiana*, 86.

116. At the time, "Carmichael's Collegians" consisted of a piano, drums, saxophone, cornet, trombone, and banjo.

117. Schiedt, *The Jazz State of Indiana*, 93.

118. Carmichael, *The Stardust Road and Sometimes I Wonder*, 47.

119. Lion, *Bix*, 71, 73. Carmichael also sought to make Kappa Sigma itself the recognizable jazz fraternity on campus and recruited for his band largely from within his fraternity. One occasional band member—himself not a member of Carmichael's fraternity—would later recall, "Hoag wanted the whole band to be Kappa Sigs!"

120. Schiedt, *The Jazz State of Indiana*, 153.

121. Carmichael, *The Stardust Road and Sometimes I Wonder*, 77.

122. Wells, *Being Lucky*, 33.

Conclusion

1. Mary B. Schoen-Nazzaro, "Plato and Aristotle on the Ends of Music," *Laval Théologique et Philosophique* 34, no. 3 (1978): 264; Plato, *The Republic of Plato*, trans. Allan Bloom, 3rd ed. (New York: Basic Books, 2016).

2. Clark, *God—or Gorilla: Images of Evolution in the Jazz Age*, 16.

3. "Jazz Is Nearing Its End, Says Musical Editor," *Detroit News*, March 28, 1931.

4. Mark Katz, *Capturing Sound: How Technology Has Changed Music* (Berkeley: University of California Press, 2004), 67.

5. McGinty, *A Documentary History of the National Association of Negro Musicians*, 52.

6. Earhart, "Is Instrumental Music in Public Schools Justified by the Actual Results? (Concluded)," 39.

7. Reginald T. Buckner, "A History of Music Education in the Black Community of Kansas City, Kansas, 1905–1954," *Journal of Research in Music Education* 30, no. 2 (1982): 104.

8. Ronald D. Cohen, "The Delinquents: Censorship and Youth Culture in Recent U.S. History," *History of Education Quarterly* 37, no. 3 (1997).

Bibliography

Archive Collections

Center for Black Music Research, Columbia College
    National Association of Negro Musicians Collection
Chicago Board of Education Archives
    Unboxed Meeting Minute Transcriptions
Chicago Symphony Orchestra Archives
    Artistic Series—Education Concert Programs
Indiana University Archives
    Dance Cards
    Mildred Valeda Daum Diary and Scrapbooks, 1919–1924
    Indiana University President's Office Correspondence, 1913–1937
    Indiana University Rules and Regulations, 1916–1929
    Jordan River Revue Records
IUPUI Archives
    Crispus Attucks Museum (Digital Collection)
Penn State University Library
    Fred Waring's America (Digital Collection)
Robert W. Woodruff Library, Atlanta University Center
    Edward T. Ware Papers
University of Chicago Special Collections Research Center
    Ernest W. Burgess Papers
University of Illinois Library
    Student Life and Culture Archives

Secondary Sources

Absher, Amy. *The Black Musician and the White City: Race and Music in Chicago, 1900–1967*. Ann Arbor: University of Michigan Press, 2014.

Anderson, James. *The Education of Blacks in the South, 1860–1935*. Chapel Hill and London: University of North Carolina Press, 1988.
Bailey, Beth L. *From Front Porch to Back Seat: Courtship in Twentieth-Century America*. Baltimore, MD: Johns Hopkins University Press, 1989.
Barlow, William. *Voice Over: The Making of Black Radio*. Philadelphia: Temple University Press, 1998.
Bender, Daniel E. *American Abyss: Savagery and Civilization in the Age of Industry*. Ithaca, NY and London: Cornell University Press, 2011.
Berglund, Donald H. "A Study of the Life and Work of Frederick Stock During the Time He Served as Musical Director of the Chicago Symphony Orchestra, with Particular Reference to His Influence on Music Education." PhD, Northwestern University, 1955.
Blair, Cynthia M. *I've Got to Make My Livin': Black Women's Sex Work in Turn-of-the-Century Chicago*. Chicago and London: University of Chicago Press, 2010.
Brinkley, Alan. *The End of Reform: New Deal Liberalism in Recession and War*. New York: Knopf Doubleday, 2011.
Brundage, W. Fitzhugh, ed. *Beyond Blackface: African Americans and the Creation of American Popular Culture, 1890–1930*. Chapel Hill: University of North Carolina Press, 2011.
Buckner, Reginald T. "A History of Music Education in the Black Community of Kansas City, Kansas, 1905–1954." *Journal of Research in Music Education* 30, no. 2 (1982): 91–106.
Burkholder, Zoe. *Color in the Classroom: How American Schools Taught Race, 1900–1954*. New York: Oxford University Press, 2011.
———. *An African American Dilemma: A History of School Integration and Civil Rights in the North*. New York: Oxford University Press, 2021.
Burton, Ralph. *Remembering Bix: A Memoir of the Jazz Age*. Cambridge, MA: Da Capo Press, 1974, 2000.
Carmichael, Hoagy. *The Stardust Road and Sometimes I Wonder: The Autobiography of Hoagy Carmichael*. New York: Da Capo, (1946, 1965) 1999.
Carney, Court. *Cuttin' Up: How Early Jazz Got America's Ear*. Lawrence: University of Kansas Press, 2009.
Chaddock, Katherine Elise. *The Multi-Talented Mr. Erskine: Shaping Mass Culture through Great Books and Fine Music*. New York: Palgrave Macmillan, 2012.
Chauncey, George. *Gay New York: Gender, Urban Culture, and the Making of the Gay Male World, 1890–1940*. New York: Basic Books, 1995.
Churchill, David. "Making Broad Shoulders: Body-Building and Physical Culture in Chicago, 1890–1920." *History of Education Quarterly* 48, no. 3 (2008): 341–70.
Churchwell, Sarah B. *Careless People: Murder, Mayhem and the Invention of the Great Gatsby*. New York: Penguin Books, 2013.

Chuck, Workman. "Tribute to Jimmy Coe." *NUVO*, February 25, 2004, 3.
Clark, Constance Areson. *God—or Gorilla: Images of Evolution in the Jazz Age*. Baltimore, MD: Johns Hopkins University Press, 2008.
Clark, Daniel A. *Creating the College Man: American Mass Magazines and Middle-Class Manhood, 1890-1915*. Madison: University of Wisconsin Press, 2010.
Coben, Stanley. *Rebellion against Victorianism: The Impetus for Cultural Change in 1920s America*. New York and Oxford: Oxford University Press, 1991.
Cohen, Lizabeth. *Making a New Deal: Industrial Workers in Chicago, 1919-1939*. Cambridge, UK: Cambridge University Press, 2008.
Cohen, Ronald D. "The Delinquents: Censorship and Youth Culture in Recent U.S. History." *History of Education Quarterly* 37, no. 3 (1997): 251-70.
Collier, James Lincoln. *The Reception of Jazz in America: A New View*. Brooklyn, NY: Institute for Studies in American Music, 1988.
Crawford, Richard. *America's Musical Life: A History*. New York: Norton, 2001.
Curtis, Susan. "Black Creativity and Black Stereotype: Rethinking Twentieth Century Popular Music in America." In *Beyond Blackface: African American and the Creation of American Popular Culture, 1890-1930*, edited by W. Fitzhugh Brundage, 124-46. Chapel Hill: University of North Carolina Press, 211.
Day, Gary. *Varieties of Victorianism: The Uses of a Past*. New York: Palgrave Macmillan 1998.
Determeyer, Eddy. *Rhythm Is Our Business: Jimmie Lunceford and the Harlem Express*. Ann Arbor: University of Michigan Press, 2009.
Dixson, Adrienne D. "The Fire This Time: Jazz, Research, and Critical Race Theory." Chap. 11 In *Critical Race Theory in Education: All God's Children Got a Song*, edited by Adrienne D. Dixon and Celia K. Rousseau, 213-30. New York: Routledge, 2006.
Dumenil, Lynn. *The Modern Temper: American Culture and Society in the 1920s*. New York: Hill and Wang, 1995.
Dupree, Mary Herron. " 'Jazz,' the Critics, and American Art Music in the 1920s." *American Music* 4, no. 3 (1986): 287-301.
Early, Gerald. "Three Notes toward a Cultural Definition of the Harlem Renaissance." *Callaloo* 14, no. 1 (1991): 136-49.
Evans, Stephanie Y. *Black Women in the Ivory Tower, 1850-1954: An Intellectual History*. Gainesville: University Press of Florida, 2007.
Fass, Paula S. *The Damned and the Beautiful: American Youth in the 1920's*. New York: Oxford University Press, 1977.
Filene, Peter G. *Him/Her/Self: Gender Identities in Modern America*. 3rd ed. Baltimore, MD: Johns Hopkins University Press, (1974) 1998. "Folk Dancing Versus Jazz." *Oregonia*, June 28, 1920, 6.
Floyd, Samuel A., Jr. "The Invisibility and Fame of Harry T. Burleigh: Retrospect and Prospect." *Black Music Research Journal* 24, no. 2 (2004): 179-94.

Franklin, Barry, and Gary McCulloch, eds. *The Death of the Comprehensive High School?: Historical, Contemporary, and Comparative Perspectives.* New York: Palgrave Macmillan, 2007.

Gerstle, Gary. *American Crucible: Race and Nation in the Twentieth Century.* Princeton, NJ and Oxford, UK: Princeton University Press, 2002.

Gilpin, Patrick, and Marybeth Gasman. *Charles S. Johnson: Leadership beyond the Veil in the Age of Jim Crow.* Albany: State University of New York Press, 2003.

Giordano, Ralph G. *Social Dancing in America: A History and Reference.* Westport, CT: Greenwood, 2007.

———. *Social Dancing in America: A History and Reference.* Westport, CT: Greenwood, 2007.

Gordon, Linda. *The Second Coming of the KKK: The Ku Klux Klan of the 1920s and the American Political Tradition.* New York and London: Liveright, 2017.

Gordon, Lynn D. *Gender and Higher Education in the Progressive Era.* New Haven, CT and London: Yale University Press, 1990.

Graves, Karen. *Girls' Schooling during the Progressive Era: From Female Scholar to Domesticated Citizen.* New York and London: Garland, 1998.

Grossman, James R. *Land of Hope: Chicago: Black Southerners, and the Great Migration.* Chicago: University of Chicago Press, 1991.

Handlin, Oscar and Mary. *The American College and American Culture: Socialization as a Function of Higher Education.* Berkeley, CA: Carnegie Commission on Higher Education, 1970.

Hankins, Barry. *Jesus and Gin: Evangelicalism, the Roaring Twenties and Today's Culture Wars.* New York: Palgrave Macmillan, 2010.

Harcourt, Felix. *Ku Klux Kulture: America and the Klan in the 1920s.* Chicago, IL and London: University of Chicago Press, 2017.

Hartman, Andrew. *A War for the Soul of America: A History of the Culture Wars.* 2nd ed. Chicago, IL and London: University of Chicago Press, 2019.

Hersch, Charles. *Subversive Sounds: Race and the Birth of Jazz in New Orleans.* Chicago, IL and London: University of Chicago Press, 2008.

Hine, Thomas. *The Rise and Fall of the American Teenager.* New York: HarperCollins, 2000.

Hixson, Jerome. *Past Perfect: Recollections of Jerome Hixson.* Greencastle, IN: DePauw University, 1982.

Hoekema, David A. *Campus Rules and Moral Community: In Place of in Loco Parentis.* Lanham, MD: Rowman & Littlefield, 1994.

Horowitz, Helen Lefkowitz. *Alma Mater: Design and Experience in the Women's Colleges from Their Nineteenth-Century Beginnings to the 1930s.* 2nd ed. Amherst: University of Massachusetts Press, 1993.

———. *Campus Life: Undergraduate Cultures from the End of the Eighteenth Century to the Present.* New York: Knopf Doubleday, 1987.

Hutcheson, Philo. *A People's History of American Higher Education*. New York and London: Taylor & Francis, 2019.
"Indiana Avenue and Beyond: A History and Heritage Reflecting a Community of Jazz in Indiana." 2011. http://jazzindianaavenue.wordpress.com/.
Katz, Mark. *Capturing Sound: How Technology Has Changed Music*. Berkeley: University of California Press, 2004.
Keene, James A. *A History of Music Education in the United States*. 2nd ed. Centennial, CO: Glenbridge, 2009.
Kendall, Elaine. *"Peculiar Institutions": An Informal History of the Seven Sister Colleges*. New York: G. P. Putnam, 1976.
Kenney, William. *Chicago Jazz: A Cultural History*. New York and Oxford, UK: Oxford University Press, 1993.
———. *Jazz on the River*. Chicago, IL: University of Chicago Press, 2005.
Krug, Edward A. *The Shaping of the American High School: Volume 2, 1920–1941*. Madison: University of Wisconsin Press, 1972.
Lawson, Ashley. "Making the Most of the Middle: Zelda Fitzgerald and Dawn Powell in College Humor." *Journal of Modern Periodical Studies* 9, no. 2 (2019): 200–19.
Laats, Adam. *Fundamentalism and Education in the Scopes Era: God, Darwin, and the Roots of America's Culture Wars*. New York: Palgrave Macmillan, 2012.
———. *The Other School Reformers: Conservative Activism in American Education*. Cambridge, MA: Harvard University Press, 2015.
Leonard, Neil. *Jazz and the White Americans: The Acceptance of a New Art Form*. Chicago, IL: University of Chicago Press, (1962) 1970.
Levine, David. *The American College and Culture of Aspiration 1915–1940*. Ithaca, NY: Cornell University Press, 1986.
Lion, Jean Pierre. *Bix: The Definitive Biography of a Jazz Legend*. Translated by Gabriella Page-Fort. New York: Continuum International, 2005.
Loss, Christopher P. *Between Citizens and the State: The Politics of American Higher Education in the 20th Century*. Princeton, NJ and Oxford, UK: Princeton University Press, 2012.
Lucas, Christopher J. *American Higher Education: A History*. New York: Palgrave Macmillan, 2016.
MacNamara, Thomas. *Birth Control and American Modernity: A History of Popular Ideas*. Cambridge, UK: Cambridge University Press, 2018.
Mark, Michael L., and Charles L. Gary. *A History of American Music Education*. Lanham, MD: Rowman and Littlefield Education, 2007.
Marsden, George M. *Fundamentalism and American Culture*. 2nd ed. Gary, NC: Oxford University Press, (1982) 2006.
Martin, Abe. "The Campus Scout." *Daily Illini*, January 19, 1917, 5.
May, Henry F. "Shifting Perspectives on the 1920s." *Mississippi Valley Historical Review* 43, no. 3 (December 1956): 405–27.

May, Lissa Fleming. "Early Musical Development of Selected African-American Jazz Musicians in Indianapolis in the 1930's and 1940's." *Journal of Historical Research in Music Education* 27, no. 1 (2005): 21–32.
McCann, Paul. "Performing Primitivism: Disarming the Social Threat of Jazz in Narrative Fiction of the Early Twenties." *Journal of Popular Culture* 41, no. 4 (2008): 658–75.
McClellan, B. Edward. *Moral Education in America: Schools and the Shaping of Character since Colonial Times*. New York: Teachers College Press, 1999.
McGerr, Michael. *A Fierce Discontent: The Rise and Fall of the Progressive Movement in America*. Oxford, UK and New York: Oxford University Press, 2003.
McGinty, Doris Evans, ed. *A Documentary History of the National Association of Negro Musicians*. Chicago, IL: Center for Black Music Research, 2004.
McGirr, Lisa. *The War on Alcohol: Prohibition and the Rise of the American State*. New York and London: W. W. Norton, 2016.
Merriam, Alan, and Fradley Garner. "Jazz-the Word." *Ethnomusicology* 12, no. 3 (1968): 373–96.
Miller, Nathan. *New World Coming: The 1920s and the Making of Modern America*. New York: Scribner, 2003.
Mintz, Steven. *Huck's Raft: A History of American Childhood*. Cambridge, MA and London: Harvard University Press, 2004.
Mirel, Jeffrey. *Patriotic Pluralism: Americanization, Education, and European Immigrants*. Cambridge, MA and London: Harvard University Press, 2010.
Mixon, Anita J. "Women Speaking in and for Institutions: A Rhetorical History of the Politics of Respectability in Black Chicago, 1919–1939." PhD, University of Illinois at Urbana–Champaign, 2017.
Moran, Jeffrey P. *Teaching Sex: The Shaping of Adolescence in the 20th Century*. Cambridge, MA and London: Harvard University Press, 2000.
Morris, Aldon. *The Scholar Denied: W. E. B. Du Bois and the Birth of Modern Sociology*. Berkeley and Los Angeles: University of California Press, 2017.
Nash, Roderick. *The Nervous Generation: American Thought, 1917–1930*. Chicago, IL: Rand McNally, 1970.
National Center for Education Statistics. *Digest of Education Statistics*. Washington, DC: U.S. Department of Education, 1998.
———. *The Traditionally Black Institutions of Higher Education, 1860 to 1982*. Washington, DC: U.S. Department of Education, 1994.
Nelson, Lawrence J. *Rumors of Indiscretion: The University of Missouri "Sex Questionnaire" Scandal in the Jazz Age*. Columbia and London: University of Missouri Press, 2003.
Nettl, Bruno. *Heartland Excursions: Ethnomusicological Reflections on Schools of Music*. Urbana and Chicago: University of Illinois Press, 1995.
Odom, Mary E. *Delinquent Daughters: Protecting and Policing Adolescent Female Sexuality in the United States, 1885–1920*. Chapel Hill: University of North Carolina Press, 1995.

Ogren, Kathy J. *The Jazz Revolution: Twenties America and the Meaning of Jazz.* New York: Oxford University Press, 1989.
Ogren, Christine A., and Mark A. VanOverbeke. *Rethinking Campus Life: New Perspectives on the History of College Students in the United States.* Cham, Switzerland: Springer, 2018.Osgood, Robert L. *The History of Special Education: A Struggle for Equality in American Public Schools.* Westport, CT: Praeger, 2008.
Pacyga, Dominic A., and Ellen Skerrett. *Chicago, City of Neighborhoods: Histories & Tours.* Chicago, IL: Loyola University Press, 1986.
Parrenas, Rhacel Salazar. " 'White Trash' Meets the 'Little Brown Monkeys': The Taxi Dance Hall as a Site of Interracial and Gender Alliances between White Working Class Women and Filipino Immigrant Men in the 1920s and 30s." *Amerasia Journal* 24, no. 2 (1998): 115.
Patterson, Willis Charles. "A History of the National Association of Negro Musicians (N.A.N.M.): The First Quarter Century, 1919-1943." PhD, Wayne State University, 1993.
Peretti, Burton W. *The Creation of Jazz: Music, Race, and Culture in Urban America.* Urbana: University of Illinois Press, 1992.
Pierce, Richard B. *Polite Protest: The Political Economy of Race in Indianapolis.* Bloomington: Indiana University Press, 2006.
Postel, Charles. *The Populist Vision.* Oxford, UK and New York: Oxford University Press, 2007.
Putnam, Lara. *Radical Moves: Caribbean Migrants and the Politics of Race in the Jazz Age.* Chapel Hill: University of North Carolina Press, 2013.
Ramsey, Paul. *Bilingual Public Schooling in the United States: A History of America's "Polyglot Boardinghouse."* New York: Palgrave Macmillan, 2010.
Reuben, Julie. *The Making of the Modern University: Intellectual Transformation and the Marginalization of Morality.* Chicago, IL and London: University of Chicago Press, 1996.
Richardson, Joe M. *A History of Fisk University, 1865-1946.* Tuscaloosa: University of Alabama Press, 2002, 1980.
Rousmaniere, Kate. *City Teachers: Teaching and School Reform in Historical Perspective.* New York: Teachers College Press, 1997.
Ruis, A. R. *Eating to Learn, Learning to Eat: The Origins of School Lunch in the United States.* New Brunswick, NJ and London: Rutgers University Press, 2017.
Ryan, Erica. *When the World Broke in Two: The Roaring Twenties and the Dawn of America's Culture Wars.* Santa Barbara, CA: Praegar, 2018.
Schenbeck, Lawrence. "Music, Gender and 'Uplift' in the Chicago Defender." *Musical Quarterly* 81, no. 3 (Autumn 1997): 344-70.
———. *Racial Uplift and American Music, 1878-1943.* Jackson: University Press of Mississippi, 2012.
Schiedt, Duncan P. *The Jazz State of Indiana.* Pittsboro, IN: Self-published, 1977.

Schlereth, Thomas J. *Victorian America: Transformations in Everyday Life.* New York: Harper Collins, 1991.
Schneider, Mark Robert. *"We Return Fighting": The Civil Rights Movement in the Jazz Age.* Boston, MA: Northeastern University Press, 2002.
Schoen-Nazzaro, Mary B. "Plato and Aristotle on the Ends of Music." *Laval Théologique et Philosophique* 34, no. 3 (1978): 261–73.
Schrum, Kelly. *Some Wore Bobby Sox: The Emergence of Teenage Girls' Culture, 1920–1945.* New York: Palgrave Macmillan, 2004.
Schuller, Gunther. *Early Jazz: Its Roots and Musical Development.* New York and Oxford, UK: Oxford University Press, 1968.
Selig, Diana. *Americans All: The Cultural Gifts Movement.* Cambridge, MA and London: Harvard University Press, 2008.
Sengstock, Charles A. *That Toddlin Town: Chicago's White Dance Bands and Orchestras, 1900–1950.* Urbana and Chicago: University of Chicago Press, 2004.
Shapiro, Nat, and Nat Hentoff, eds. *Hear Me Talkin' to Ya: The Story of Jazz as Told by the Men Who Made It.* New York: Dover Publications, 1955.
Sivulka, Juliann. *Soap, Sex, and Cigarettes: A Cultural History of American Advertising.* 2nd ed. Boston, MA: Wadsworth Press, (1998), 2012.
Smith, Carl. *Urban Disorder and the Shape of Belief: The Great Chicago Fire, the Haymarket Bomb, and the Model Town of Pullman.* Chicago, IL and London: University of Chicago Press, 2007.
Smith, Jason Scott. "The Strange History of the Decade: Modernity, Nostalgia, and the Perils of Periodization." *Journal of Social History* 32, no. 2 (1998): 263–85.
Sollors, Werner. *Ethnic Modernism.* Cambridge, MA and London: Harvard University Press, 2008.
Solomon, Barbara. *In the Company of Educated Women.* New Haven, CT: Yale University Press, 1985.
Southern, Eileen. *The Music of Black Americans: A History.* New York: W. W. Norton, (1971, 1983), 1997.
Stearns, Marshall and Jean. *Jazz Dance: The Story of American Vernacular Dance.* New York: G. Schirmer, (1964) 1979.
Steele, Kyle P. *Making a Mass Institution: Indianapolis and the American High School.* New Brunswick, Camden, and Newark, NJ, and London: Rutgers University Press, 2020.
Sudhalter, Richard M. *Stardust Melody: The Life and Music of Hoagy Carmichael.* New York: Oxford University Press, 2003.
Sudhalter, Richard M., and Philip R. Evans. *Bix: Man & Legend.* New Rochelle, NY: Arlington House, 1974.
Susman, Warren. *Culture as History: The Transformation of American Society in the Twentieth Century.* 2nd ed. Washington, DC and London: Smithsonian, 2003.
Syrett, Nicholas L. *The Company He Keeps: A History of White College Fraternities.* Chapel Hill: University of North Carolina Press, 2009.

Thelin, John R. *A History of American Higher Education*. 3rd ed. Baltimore, MD: Johns Hopkins University Press, (2014) 2019.
Tomko, Linda J. "*Fete Accompli*: Gender, "Folk-Dance," and Progressive-Era Political Ideals in New York City." In *Corporealities*, edited by Susan Leigh Foster, 155–76. London: Routledge, 1996.
Turpin, Andrea. *A New Moral Vision: Gender, Religion, and the Changing Purposes of American Higher Education, 1837–1917*. Ithaca, NY: Cornell University Press, 2016.
Tyack, David. *The One Best System: A History of American Urban Education*. Cambridge, MA and London: Harvard University Press, 1974.
Vaillant, Derek. *Sounds of Reform: Progressivism and Music in Chicago, 1873–1935*. Chapel Hill and London: University of North Carolina Press, 2004.
Wagner, Anne Louise. *Adversaries of Dance: From the Puritans to the Present*. Urbana: University of Illinois Press, 1997.
Walton, Lester A., L. H. White, A. W. K., and Lucien H. White. "Black-Music Concerts in Carnegie Hall, 1912–1915." *Black Perspective in Music* 6, no. 1 (1978): 71–88.
Wells, Herman B. *Being Lucky: Reminiscences and Reflections*. Bloomington: Indiana University Press, 1980.
Carl Withers. *Plainville, USA*. New York: Columbia University Press, (1945) 1971.
Wolfe, Brendan. *Finding Bix: The Life and Afterlife of a Jazz Legend*. Iowa City: University of Iowa Press, 2017.
Wolters, Raymond. *The New Negro on Campus: Black College Rebellions of the 1920s*. Princeton, NJ: Princeton University Press, 1975.
Wright, William. *Harvard's Secret Court: The Savage 1920 Purge of Campus Homosexuals*. New York: St. Martin's, 2005.
Zimmerman, Jonathan. "'Each "Race" Could Have Its Heroes Sung': Ethnicity and the History Wars in the 1920s." *Journal of American History* 87, no. 1 (2000): 92–111.
———. *Whose America? Culture Wars in the Public Schools*. 2nd ed. Chicago, IL and London: Chicago University Press, 2022.
Zinar, Ruth. "Racial Bigotry and Stereotypes in Music Books Recommended for Use by Children." *Black Perspective in Music* 3, no. 1 (Spring 1975): 33–39.

Published Primary Sources

"39 Bodies Taken from Club Debris; Looter Shot Down." *Washington Post*, July 6, 1925, 1.
"43rd Body Removed from Ruins of Club." *Washington Post*, July 7, 1925, 3.

"98% of School Children Good, Mortenson Says." *Chicago Daily Tribune*, January 27, 1922, 2.
"Ex-Cited." "Advice—Roommate's Jazz Music." *Daily Illini*, February 25, 1917, 5.
"Active Chapter." *Tau Topics*, May, 1927, 1.
"Ad—'Colored People Don't Want Classic Music!'" *The Crisis*, January 1922, 139.
"Ad—Are You Fighting Jazz and Cheap Popular Music?" *Music Supervisors' Journal* 9, no. 1 (1922): 28.
"Ad—Be Popular! Play Jazz on the 'Sax.'" *College Humor*, November 1925, 113.
"Ad—Brunswick Records." *Ohio State Lantern*, January 18, 1923, 2.
"Ad—Dance Records You Can't Be Without." *Daily Illini*, November 15, 1919, 7.
"Ad—Dundee Woolen Mills." *Puget Sound Trail*, February 27, 1924, 4.
"Ad—Full of Jazz and Ginger." *Cornell Daily Sun*, April 18, 1921, 4.
"Ad—Hickey's Lyceum Music Store." *Cornell Daily Sun*, September 26, 1924, 5.
"Ad—Hite Brothers Shoe Shining Parlor." *Daily Illini*, December 10, 1919, 8.
"Ad—Play Jazz in a Week on Your Buescher Saxophone." *College Humor*, October 1925, 109.
"Ad—Play Right Away on This Jazzy Sax." *College Humor*, Holiday [December] 1924, 80.
"Ad—Post Prom Dance." *Indiana Daily Student*, April 16, 1926.
"Ad—Test Your Talent Free on a Buescher Saxophone." *College Humor*, November 1925, 126.
"Ad—The Original New Orleans Creole Band." *Daily Illini*, November 16, 1917.
"Ad—Who Else Wants to Play Jazz?" *College Humor*, July 1925, 123.
"Ad—You'd Better Look into This Paul Whiteman Matter!" *Ohio State Lantern*, December 6, 1929, 3.
Adams, Wellington A. "Conference of Colored Musicians at Dunbar." *Washington Bee*, May 17, 1919, 2.
Allen, Clarence G. "Negro Musicians Urge against Perversion of Their Songs, at Second Convention." *Musical America*, August 7, 1920, 4.
"Alpha Phi Alpha Has Pretty Dance." *Indianapolis Recorder*, May 14, 1932, 6.
Angell, Robert Cooley. *The Campus: A Study of Contemporary Undergraduate Life in the American University*. New York and London: D. Appleton, 1928.
Ator, Joe. "Tropical Sky and Desert Sands Carry Prom Dancers to Orient." *Daily Illini*, December 9, 1922, 1.
"Attucks Organ Purchasing Plan Made." *Indianapolis Recorder*, May 28, 1932, 1.
Austin City High School, ed. *The Maroon and White*. Chicago, IL: Austin City High School, 1929.
———. *The Maroon and White*. Chicago, IL: Austin City High School, 1924.
Bailey, W. M., and I. W. Wheeler. "The Feeding Habits of Pseudomyrmine and Other Ants." *Transactions of the American Philosophical Society, New Series* 22, no. 4 (1920): 235–79.

Baker, Joseph E. "Plato as a Contemporary Essayist." *Classical Journal* 22, no. 3 (1926): 210–20.
"Ban Jazz Dancing and Auto Spooning." *Washington Post*, November 19, 1921, 1.
Bargelt, Louise James. "Doctor Evolves Rest Cure for Jazz Age Child." *Chicago Daily Tribune*, December 9, 1923, 14.
"The 'Barn Social.'" *The Scroll*, March 1927, 8.
Beanpot, Boston. "Essential Parts of a Fraternity." *College Humor*, October 1925, 75.
Birchard, C. C. "What about the Saxophone?" *Music Supervisors' Journal* 12, no. 1 (1925): 56–57.
Birge, Abe Martin. "A Postlude by Abe Martin." *Music Supervisors' Journal* 7, no. 4 (March 1921): 4.
"Bodies of 12 Found; 17 Injured in Ruins of Boston Building." *Washington Post*, July 5, 1925, 1.
"Both Jazz Music and Jazz Dancing Barred from All Louisville Episcopal Churches." *New York Times*, September 19, 1921, 16.
Bowen, George Oscar. "First Things First." *Music Supervisors' Journal* 14, no. 5 (1928): 19, 21, 23, 25, 27, 29, 31, 33.
Bray, Mabel. "The Correlation of the Singing Lesson and the Listening Lesson." Paper presented at the Sixteenth Annual Meeting of the Music Supervisors' National Conference, April 9–13, 1923.
Brockett, Alice. *The Reveille*. Franklin, OH and Denver, CO: Eldridge Entertainment House, 1922.
Brockett, E. B. "Instrumental Music in the High School." Paper presented at the Proceedings of the High School Conference, University of Illinois, Urbana, 1921.
Brown, J. Harold. "In the Music World." *Indianapolis Recorder*, December 29, 1928, 5.
———. "In the Music World." *Indianapolis Recorder*, January 19, 1929, 5.
Brown, Sterling A. "Negro Character as Seen by White Authors." *Journal of Negro Education* 2, no. 2 (1933): 179–203.
Burchenal, Elizabeth. *Folk-Dances and Singing Games: Twenty-Six Folk-Dances of Norway, Sweden, Denmark, Russia, Bohemia, Hungary, Italy, England, Scotland and Ireland, with the Music, Full Directions for Performance, and Numerous Illustrations, Volume 1*. New York: G. Schirmer, 1909.
———. "Folk Dancing." Paper presented at the Music Supervisor's National Conference Meeting, 1918.
———. "Reviving the Folk Dance." *National Education Association Journal* 15 (1926): 241.
Butler, Eloise. "Helen C. Laster and Cornell A. Talley in Joint Recital." *Indianapolis Recorder*, June 4, 1932, 6.
Butler, Eloise Keller. "Mother's Day Program Was Great Success." *Indianapolis Recorder*, May 14, 1932, 1.

Carr, Raymond Norman. *Building the School Orchestra: A Guide for Leaders.* Elkhart, IN: C. G. Conn, 1923.
"Cartoon—Will Our Dance Orchestras Come to This?" *Etude*, May 1925, 322.
Cassill, R. V. "Afterword." In *The Plastic Age*, 333–43. Carbondale, IL: Southern Illinois University Press, 1980.
Cayton, Madge R. "The Origin of Jazz." *Cayton's Monthly*, February 1, 1921.
Chicago College of Dental Surgery. *Dentos*. Chicago, IL: Chicago College of Dental Surgery, 1926.
"Church Notes." *Indianapolis Recorder*, May 28, 1932, 8.
"City Wide Open, Youth Periled, Report Asserts." *Chicago Daily Tribune*, March 18, 1928, 12.
Clark, Frances Elliott. "Music in Education (Concluded)." *Music Supervisors' Journal* 5, no. 2 (1918): 12–18.
Clark University. *Pasticcio*. Atlanta, GA, 1926.
"Class Notes." *Ariston*, April 1921, 20.
Cobb, B. B. "Music as an Essential." *Music Supervisors' Journal* 9, no. 4 (1923): 18, 20, 22, 24.
Columns, Washington. "How to Avoid Petting Parties." *College Humor*, March 1925, 84.
Cooke, James F. "June [Editorial]." *Etude*, June 1924, 369.
———. "Where the Etude Stands on Jazz." *Etude*, August 1924, 515.
———. "What Jazz Is Leading America?: Part II of a Symposium Which Has Already Attracted National Attention." *Etude*, September 1924, 595–96.
"Coonskin Coat Comes in for College Censure." *Chicago Daily Tribune*, March 18, 1927, 29.
Cressey, Paul Goalby. *The Taxi-Dance Hall: A Sociological Study in Commercialized Recreation and City Life*. Chicago, IL: University of Chicago Press, (1932) 2008.
Crispus Attucks High School. *The Attucks: Crispus Attucks High School Yearbook*. Indianapolis, IN: Crispus Attucks High School, 1931.
———. *The Attucks: Crispus Attucks High School Yearbook*. Indianapolis, IN: Crispus Attucks High School, 1933.
———. *The Attucks: Crispus Attucks High School Yearbook*. Indianapolis, IN: Crispus Attucks High School, 1936.
"Current Topics." *Music Supervisors Journal* 9, no. 3 (1923): 38–41.
"Damrosch Assails Jazz." *New York Times*, April 17, 1928.
"Dance Ban Stands." *Milwaukee Journal*, May 18, 1912, 1.
"Dance Not the Only Reason Baylor Women Can't Go to Fair Says Prexy." *Daily Lariat*, October 4 1924, 1.
"Dancing." *Greater Fisk Herald*, December 1926.
Danovsky, Evelyn. "Melody in F." *Flower Echo*, October 31, 1933, 4.

"Dean Talbot of U. Of C. To Quit Her Post." *Chicago Daily Tribune*, April 1, 1925, 25.

"Declares Jazz Lowers Tastes." *Los Angeles Times*, August 14, 1921, 14.

Dirge, Washington. "Fraternity Meeting." *College Humor*, August 1925, 64.

Dixon, Maenelle. "Spelman and Morehouse Get Acquainted." *Campus Mirror*, October 1929, 7.

Dooley, Roy. "500 Prom Couples Celebrate Amid Wintry Setting." *Daily Illini*, December 1, 1925, 1.

"Duke Ellington Calls Swing 'Emotional Bounce of Jazz.'" 6, *Indiana Daily Student*, October 13, 1939, 2.

Dunn, J. P. "Review." *Mississippi Valley Historical Review* 9, no. 3 (1922): 257–59.

Earhart, Will. "Art in Life and Musical Art for the Child." Paper presented at the Journal of the Proceedings of the Annual Meeting of the Music Supervisors' National Conference—Twenty-Second Year, [May?] 1929.

———. "Factors of Musical Appeal and Responses of Pupils to Them." *Music Supervisors' Journal* 17, no. 2 (1930): 18–24.

———. "Is Instrumental Music in Public Schools Justified by the Actual Results? (Concluded)." *Music Supervisors' Journal* 8, no. 2 (1921): 36–40.

———. "The Reveille by Alice W. Brockett [Review]." *Music Supervisors' Journal* 9, no. 2 (1922): 37–38.

"Editorial—The Ragtime Craze." *Daily Iowan*, May 9, 1918, 2.

"Educator Says Movies and Jazz Retard Student." *Chicago Daily Tribune*, April 8, 1922, 15.

"Edward Moore, Noted Critic and Musician, Dies." *Chicago Daily Tribune*, October 7, 1935, 5.

Egloff, Andrew, and Abbott Rainer. "The Polish Peasant in Oberlin and Chicago: The Intellectual Trajectory of W. I. Thomas." *American Sociologist* 39, no. 4 (December 2008): 217–58.

Elliot, Gilbert. "Our Musical Kinship with the Spaniards." *Musical Quarterly* 8, no. 3 (1922): 413–18.

Ellis, William T. "Children Test for Jazz Civilization." *Dallas Morning News*, January 1, 1921, 10.

Elson, Louis C. *The National Music of America and Its Sources*. Boston, MA: L. C. Page, (1924) 1899.

Engel, Carl. *Discords Mingled: Essays on Music*. Edited by Carl Engel. Freeport, NY: Books for Libraries Free Press, (1931) 1967.

———. "Views and Reviews." *Musical Quarterly* 8, no. 4 (1922): 611–32.

Epstein, Dana. "Frederick Stock and American Music." *American Music* 10, no. 1 (1992): 20–52.

Erskine, John. "De-Centralizing Our Music." *Music Supervisors Journal* 16, no. 5 (1930): 21, 23, 25, 27, 29, 31, 33.

———. "Give Music a Larger Place in Education." *Music Supervisors Journal* 17, no. 4 (March 1931): 17–18, 29.
"Et Tu." "Confessions of a College Cynic." *Flamingo*, January 1923.
Evans, Judge Ben B., and Lindsey Wainwright. *The Revolt of Modern Youth.* New York: Boni and Liveright, 1925.
Faulkner, Anne Shaw. "We Need a Universal Language." *Ladies Home Journal*, November 1919, 37.
———. *What We Hear in Music: A Course of Study.* Camden, NJ: Victor Talking Machine, 1924.
"Fears Colleges' Moral Tone: Dean Marion Talbot Writes They, Promote Race Suicide." *Chicago Daily Tribune*, April 21, 1910, 1.
"Finds Delusion of Wildness in Modern Youth." *Chicago Daily Tribune*, February 19, 1926, 21.
"First Shipment of Decorations for Prom Arranged in Men's Gym." *Indiana Daily Student*, April 15, 1926, 2.
Fischer, William Arms. "The Radio and Music." *Music Supervisors' Journal* 12, no. 3 (1926): 8, 10, 12, 14, 16, 67–42.
Fiske, Christabel F. "Problems in the Teaching of Poetry." *English Journal* 12, no. 8 (1923): 533–44.
Fitzgerald, F. Scott. *Flappers and Philosophers.* Edited by James L. W. West III. Cambridge, UK: Cambridge University Press, (1930) 2012.
———. *Tales of the Jazz Age.* New York: Charles Scribner's, 1922.
Flanagan, Thomas Jefferson. "Farewell." *The Scroll*, April 1925, 3–4.
———. "Honey, Can You "Charleston"?" *The Scroll*, January 1926, 8.
"Folk Dancing versus Jazz." *Oregonia*, June 28, 1920, 6.
"For More but Smaller High Schools." *Chicago Daily Tribune*, February 2, 1922, 8.
Forbes, Genevieve. "Copyright Bar Stirs Radio Fans' Static." *Chicago Daily Tribune*, April 15, 1923, 17.
———. "Mortenson Asks Parents to Curb Student Revels." *Chicago Daily Tribune*, January 26, 1922.
"Former University Man Dies in East." *Daily Iowan*, August 8, 1931, 3.
"Frank Trumbauer's Band—King of Charleston Music." *Indiana Daily Student*, April 10, 1926.
"Fraternity Men Aid Negro Jazz Artist's Rise to Local Fame." *Columbia Evening Missourian*, October 3. 1921, 1.
"Fred Waring and Orchestra Pay Visit to House." *Phi Kappa News*, November 1930, 2.
Freer, Louise. "Modern Tendencies in Physical Education." Paper presented at the Proceedings of the High School Conference, University of Illinois Urbana, November 1921.
Frivol, Iowa. "Very Little Difference." *College Humor*, July 1925, 93.
Fullerton, C. A. "Music in Rural Communities." *Music Supervisors' Journal* 14, no. 2 (1927): 35, 37, 39, 41, 43, 47, 49, 51, 53.

Gaboon, Hamilton Royal. "Joke—Latest Dance Steps." *College Humor*, September 1925, 28.

"Get 'em Young, Teach 'em Grace, Urges Pavlova." *Chicago Daily Tribune*, March 27, 1922, 12.

Gilbert, Russell. "Deportment at the Piano." *Etude*, March, 1925, 166.

Gilbert, Thelma. "The Negro in Music." *Spelman Messenger*, February 1927, 16–18.

"Girls Seek Risque, Thrive on Thrills but Believe Situation Unalarming." *Ohio State Lantern*, January 10, 1922, 1, 4.

Glenn, Mabelle. "The Symphony Orchestra in the Public School: The Kansas City (Mo.) Plan." *Music Supervisors' Journal* 10, no. 3 (1924): 42–44.

Graham, Otto. "The Development of Instrumental Music." Paper presented at the Proceedings of the High School Conference, 1922.

Grant, Henry L. "Individualism and Organization." *Negro Musician* 1, no. 3 (June 1921): 3.

Gulick, Luther H. "Preface." In *Folk-Dances and Singing Games: Twenty-Six Folk-Dances of Norway, Sweden, Denmark, Russia, Bohemia, Hungary, Italy, England, Scotland and Ireland, with the Music, Full Directions for Performance, and Numerous Illustrations, Volume 1*, edited by Elizabeth Burchenal, vii. New York: G. Schirmer, 1909.

Gunn, Glenn Dillard. "Stock Stirs Spark of Harmony in Souls of Rising Generation." *Chicago Herald and Examiner*, January 28, 1923.

"Hallowe'en Party Big Event of Year." *Eastern Progress*, November 7, 1922, 1.

Hamilton, Clarence G. "The Teacher's Round Table." *Etude*, December 1927, 913.

———. "The Teacher's Round Table." *Etude*, August 1924, 531.

Hamilton Royal Gaboon. "Joke—Age of Elizabeth." *College Humor*, August 1925, 61.

Harper, Robert H., ed. *Annual of Louisiana 76th Conference of the Methodist Episcopal Church, South*, 1921.

Harreld, Mrs. Kemper. "Music in the Home." *Spelman Messenger*, January 1927, 14–15.

"Harry Burleigh Bewails Misuse of Folk Songs." *Chicago Defender*, November 18, 1922, 8.

Hart, James. "Jazz Jargon." *American Speech* 7, no. 4 (1932): 241–54.

Hawes, Joseph. *Children between the Wars: American Childhood, 1920–1940*. New York: Twayne Publishers, 1997.

"Heaven Protect Jazz!" *Daily Illini*, January 22, 1921, 4.

"Hen Parties." *The Scroll*, November 1926, 12.

Herrick, Genevieve Forbes. "Rush to Defense of Co-Eds." *Chicago Daily Tribune*, September 15, 1926, 1.

Hewitt, Joseph William. "The Humor of the Greek Anthology." *Classical Journal* 17, no. 2 (1921): 66–76.

"High Lights of the Convention." *Music Supervisors' Journal* 8, no. 5 (1922): 12, 14, 16.

Hilderbrant, Edith. "Music Memory Contests." *School Review*, April 1922, 300–06.
"Holds Jazz and Girls Wreck Scholarship." *New York Times*, June 30, 1928, 24.
"Holds Jazz Upsets Life at College." *Los Angeles Times*, January 5, 1926, 5.
Holmes, Ethelyn. "Negro Music and Composers." *The Scroll*, April 1925, 6.
Holt, Nora Douglas. "Musicians Organize National Association." *Chicago Defender*, August 9, 1919, 15.
Indiana University. *Arbutus*. Bloomington: Indiana University, 1925.
———. *Arbutus*. Bloomington: Indiana University, 1926.
Innes, Frederick Neil. "The Musical Possibilities of the Wind Band." *Music Supervisors' Journal* 10, no. 5 (1924): 40, 42–45, 62–64.
"Irate at Fraternity Din." *New York Times*, November 19, 1926, 10.
"Is Music Related to School Life?" *Music Supervisors' Journal* 8, no. 2 (1921): 26.
"J. Harold Brown Resigns from Attucks." *Indianapolis Recorder*, October 13, 1934, 1, 7.
Jackson, O. E. "Our Prospects in the Realm of Music." *Athenaeum*, November 1924, 54–55.
"Jazz Band Hold Snappy Practice for Chicago Game." *Daily Illini*, February 28, 1919, 1.
"Jazz Country 'Jazz Mad.'" *The Evening World*, March 14, 1922.
"Jazz Gives Woman Goiter, Physican Finds." *Chicago Daily Tribune*, June 26, 1927, 12.
"Jazz Is Nearing Its End, Says Musical Editor." *Detroit News*, March 28, 1931.
"Jazz Is Popular Revenge on Music." *Norwalk Hour*, November 8, 1926, 8.
"Jazz Music in High School Class in Typewriting." *Ogden Standard* (Ogden, UT), November 18, 1919.
"Jazz Receives Censure by Old Fiddlers Who Contested in Ithaca Yesterday." *Cornell Daily Sun*, May 4, 1926, 2.
"Jazz, Steam Whistle Equally Melodious, Prof. Morgan Asserts." 1, *Indiana Daily Student*, October 30, 1924.
Johnson, Charles S. "Jazz Poetry and Blues." *Fisk Herald*, May 1930, 14–16.
Johnson, Guy B. "A Sociological Interpretation of the New Ku Klux Movement." *Journal of Social Forces* 1, no. 4 (1923): 440–45.
"Joke—Have You Heard from Mary?" *Trintonian*, June 8, 1920, 4.
"Joke—This Jazz Age." *College Humor*, Winter (January) 1925, 25.
Jones, Anna L. "An Evaluation of the Art of Dancing." *Greater Fisk Herald*, April/May 1926, 14.
Juggler, Notre Dame. "Clairvoyant." *College Humor*, September 1925, 17.
———. "Joke—Jolly Party." *College Humor*, October, 1925, 74.
———. "Joke—Rented Land and Wheat." *College Humor*, October 1925, 74.
"Junior Prom Date Set for December 6." *Daily Illini*, November 13, 1929, 1.
"Junior Prom Debt of Long Standing at Last Wiped Out." *Ohio State Lantern*, January 9, 1922, 1.

"Junior Prom Tickets Go on Sale Today-Prize Poster Is Picked." *Daily Illini*, March 5, 1919, 8.
"Kansas Federation Denounces Church Music." *Herald* (Hayti, MO), December 9, 1920.
"Kissing Is O.K. for Young Folks, Physician Says." *Chicago Daily Tribune*, March 16, 1922.
"Kiwanis Will Visit High School." *El Paso Herald*, April 15, 1919.
L.E.B. "Here's to the Prom." *Phoenix*, January 1925, 10.
Lambin, Leroy E. Bowman and Maria Ward. "Evidences of Social Relations as Seen in Types of New York City Dance Halls." *Journal of Social Forces* 3, no. 2 (1925): 286–91.
Levy, Heniot. "Curbing the Music Student's Mania for Speed." *Etude*, March 1925, 161–62.
Lewis, Rev. Franklin F. *Five Reasons Why Methodists Don't Dance*. Chicago: Glad Tidings, 1921.
"List Jazz Dance Halls of City as Morally Unfair." *Chicago Daily Tribune*, February 20, 1922, 2.
"Lock N.U. 'Frat' for Wild Party." *Chicago Daily Tribune*, September 7, 1925, 1.
"A Look into the Lurid Limelight of Our Most Syncopated Cities." *College Humor*, Winter (January) 1925, 58–59.
Loyola University. *Loyolan*. Chicago, IL: Loyola University, 1924.
———. *Loyolan*. Chicago, IL: Loyola University, 1926.
Lunceford, James M. "Has the Athletic Council Succeeded." *Greater Fisk Herald*, June 1926, 9.
Manchester, Arthur L. "Music Education, a Musical America, the American Composer, a Sequence." *Musical Quarterly* 10, no. 4 (1924): 587–95.
Mannes, David. *Music Is My Faith: An Autobiography*. New York: W.W. Norton, 1938.
McMahon, John R. "Our Jazz-Spotted Middle West." *Ladies Home Journal*, February 1922, 38, 181.
Meima, Ralph C. "Literature and Life." *Anchor*, January 24, 1921, 2.
"A Message to Midwest Band and Orchestra Contest Participants." *Music Supervisors' Journal* 11, no. 5 (1925): 69–71.
"Methodist Favors Dancing." *New York Times*, February 6, 1920, 25.
"Methodists Lift Amusements Ban." *Illinois Fiery Cross*, 1924, 7.
Moore, Edward. "Fashion Turns Its Thumb Down on Jazz Rhythm." *Chicago Daily Tribune*, November 25, 1921, F1.
———. "In Which the Music Critic Is Instructed as to His Plain Duty." *Chicago Daily Tribune*, December 18, 1921, F1.
———. "Where Are the Popular Tunes of Yesteryear?" *Chicago Daily Tribune*, October 23, 1921, F1.
"Mortenson to Quit Schools." *Chicago Daily Tribune*, August 29, 1923, 1.
"Music." *The Greater Fisk Herald*, March 1927, 22–23.

"Music Contest Creates Interest." *Oregonian*, February 16, 1921, 9.
"Musical Notes." *Phoenix*, November, 1928, 4–5.
"Musicians Organize." *New York Age*, May 17, 1919, 6.
"Negro Spirituals of African Origin." *Spelman Messenger*, January 1930, 59–60.
"Net $682 in Jazz Carnival." *Evening Missourian* (Columbia), April 2, 1920.
"New Victrola." *Sigmagram*, April 1926, 2.
"News of the Day through the Eye of the Camera." *Chicago Daily Tribune*, January 27, 1922, 26.
Newsome, Maurice E. "They Call It Dancing." *Greater Fisk Herald*, December 1926, 16.
"Notes of Higher Culture at Indiana University: on Immorality." *Vagabond*, 1924, 2.
Nunn, William. "Has the Negro Church Been Weighed in the Balance and Found Wanting?" *Pittsburgh Courier*, October 2, 1926, 9.
Oakes, John. "Goose Stepping." *Scroll*, January 1926, 9.
Ohio State Lantern. "Jazz Hounds." *Daily Illini*, January 17, 1920, 4.
" 'Old Question,' Says Symphony Director, Branding Jazz Music as Temporary Craze." *Indiana Daily Student*, February 6, 1925, 1.
"On Fraternities." *Vagabond*, March, n.d., 22–24.
"Opera Manager Urges Students to Hear 'Aida.' " *Marshall News*, December 9, 1924, 1.
"Opinions Vary on Meaning of Preston Creed: Leaders Ponder at Last Rites Are Held." *Chicago Daily Tribune*, April 16, 1925, 6.
"Others' Opinions." *Daily Illini*, December 3, 1924, 4.
"Over One-Half Attucks Seniors Wish to Become Public School Teachers." *Indianapolis Recorder*, July 8, 1933, 1.
Panurge, Sir Polonius. "The End of the Jazz Age." *Vagabond*, Autumn, 1924, 22–27.
"Parents Back Mortenson in Fight on 'Petting.' " *Chicago Daily Tribune*, March 21, 1922, 1.
"Parents Back Mortenson in Jazz Crusade." *Chicago Daily Tribune*, January 29, 1922, 5.
Park, Robert E. "The Natural History of the Newspaper." *American Journal of Sociology* 29, no. 3 (1923): 273–89.
Parker, Thelma. "Shortridge Teachers Are Proud of 'Bobs.' " *Shortridge Daily Echo*, September 21, 1927, 1.
Patrick, G. T. W. "Can the Sentiment of Patriotism Be Refunded?" *American Journal of Sociology* 30, no. 5 (1925): 569–84.
"Paul Whiteman, Carded for Program Here April 17, Is Uplifter of Present Day Jazz." *Indiana Daily Student*, April 10, 1925.
Pepsus, Sam. "Diarist Awaits Whiteman at Stair Landing; Dines with Him on Frankfurters and Onions." *Indiana Daily Student*, April 18, 1925.
Peyton, Dave. "The Musical Bunch—Interested Music Teachers." *Chicago Defender*, July 17, 1926, 6.

———. "The Musical Bunch: Things in General." *Chicago Defender*, October 29, 1927, 8.
"Philip Yarrow, Vice Crusader, Is Dead at 82." *Chicago Daily Tribune*, June 16, 1954, C7.
"Pickwick Pier Rotten, Asserts Gen. Goethals." *Washington Post*, August 3, 1925, 3.
"Plan 'Sings' as Jazz Antidote among Youth." *Chicago Daily Tribune*, June 9, 1924, 5.
"Plans Are Completed for Indiana's Premier Social Activity." *Indiana Daily Student*, April 16, 1926.
Plato. *The Republic of Plato*. Translated by Allan Bloom. 3rd ed. New York: Basic Books, 2016. 1968.
"Play 'Jazz' on the Saxophone." *College Humor*, August 1925, 121.
Prehn, Professor. "Joke—'Shots Follow Dance.'" *Prehn's Bonmots*, February 12, 1930, 8.
"Prom with Inspiring Beauty Caps Social Season on Campus." *Indiana Daily Student*, April 17, 1926.
"Put Snuggle Dance All up to the Girls." *New York Times*, August 22, 1922, 1.
Rawlins, E. Elliot. "Keeping Fit: the Intoxication of Jazz." *New York Amsterdam News*, April 11, 1923, 16.
———. "Keeping Fit: Jazz-a Drug." *New York Amsterdam News*, April 1, 1925.
"The Rhythm of the Age." *Chicago Daily Tribune*, October 23, 1927, 10.
Riley, R. W. "The Attitude of a New Student." *Maroon Tiger*, November 1926, 5.
Rowsey, Frank. "The Younger Set." *College Humor*, March 1925, 68–71, 109, 11.
Rue, Larry. "Trieste Has Guaranteed Cure for Jazz Habit." *Chicago Daily Tribune*, April 9, 1922, F17.
Ruggles, Wesley. "*The Plastic Age*." Los Angeles, CA: B. P. Schulberg Productions, 1925.
Schell, Harry O. "The Social Problem of Atlanta University." *The Scroll*, November 1926, 11–12.
Scholes, Percy. *Music: The Child and the Masterpiece*. Oxford, UK: Oxford University Press, 1935.
"School Board Bans Teaching Language of Hun: Favors Superintendent's Idea Regarding German in Elementary Work." *Chicago Daily Tribune*, September 7, 1918, 9.
"School Official Says He Hears Too Much Jazz." *Chicago Daily Tribune*, February 11, 1927, 16.
Scott, Emmett J. "Initial Conference of Negro Musicians and Artists." *Tuskegee Student*, June 28, 1919, 4.
Seegers, J. C. "Teaching Music Appreciation by Means of the Music-Memory Contest." *Elementary School Journal* 26, no. 3 (1925): 215–23.
Shaw, Herbert. "Dancing at Fisk." *Greater Fisk Herald*, October, 1926, 12–13.
Sleezer, Margaret M. "Student Citizenship at the Senn High School." *School Review* 32, no. 7 (1924): 508–20.

"Social Festivities End with Formal: Called Best Yet." *Phi Kappa News*, June 1930, 2.
"Society Notes." *Daily Illini*, November 14, 1918, 3.
"Sousa and Band Give Campus Concert Tonight." *Daily Illini*, November 5, 1925, 1.
"The Spelman Social." *Maroon Tiger*, November 1926, 3.
Starr, Clara Ellen. "Music Appreciation in the Junior High School of Detroit." *Music Supervisors' Journal* 12, no. 2 (1925): 52–56.
Stephens, Dessie. "To the Editor—Farmers and Music." *Etude*, January 1924, 59.
"Stock's Aids Move to Ruin Craze for Jazz." *Chicago Daily Tribune*, 1922, 21.
Stringham, Edwin J. "'Jazz'—an Educational Problem." *Musical Quarterly* 12, no. 2 (1926): 190–95.
"Teaches "Jazz" in Newark High School." *New York Tribune*, March 21, 1919.
Tempo. "The Era of Sock." *Vagabond* 1, no. 3 (1924): 3.
"That Wicked Jazz the Child of Old Peru?" *New York Tribune*, May 8, 1921, 7.
Thomas, Olive Coleman. "How to Create an Appreciation for Good Music in the Public Schools." *Mississippi Educational Journal for Teachers in Colored Schools* 3, no. 3 (January 1927): 59.
Thomas, William I. *The Unadjusted Girl: With Cases and Standpoint for Behavior Analysis*. Criminal Science Monographs. Vol. 4, Boston, MA: Little, Brown, 1923.
Thompson, Warren S. "Race Suicide in the United States." *Scientific Monthly* 5, no. 1 (1917): 22–35.
Thurman, Howard B. "The Message of the Spirituals." *Spelman Messenger*, October 1928, 4–12.
"To a Sophisticated Blonde." *Phoenix*, October 1925, 10.
"To Launch New Attucks Organ Campaign." *Indianapolis Recorder*, May 21, 1932, 1.
"Tomorrow's Freedom." *Scroll*, April 1927, 11–12.
Toner, Williams M. "Halltree: a Parody." *Vagabond*, 1926, 4.
"Trustees Will Permit Charlestoning at Prom." 4, *Indiana Daily Student*, March 17, 1926.
Vagabond Editorial Board. "Vagabond Editorial Board and Mission." *Vagabond*, October 1923, 33–34.
"Vows He'll Mop Floor to Keep Yarrow in Jail." *Chicago Daily Tribune*, June 28, 1931, 1.
"W. L. Lifts Old Dancing Ban in Sororities." *Daily Illini*, March 17, 1932, 1.
Wallace, Leon. "Dancers Will Revel in Starry Phantasmagoria of Harmonies, Colors at Fifth Prom Tonight." *Indiana Daily Student*, May 1, 1925.
Walton, Lester A. "Concert at Carnegie Hall." *New York Age*, May 9, 1912, 6.
Webster, W. F. "Music and the Sacred Seven." *Music Supervisors' Journal* 13, no. 5 (1927): 33, 35, 37, 39, 43, 45.
"Whiteman Makes His Work Play and Keeps Jocularity Abounding." *Indiana Daily Student*, April 14, 1925.

"Whiteman Orchestra to Be Advertised by Cross-Word Contest." *Indiana Daily Student*, March 28, 1925, 4.
"Whiteman Program Traces Jazz through Stages of Development." *Indiana Daily Student*, April 18, 1925.
"Whiteman to Arrive Early to Spend Day on Indiana Campus." *Indiana Daily Student*, April 11, 1925.
Widow, Cornell. "Lager Rhythms." *College Humor*, October 1925, 84.
Williams, Martin. "Jazz: What Happened in Kansas City?" *American Music* 3, no. 2 (1985): 171–79.
"Women Condemn Jazz Tunes on U. Of C. Campus." *Chicago Daily Tribune*, March 8, 1922, 9.
"Women Deans Open Fight on Jazz in Dancing." *Chicago Daily Tribune*, November 20, 1921, 17.
"Work Assails Spirit of Jazz." *Los Angeles Times*, June 16, 1925, 4.
Work, John W. "The Negro's Contribution to Music." *Fisk Herald*, May 1930, 12–13.
Yarrow, Phillip, ed. *Fighting the Debauchery of Our Girls and Boys*. Chicago: Self-published, 1923.

Index

Adams, Samuel Hopkins, 137
Adams, Wellington A., 68
Addams, Jane, 31–32
Alinsky, Saul, 19–24
Amherst College, 127–28
Anderson, Marion, 70, 73–74
Armstrong, Louis, 2, 14, 87, 88, 132
Atlanta University, 96–99, 114–15

Bailey, Buster, 14
Baker, Joseph E., 102
Baylor University, 120
Bechet, Sidney, 14
Beiderbecke, Bix, 1–2, 9, 87–88, 111, 132, 138
Blues, 14, 59, 63, 69, 78, 105
books (selected): *A Night in a Moorish Harem*, 34; *Fighting the Debauchery of Our Girls and Boys*, 34; *The Polish Peasant in Europe in America*, 101; *The Unadjusted Girl*, 101; *This Side of Paradise*, 137; *Unforbidden Fruit*, 137
Brown, J. Harold, 74–78, 80
Brown University, 108
Burchenal, Elizabeth, 51–53
Burleigh, Henry (Harry) T., 63, 64, 73–74, 97
Butler College, 88

Carmichael, Hoagy, 2, 10, 12, 130–33, 178n108
Carnegie Hall, 63–66
Carnegie Institute of Technology, 123
Carruthers, Earl, 138
Chicago, 1, 2, 7, 9, 10, 11, 13–38, 39, 50, 54, 57, 67, 69, 80–89 passim, 99–102, 120, 122, 124, 132, 138
Chicago Civic Opera (COO), 35–36
Chicago College of Dental University, 22
Chicago Defender, 26, 74, 77, 80, 151n63
Chicago Public Schools, 26–28
Chicago Symphony Orchestra, 17–18, 36
clothing, 3, 16, 17, 21, 23, 27–30, 34–35, 49, 52, 54, 83, 101, 108, 116, 118, 123, 128–29, 136, 139
Cincinnati, 78
Coleridge-Taylor, Samuel, 64
College Humor, 21, 89–91, 125
College of Puget Sound, 93
Colored Music School Settlement, 63–66
Columbia University, 103–104, 124
comic songs, 59
Concordia University Chicago, 121
Cook, Will Marion, 69

Cooke, James F., 3, 135–36. (See also *The Etude*)
Cornell University, 90, 93
Cressey, Paul, 22–24, 31
Crispus Attucks High School 61–62, 74–75, 77–78, 136
culture wars 3, 6, 100

Dallas, 8, 76, 120
dancing, 5–7, 11–13, 15–24, 27–37, 40–41, 47, 50, 53, 59, 74, 83, 88–139 passim; ballroom
dancing, 13; black bottom, 16, 35, 108; cabaret, 20, 27, 63, 90; cake walk, 86; camel-walk, 101; Charleston, 5, 16, 30, 35, 108, 111, 112, 115, 116, 122, 139; dance hall, 2, 5, 14–16, 19–58 passim, 85, 88, 103, 108, 110, 130, 131, 138; folk dance, 50–53, 138; foxtrot, 19, 74, 115, 125; high school and college dances, 2, 11, 12, 22, 27, 86, 93, 94, 98, 108–15, 119–37 passim; prom, 22, 94, 109–13, 115; quickstep, 108; sarabande, 40–41; shimmy, 13, 16, 35, 42, 91, 93, 101, 107, 108, 137; tango, 108; toddle, 101; waltz, 18, 37, 41, 50, 108
dating, 115–16, 122, 129
Deans of students, 99, 123; Clark, Thomas Arkle, 119; Deans of men 11, 99, 124, 126, 137;
Deans of women 13, 98–99, 117–18, 126, 137; Talbot, Marion, 118–19
Denison University, 95
DePauw University, 120–21
Des Moines University, 103
Detroit, 21, 55, 88, 135
Dett, R. Nathaniel, 64, 65, 72, 97
Diton, Carl, 68, 72, 97
Dreamland Ballroom, 14, 19, 20, 23

drinking, 2, 6, 19, 20, 26, 28, 32, 59, 87, 90, 96, 107, 108, 109, 113, 116, 122, 128–29, 137, 139
driving, 15, 27, 28, 54, 117, 121, 131
drugs 132, 139. (*See also* smoking)
Du Bois, W. E. B., 63, 105, 114, 163n83
Dunbar Music Festival, 66–67, 71
DuValle, Reginald, 130

Earhart, Will, 42–44, 137–38
East coast 2, 10
education: culture, 9; curricular, 5, 9, 10, 18, 48–49, 54, 56, 77, 80, 138; dance education, 50–51, 108, 118; extra-curricular, 5, 17–18, 66–67, 70, 72, 79, 80, 93, 94, 120, 127; moral
education, 106; music education, 36, 39–44, 48, 52–53, 56–57, 63, 65–68, 70–79, 103, 105, 135, 137, 138; Music Memory Contest, 18, 55–56; policies 10, 27, 54, 62, 97–99, 109, 111–14, 117–21, 126–28; role in society 3, 4, 8, 9, 10, 39–43, 70
Elgar, Charles, 19
Engel, Carl, 40–43
Erskine, John, 103–104
The Etude 3, 42, 46, 47, 48, 57, 135. (*See also* Cooke, James F.)
Europe, James Reese, 64
European Classical Music, 12, 25, 40–42, 46, 49, 52, 54–57, 60, 63–72, 75, 77, 97, 98, 103, 135, 136. (*See also* Western Classical Music)
Evangelicalism: Christians, 6, 106; colleges 12, 84, 133, 137

Fisk University, 14, 74–76, 79, 96–99, 105, 113–14
Fitzgerald, F. Scott, 115–16, 126, 137

Folk music, 12, 18, 26, 48, 63, 66, 72, 73, 74, 77. (*See also* dancing)
Frank Trumbauer Orchestra, 111

Gaelic Park Ballroom, 23
gambling, 32
gender, 6, 10, 20–24, 29, 30, 33–35, 49, 50, 90–137 passim; body, 6, 29, 35, 49, 50, 92, 108, 115, 116, 119, 123, 128, 129; roles 3, 17, 29, 95, 116, 117, 128. (*See also* sex)
Goodman, Benny, 58
Gospel music, 69
Grant, Henry L., 66–75
Greek life 12, 21, 90, 96, 111, 123–31; fraternities, 21, 85, 87, 88–91, 95, 96, 108–10, 114, 116, 120–33, 137; sororities, 89, 96, 109, 114, 123–28, 131, 132
Gulick, Dr. Luther, 51

Hardin, Lil, 14
Harvard University, 94, 100
Handy, W. C., 69
Hayes, Roland, 64, 74
Hilderbrant, Edith L., 16–17, 19, 21
Hip-hop, 135, 138
Hope College, 94
Howard University, 66–67
Humor 89–91, 112, 125, 166n29, 169n75
Hughes, Langston, 105
Hunter, Alberta, 14

Illinois, 16, 54
Illinois Vigilance Association, 32. (*See also* Yarrow, Rev. Philip)
Indiana, 106
Indiana University, 21, 22, 42, 86–89, 95, 96, 101, 109–13, 117, 118, 124, 126–33

Indianapolis, 42, 49, 55, 60, 61, 62, 74–78, 80, 88, 130, 132, 133
instruments, 3, 18, 55, 57, 59, 91, 92, 131; banjo, 90, 131; clarinet, 14; cymbal, 57; fiddle, 58; French horn, 131; gong, 57; organ, 75; piano, 7, 12, 51, 57, 68, 76, 78, 87, 89, 98, 104, 107, 130, 131, 133; percussion, 46, 101; saxophone, 14, 62, 85, 91, 92, 99, 111, 124, 131; snare drum, 57; trumpet, 1, 2, 111, 131, 132; trombone, 7, 131; violin, 63, 65, 67, 131
Iowa, 1, 50, 60
Iowa State Teachers College, 52

Jackson, 77
jazz: advertisements, 91, 92, 93; chording, 57; history of, 7, 14, 25–26, 41, 46, 63, 119, 141n10, 144n25; impact on health, 24, 25, 35, 43, 62, 63, 77; "Jazz Age," 2, 3, 5, 9, 12, 30, 31, 47, 70, 90, 102, 104, 106, 123, 135; lifestyle, 6, 9; religious response to, 31, 32, 33, 120, 121, 122, 123; sexualized nature of, 16, 108; student opposition to, 5, 11, 84, 85, 93, 94, 95, 96, 109, 113
Johnson, Charles S., 104, 105
Johnson, Guy B., 105
Johnson, Lola, 71
Jones, Isham, 58, 122
Julliard School, 104
Juvenile Protection Association (JPA), 23, 31–32

Kansas City, 54, 138
Ku Klux Klan (KKK), 6, 40, 61, 105–106, 171n14. (*See also* race)
Kynard, Charles, 138

Lane, Russell, 61–62, 77, 136
Lemon, Lillian, 76
Los Angeles, 7
Louisville, 33, 39
Lowry, Charles D., 31
Loyola University, 22, 85, 121–22
Lunceford, Jimmie, 78–79, 99

Mann Act 102
Mannes, David, 63–66
Marshall, Harriet Gibbs, 66, 68, 72, 73
Memphis, 14, 79
Miami University, 88
Midwest, 7, 10, 37, 87, 88, 96, 109, 137
Milhaud, Darius, 72
Miller, Edwin L., 21
Mississippi, 14
Missouri, 33, 53, 117
modernity 5, 6, 8, 9, 16, 27, 31, 43, 46, 47, 53, 63, 79, 94, 95, 101, 106, 119, 130, 133, 139, 142n12; modernism 3, 105
Moore, Edward, 25, 26
morality, 3, 6, 10, 11, 15–35 passim, 49–59 passim, 75, 91, 93–112 passim, 118, 119, 122, 123, 133–39 passim
Morehouse College, 96, 98, 113, 114, 115
Mortenson, Peter A., 26, 27, 28, 29, 30, 31, 34, 37
Morton, Jelly Roll, 7
Mount Holyoke College, 127, 128
movies, 15, 35, 85, 101, 117; *Plastic Age*, 107, 108, 137, 171–72n2; *The Collegians*, 137; *Young Man with a Horn*, 2
Music Supervisors' Journal, 54, 57, 76, 104
Music Supervisors' National Conference, 11, 40, 60, 70

Nashville, 21, 40, 99, 113
National Association for the Advancement of Colored People (NAACP), 7, 8, 69
National Association of Negro Musicians (NANM), 59, 60, 66–77, 80, 136
New Orleans, 7, 14, 84
New York City, 2, 50, 51, 53, 63, 65, 73, 87, 88, 91, 124
New Jersey, 46, 49, 55, 123
New Orleans Rhythm Kings, 122
Northwestern University, 32, 118, 122, 124

Ogden, 49
The Ohio State University, 95, 110, 116
Oliver, King 14
Ory, "Kid," 7
O'Shea, Michael Vincent, 15–16, 35

Pace, Harry, 59
Pennsylvania State University (Penn State), 87, 88, 99, 119
Peyton, Dave, 26
phonograph, 8, 24, 54, 55, 59, 84, 85, 92, 125, 127; phonodiscs, 5. (*See also* Victor Talking Machine Company)
pledge cards, 28
Pittsburgh, 8, 21, 63, 137
Portland, 51, 55
Princeton University, 126
Progressive Era, 58, 118

race 3, 5–15, 17–19, 24–26, 36–37, 39–42, 45–46, 48–49, 52, 57–60, 63–65, 69, 71, 76, 78, 83–84, 88–90, 96–97, 101, 103–105, 109, 113, 115–16, 118–19, 130, 133, 135–36; education inequities, 61, 66; financial privilege, 56,

133; hypersexualized blackness, 7, 37, 39, 58, 77. (*See also* sex); primitiveness, 7, 45, 46, 47, 48, 58, 73; "race suicide," 118–19; racial pride, 24, 26, 60, 67, 71, 74, 75, 77, 80, 81, 97, 105; representation, 71–72, 80; riot, 69; stereotypes, 7, 13, 15, 40, 42, 45, 46, 47, 48, 63, 65, 76, 89, 110, 114, 135; white superiority, 84, 118–19. (*See also* Ku Klux Klan)
radio, 8, 19, 31, 57, 69, 84, 99, 117, 145n32, 149n27
ragtime, 12, 16, 43, 59, 63, 64–66, 77, 78, 98, 130, 138, 144–45n31, 163–64n77
records, 1, 2, 8, 54, 59, 84, 92, 127. (*See also* phonograph)
The Reveille, 43–45
riverboats, 1, 7, 138
Robeson, Paul, 74
rock n' roll, 135, 138

Seattle 45
sex 5, 6, 7, 17, 20–25, 34–35, 39, 91, 96, 101, 112, 113, 116, 117; "petting," 6, 24, 26, 28, 91, 107, 108, 116, 122, 123, 139; physical affection, 23, 29, 33, 95, 96, 116, 123, 128; prostitution, 6, 22, 96, 102, 116, 129; sexuality, 11, 17, 23, 25, 28, 29, 30, 33, 34, 35, 37, 39, 91, 92, 98, 109, 113, 114, 116, 117, 128. (*See also* race)
Simmons, Alice C., 67
slang, 16
Smith College, 99, 127–28
smoking 27, 28, 101, 107, 108, 116, 132. (*See also* drugs)
Sousa, John Philip, 89
South, 7, 10, 37, 45, 76, 84, 96
Spelman College, 97–98, 113–15
Spelman High School, 78

Spirituals, 5, 11, 12, 60, 63–68, 71–78, 80, 97, 105, 136, 159n2
Spokane, 54
St. Catherine's University, 121
Still, William Grant, 69
Stock, Frederick, 17–19, 31, 36
Stowe, Lyman Beecher 63

Texas 42, 46, 54, 115, 120
Thomas, Olive Coleman, 77
Thomas, William I., 101–102
Trinity College, 115
Tuskegee University, 67, 98

University of California, Berkeley, 125–26
University of Chicago, 19, 21–24, 31, 85, 86, 93, 101–102, 109,110, 116, 118, 119, 123, 132
University of Colorado, 83
University of Illinois at Urbana-Champaign, 3, 49, 84–85, 87, 89, 90, 93–95, 102, 106, 109–10, 113, 119, 122, 124–27
University of Iowa, 85, 88, 103
University of Massachusetts, 110
University of Michigan, 88, 110
University of Minnesota, 93, 123
University of Missouri, 89, 117
University of Notre Dame, 122
University of Wisconsin, 110

Vassar College, 101
Victorianism, 3, 5, 6, 9, 47, 100, 102, 117, 118, 136, 137, 139
Victor Talking Machine Company, 3, 50, 87; Victor Victrola, 54, 98, 125–27. (*See also* phonograph)

Waring, Fred, 58, 87
Washington Conservatory of Music, 66, 76
Washington D.C., 66–71, 75

Weinberger, Constance, 19
Wellesley College, 57, 118
Wells, Herman B, 21–22, 131, 133
Wesleyan University, 100, 101
Western Classical Music, 69. (*See also* European Classical Music)
Wheaton, 31
Wheaton College, 119, 120
White Ballroom, 20, 21, 23
White, Clarence Cameron, 67
Whiteman, Paul, 2, 57, 58, 86, 87, 88, 92, 95, 103, 165n13
Work, John W., 74

Yarrow, Rev. Philip, 32–35. (*See also* Illinois Vigilance Association)

www.ingramcontent.com/pod-product-compliance
Lightning Source LLC
Chambersburg PA
CBHW020654230426
43665CB00008B/435